SAVORY
Bites

MEALS YOU CAN MAKE

SAVORY

Bites

IN YOUR CUPCAKE PAN

HOLLIS WILDER

Photographs by Tina Rupp

STEWART, TABORI & CHANG | NEW YORK

Published in 2013 by Stewart, Tabori & Chang
An imprint of ABRAMS

Cataloging-in-Publication Data has been
applied for and may be obtained from the
Library of Congress.

ISBN: 978-1-61769-019-8

EDITOR: Dervla Kelly
DESIGNER: Laura Palese
PRODUCTION MANAGER: Tina Cameron

Printed and bound in the U.S.A.

10 9 8 7 6 5 4 3 2

Stewart, Tabori & Chang books are available
at special discounts when purchased in
quantity for premiums and promotions
as well as fundraising or educational
use. Special editions can also be created
to specification. For details, contact
specialsales@abramsbooks.com or the
address below.

THE ART OF BOOKS SINCE 1949

115 West 18th Street
New York, NY 10011
www.abramsbooks.com

CONTENTS

PREFACE

I've always been surrounded by the wonderful scents of food wafting through the house, whether it was bread baking, pies and cakes waiting to be frosted, or a hearty goulash ready to be pounced upon.

Food and I have always been on the same stage from the very beginning. My grandfather proudly showed me off right alongside his cinnamon rolls, which he says were the size of my head. At my family's annual Turtle Stew Block Party, I was always the referee for the turtle races (but was hesitant to eat them after the race!).

My father's family, the Maiers clan, lived in the city; in a world of cocktails, big gems, golf, tennis, and boating. I was never offered a children's menu and was encouraged to eat whatever adult meal was being prepared.

My mother's relatives, the Tobias family, were hard-working sugar beet, corn, and navy bean farmers. They grew glorious gardens of flowers, herbs, vegetables, and every berry you could think of. Glass jars of Grandmother Hazel's green beans, tomatoes, beets, pickles, onion and corn relish, currant jelly, gooseberries, and rhubarb were the condiments of my life from early on. These were my epicurean beginnings.

From my two very different families, I learned how to bring people together with food.

When my parents retired in 1982, they purchased a restaurant in Brattleboro, Vermont. The restaurant was Autumn Winds and specialized in "nouvelle cuisine." I washed dishes, cleaned the bakery in the basement, and watched as bread and gâteaux were made from scratch along with demiglace, cassoulet, and other wonders. I continued to wash dishes until I graduated to cleaning up after the chefs, then prepping vegetables in perfect cuts that would later become glorious food.

Later, I was a partner at T. J. Buckleys, a 1920s- to 1940s-era dining car restaurant in Brattleboro, Vermont. This experience provided me with invaluable exposure to the culinary world. Handpicked, locally grown ingredients were purchased daily. Attention to detail was paramount, and it was at Buckleys that I learned how to listen to the people I was cooking for.

My Clients

Later in my life, I moved to California with the intention of becoming an actress, but after three months of acting classes I realized I would have to sell my soul in order to make that dream a reality. I took many odd jobs: photography assistant, personal shopper, babysitter. Then I had an idea: I hired a food agent who sent me on calls to make meals for people who were looking for private chefs. I made food for the Cruise-Kidman family, Warren Beatty, Annette Benning, and the Shriver-Schwarzeneggers, among other Hollywood stars. I started cooking for the toddlers of celebrities, who had special eating requirements (some were lactose intolerant, some could only eat organic food). Then I got my big break. My boyfriend's next-door neighbor just so happened to be Max Mutchnick, creator of the TV hit *Will & Grace*. Together we created a lunchtime ritual, which spanned the life of the show. Unlike other shows, where the writers would disappear into their offices to eat their bagged lunches alone, we dined as a "family" at one table. What the writers wanted, plain and simple, were meals that reminded them of home, and every afternoon I offered a buffet of food that did just that. As my career boomed, I began work as a caterer for the cast and crew of a variety of TV shows.

One of my most beloved clients was Jay Leno, host of *The Tonight Show*. I liked cooking for him not because he phoned me directly when he wanted me to prepare something for him and his wife or family and friends, nor because he personally made all of the arrangements for each menu with me. It's not even because he met me in the carport and insisted on carrying the food in from my car, and not because he is a kind, gentle, engaging human being. I adored cooking for him because he kept magazines in his oven!

I fed quite a few clients with opinionated palates while working in California. I created my chili cornbread bake (page 62) for Kevin Costner. This mini savory meal was a perfect complement to the Zone Diet popular at that time, so it became a staple at many of my celebrity dinner parties and luncheons. The *Queer Eye for the Straight Guy* team enjoyed savory pasta bites; Michael Jackson and his entourage liked the lasagna I prepared as an in-flight meal on Jackson's private jet; and Michael Eisner preferred roasted vegetable terrines (page 95). The *Will & Grace* creators and writers were fans of all of my Mexican-inspired savory bites, such as the Chicken Tamale Pies (page 166) and Flank Steak Mexican Bake (188), and many of the flavors in this book were pulled from dishes I created while working on that show.

Cupcake Champion

The game changer occurred when my family moved to Orlando, Florida. Wanting to leave my mark in some way, I opened my cupcakery, SweetByHolly—there were no other cupcake shops in sight! Later, I was cast on *Cupcake Wars* after producers viewed the three-minute Flip-camera video I'd submitted. Little did I know, after spending years in L.A., that the Food Network would find me in Florida, of all places.

I think it was the savory addition of salmon to the traditionally sweet lemon cupcake that wowed the judges on *Cupcake Wars*—it even wowed me! This small bite garnered me a win on the show, which then led to another win with my Crystallized Ginger Olive Oil Cupcakes with Lime Buttercream, Opal Basil, Mint, and Lime Zest, making me the first two-time winner of *Cupcake Wars*.

Those opportunities led me to experiment with all of the possibilities the cupcake pan offers. You could say my whole concept of mini savory meals started with those lemon-and-salmon cupcakes; the Lemon-Scented Cakes with Salmon, Caper & Lemon Topping on page 139 is a tasty variation of that prize-winning cupcake.

After that, all of the sweet cupcakes I made were extraordinary mini confections, and my SweetByHolly shops grew to be a success—but I was not content to be yet another cute cupcake-maker. I wanted to have a long-lasting relationship with the classic American cupcake pan but shake things up at the same time. Enter the savory cupcake. These cute and portable temptations utilize semi-homemade ingredients to create delicious meals that impress both family and friends.

Remember, it's not what it is; it's what it can become. What once was sweet is now savory. Everything old is new again. There really are countless uses for the cupcake pan. So open up your mind and pantry, and learn how to revolutionize mealtime.

INTRODUCTION

Why the Cupcake Pan?

Cupcakes can be a marvel of originality, with endless variations: simple buttercream-topped classics, pistachio-scented cakes with cardamom-infused chocolate ganache, thoughtfully crafted vegan, gluten-free options, irresistible pop-them-in-your-mouth minis. But there is one delectable twist that cupcake lovers have yet to explore: the savory cupcake. A natural evolution of the cupcake craze, savory cupcakes take the classic format and turn it on its head. Take out that pan and imagine the possibilities. Why not re-create the yummy flavors we remember from our childhoods—classic comfort foods like potpie, lasagna, meat loaf, and French toast—by reimagining them in a new format? Even better, let's add some savory bites inspired by newer family favorites, like curries from the local Indian restaurant, sushi from the place around the corner, and dishes with the irresistible bite of chiles and lemongrass from the neighborhood Thai restaurant. If you adore cupcakes, I invite you to revolutionize the family dinner, the potluck, or the elegant dinner party, while simultaneously rethinking portion size. In these self-contained packages, you can find a world of flavors shrunk down to the perfect size.

Even better, you can use the cupcake pan to your advantage financially. Small, uniform portions make it easier to avoid overeating, and they also reduce food waste. You know exactly how many portions you need for your family, so you can shop smarter and slim down the grocery bill. And since you're preparing only as much food as your family needs, you can say good-bye to the terrifying stacks of Tupperware filled with unidentifiable leftovers molding in the back of the fridge.

The cupcake pan can be used effectively to make the energizing yet flavorful meals we all want to eat. Using the pan as a palette, and cooking in smaller proportions, the home cook is able to pay more attention to flavor.

The diminished size of the meal concentrates taste so that each bite is appreciated instead of wolfed down. The savory cupcake is the perfect serving size—everything you want in the palm of your hand.

Adapt Ingredients to Your Needs

Use these recipes as a guide for creating your own personalized meals. I want you to be able to open the fridge, see which ingredients are available, and whip up a scrumptious meal for your family. Don't have Gouda? Use the mozzarella you have on hand instead. Trade fresh broccoli or cauliflower for the bag of frozen mixed vegetables all ready to go in your freezer. The recipe for pasta tarts on page 74 is a great example of how flexible the mini meal can be: It provides a main recipe that features smoked cheese and primavera sauce, then offers four delicious variations on the theme.

These recipes are also perfect candidates for the semi-homemade treatment. If you don't have the time—or energy—to prepare tomato sauce from scratch, open your favorite jarred sauce and use that instead. Choose the pre-made wrapper that most intrigues you—piecrust, lasagna noodle, puff pastry, egg roll—and combine it with a variety of ingredients.

Don't worry if you have twelve servings and only a few mouths to feed. Many of these dishes taste just as wonderful after being frozen and reheated in the oven or microwave. College students can share with roommates or freeze for quick meals between classes. Empty nesters can prepare a batch of meals and freeze the rest for the coming week. As for busy parents whose lives are always running full-steam ahead, why not double the recipe and make an extra batch of mini meals you can save for later?

Creating Family Meals

A recent experience finally connected the dots of my childhood experiences in the kitchen to my children's experience of cooking. One morning, I needed to test several of the meals in this book, so I put my children, ages eight and nine, in front of the television, an activity usually reserved for Saturday nights—at least it was a nature show!—while my hubby still slept. I was on a mission to create several meals in one day using this one-pan wonder.

By the time the show was over, I had one batch done and another one on the way into the oven. The children were getting hungry, so I whipped up mini meals for them as quickly as I could, hoping that feeding them would keep them occupied so I could concentrate on creating recipes. Well, that didn't work. I was at the point of waking up their dad when my daughter asked, "May I help? I'd like to make something."

I remembered when I was her age, hanging out in the kitchen watching my mother, who was always in a hurry to get the job done. That's why I never learned from her how to make bread; it's one of the more scientific baked goods to master and she simply didn't have the time to explain the nuances to me. However, she did teach me how to bake cakes and cookies and make other sweets like candies. My father was the savory chef in the family; from him I learned how to cook duck, make stocks and sauces, and cut homemade pasta. I enjoyed cooking with my parents and realized how much I wanted to create those fond memories with my children, too.

So, instead of keeping them out of the kitchen, I let my children help me put together a mini meal. So what if they measured an ingredient incorrectly and we had to start again? We spent all day in the kitchen together creating delicious food. I encouraged them to taste a variety of herbs and spices, citrus zests, and curries in different dishes. Right then and there, I started to infuse my children with a love of putting together flavors and textures and tastes. What started as a multitasking response to a trying day became a tradition: I was able to get dinner on the table and test recipes for this book, while the children made the bits and pieces of recipes that surprised all of us with just how tasty they were.

I have loved watching my children get a stepstool and drag it across the kitchen floor to the island or the stovetop. In the beginning, I taught them how to put bread in the toaster so they'd learn about heat. Stovetop cooking (with the heat on low) was a thrill, but I taught them to respect the flame and understand its dangers. When I introduced chopping, they started out using a plastic knife with a serrated edge to cut cucumbers, apples, and tomatoes. Their knife skills have advanced to using a paring knife, though still only under my watchful eyes. It takes them thirty-five minutes to cut three apples into a micro-fine dice, and they eat half of the pieces, but we have fun.

I hope these recipes—and the genius of the cupcake pan—will inspire you and your family to create some incredible savory meals together.

CHILDREN IN THE *Kitchen*

I teach my children about food not by telling them what is good for them or what they should eat, but by allowing them to make choices about the ingredients they use. Children know what they like to eat—just ask them—and they certainly know what they don't like, too! (My children love salmon, Brussels sprouts, spinach, peppers, tomatoes, cucumbers, and avocadoes.) When my children help me create mini meals, they select their favorite cheeses and vegetables in the colors they are attracted to. Then we line a cupcake pan with an edible wrapper, and they layer the cheese, meat, veggies, and sauce on top. When their mini meals come out of the oven, bubbling and smelling heavenly, they're excited beyond belief by this kitchen magic. They happily eat what they've cooked because they chose the ingredients, not me.

ESSENTIALS

Cupcake Pan

All of the recipes in this book were made using a 12-well classic cupcake pan. Each well will hold 4½ ounces (135 ml) of food, or ½ cup plus 1 tablespoon. All classic cupcake pans are not created equal, though. Vintage tins are smaller, and silicone molds can be larger or smaller. These recipes were not tested using Texas-size pans or mini cupcake pans, so those cannot be substituted for a classic pan. The simplest way for me to say it is: For the recipes in this book, use the size pan that your mother used to make cupcakes when you were growing up. With this essential tool, you'll have the power to make your family fresh, healthy, and delicious meals that are just the right size.

If you have an extra cupcake pan lying around, make meal preparation a bit more organized by placing each of the prepared and measured ingredients you'll need for the final dish into each well of the unused pan. When you are making savory bites that have sauces or condiments, like the Barbecued Pork Hand Pies with barbecue dipping sauce (page 192) or the Curried Vegetable Hand Pies with yogurt sauce (page 100), use the empty pan to hold the garnishes and sauces and allow your guests to serve themselves directly from the pan.

Wrappers

In most cases, the "wrappers" in this book are edible items that line the wells of the pan and hold the meal together. I used items found in pretty much every pantry for the wrappers. Your family and friends will be surprised and delighted when they see that the savory cupcake you serve them is wrapped in smoked salmon, which they can eat, rather than in a traditional paper or foil cupcake liner, which they could not! This is a "green" way to bake, as it cuts back on all the waste you'd create by using paper products. Here's a list of wrappers.

> **BACON AND CANADIAN BACON** Who doesn't love bacon? I certainly love it, and not just because it's delicious: It also happens to make an excellent wrapper. See how it's used in Pasta Bolognese al Forno (page 68).

> **BREAD** Thinly sliced sandwich breads are the perfect choice for lining cupcake pans, as you can see in the Mushroom & Potato Charlottes Topped with a Fried Egg (page 23). Most bread is too thick to fit in the cupcake pan wells, so I was ecstatic when I discovered Pepperidge Farm's Very Thin Breads, available in whole wheat and white, with thirty slices per package. If you are lucky enough to live near an excellent bakery, such as the La Brea Bakery in Los Angeles, order the Pain de Mie and ask the baker to slice it very thin.

> **EGG ROLL WRAPPERS** The egg roll wrapper is incredibly versatile. Open-faced, it gives you an edible bowl for fillings; when closed, it creates beautiful little packages. For the recipes in this book, egg roll wrappers work better than those made for wontons. While they are almost the same, the egg roll wrappers are much larger. Egg roll wrappers can be found in the refrigerated section of your grocery store and usually measure 4 inches (10 cm) square. Since you only need 12 for this recipe and most packages contain more, you can wrap the extras tightly in plastic wrap (otherwise, they'll dry out) and keep them in your fridge for up to 1 month. You can easily use them as the base for another savory meal—in fact, in some recipes, we use them in place of pie dough. The Egg Rolls with Sweet & Sour Crab (page 129) uses the open style, and the Short Ribs Braised with Mushroom, Onion & Bacon (page 182) uses the closed style.

> **EMPANADA DOUGH** A Mexican and Spanish specialty, empanadas are single-serving turnovers usually filled with a savory meat-and-vegetable filling. While traditional empanadas are certainly tasty, you'll find that their malleable dough makes a delicious wrapper for savory bites. Try it for the Beef Tamale Pies (page 189). Prepackaged empanada dough is available in the international foods section of your grocery store. I use Goya brand, which contains ten rounds per package.

> **GRAPE LEAVES, LEEKS, AND LETTUCES** Nature provides some of the best—and most delicious—wrappers, perfect for the cupcake pan. Grape leaves, leeks, and lettuces all do the job. Grape-Leaf Purses with Couscous & Lamb Stuffing (page 92) are just one of the irresistible ways to use them. Leeks can be cut into strips and used to line the wells of the pan to create a brilliant green wrapper for the Asparagus Mushroom Terrines (page 98).

> **PIE DOUGH** Handheld meat pies are portable, neat to eat, and reheatable—plus, they're just tasty! Vermont Chicken Potpies (page 159) are a great example of how to create beautiful little pies in a cupcake pan.

> **PUFF PASTRY** Puff pastry is a relative of phyllo dough (also spelled filo). The recipes in this book use puff pastry, which comes with the butter already folded into the dough. Phyllo dough, on the other hand, needs to be layered with melted butter to create a buttery crust. Puff pastry is the perfect wrapper for rich dishes like the Fig & Blue Cheese Tarts (page 44). When you use puff pastry as a wrapper, your oven temperature will need to be high, usually 400°F (205°C), to ensure that the pastry puffs as it should.

> **SAUSAGE PATTIES** Although they are always excellent for breakfast, these patties can be used to spice up meals at other times of the day, too. A sausage patty can be used whole as a base for the mini meal, or sausage can be crumbled to create a base, as in the Turkey, Apple & Sweet Potato Pies (page 176).

> **SMOKED SALMON** You wouldn't think fish would be a good wrapper, as it can become very flaky once cooked, but smoked salmon is the perfect solution if you want a seafood wrapper. Presliced to the perfect thickness, it's easy to use to line the wells of your cupcake pan, as I've done for the Smoked Salmon Egg Salad Sandwiches on Pumpernickel (page 137). It's even available cured with fresh herbs or cracked black pepper. Smoked salmon is especially salty due to the smoking process, so no additional salt is needed in recipes using this liner.

> **TORTILLAS** There are so many possibilities when using tortillas as wrappers. They're pliable and delicious, and since they are made from such basic ingredients, they adapt well to the flavor of whatever savory bites you're making. The Southwestern Beef Pies in Flour Tortillas (page 180) are a good example of the tortilla wrapper in action.

> **WAFFLES** In the breakfast world, waffles are king. They also make an excellent base for an assortment of mini meals, as you can see in the Wafflinis (page 37).

> **PLASTIC WRAP** Plastic wrap is used to line the pan when making aspics and terrines. While these dishes may sound complicated, they're really not. Aspics are simply savory

items encased in a savory gelatin. Terrines are similar to pâté in that they are compressed into a mold, but here the ingredients are chopped coarsely before being pressed into a compact form. For these chilled, no-bake items, line the wells of the cupcake pan by overlapping two long pieces of plastic wrap along the center of the pan, leaving at least a 3-inch (7.5-cm) border on all sides of the pan; this extra plastic will create handles that make it easy for you to unpan the bites. Press the plastic firmly into each well to create cups, then fill the wells with the ingredients. Cover the pan in another layer of plastic, place a second cupcake pan on top to compress the savory meals, then chill as the recipe instructs, for several hours or overnight. See the Aspics with Roasted Peppers, Eggplant & Spinach (page 122) for an example.

Unpanning Meals

There are various ways to unpan your savory bites. Mini meals made with dough wrappers, such as pie or empanada dough, puff pastry, or tortillas, will simply pop out of the pan after you have loosened the edges of each well with a table knife. Those made with cheese and eggs require a gentler approach: Use a table knife to loosen the sides and then slip the tines of a fork between the pan and each meal to lift it out. Do not invert the pan unless the recipe directs you to use this method.

The wells of the cupcake pan are lined with plastic wrap in recipes for terrines and aspics, to keep the mini meals from sticking to the pan (see "Plastic Wrap," at left, for instructions). To unpan, remove the top layer of plastic wrap, then lift up on the edges of the plastic wrap lining the wells of the pan to remove the terrines. They will pop out of the wells easily.

Ingredients

When making out your grocery list for the week, take a look at which recipes you want to make; then browse through your pantry and poke around in the fridge and freezer to see what you already have that could work just as well—and maybe even better.

One tasty point to keep in mind when purchasing ingredients: The cupcake pan makes the perfect portion size, so there's no need to sacrifice rich ingredients to cut calories. By cutting out overeating, you generally eliminate more calories than you would add by using a touch of real cream, butter, and cheese in a recipe. Yes, cheese too. This is why Europeans are so lean: They eat the real deal in small packages.

> **SMART BALANCE® OLIVE OIL SPRAY** Cooks no longer have to use butter or vegetable shortening to grease pans like their grandmothers did. I use cooking spray because it is convenient, and very little is required to coat the wells of the pan. This trims both fat and calories. Any nonstick spray works for my savory bites, but I like Smart Balance Olive Oil Spray because it's heart healthy (and vegan, by the way). I use it for all of the cupcakes at my SweetBy-Holly stores.

Silpat: **Speaking of greasing pans, one of the best items to use with sheet pans is a Silpat mat, a nonstick silicone baking mat. There are many benefits to these reusable mats, which do not have to be greased, not the least of which is reduced mess and less waste. Silpat mats are available at kitchen-supply stores.**

> **GELATIN** When I say gelatin, I'm not talking about the bright, sugary concoctions that jiggle for all they're worth. Unflavored gelatin is a thickening agent made from beef, veal, and pig proteins, and is the basis for an under-appreciated specialty: aspic (see page 13). When purchasing gelatin, make sure it is unflavored, or you might get an unpleasant surprise once the meal is prepared.

If you're looking for kosher or vegan alternatives to gelatin, try these options: Lieber's, Carmel, or KoJel kosher brands. The most common vegan substitute, agar-agar, is made from seaweed. You can make any of the aspics and other recipes in this book that call for gelatin with agar-agar instead.

> **GENERAL INGREDIENTS** In addition to the pantry staples described above, keep these fresh and canned ingredients on hand to give you plenty of options when you're feeling spontaneous.

- **Artichoke hearts, canned**
- **Beans, an assortment of canned varieties**
- **Fish, vegetable, beef, and poultry broths or bases (I use Better Than Bouillon brand)**
- **Capers**
- **Cheese, an assortment of grated and sliced types**
- **Roasted peppers**
- **Olives**
- **Pine nuts**
- **Plum tomatoes, canned**
- **Sun-dried tomatoes**

> **GOURMET GARDEN® HERBS AND OTHER AROMATICS FROM A TUBE** I love accenting meals with fresh herbs, but they aren't always available in my area and certainly not year-round. And, unfortunately, not everyone has the time or space to plant an herb garden. Instead of buying expen-sive little packets of quickly wilting basil, you can purchase a variety of commonly used herbs and aromatics—like garlic, ginger, basil, oregano, and cilantro—in squeezable tubes. Gourmet Garden's 4-ounce tubes contain twenty-three cloves of garlic, or twenty-one pieces of ginger, or three bunches of Italian herbs, basil, cilantro, or parsley. They're also gluten-free, made with organic ingredients, have no added flavors or colors, and are long-lasting (the "use by" date is printed on the cap). In addition to using them in the recipes in this book, use them to make drinks, soups, and sauces. I even spread them on bread when I make sandwiches.

And since the herbs come prechopped or pregrated in the squeezable tubes, they take away a lot of the prep work required when you're cooking with fresh aromatics and herbs—washing, chopping, stemming, mincing. They stay fresh a lot longer than the parsley languishing in the bottom of your fridge. A total win-win!

One thing to note: It's best to follow the guide on the tube to make sure you don't overseason the dish. If you're not sure about how much to use, go easy on the herb—you can always add more. Gourment Garden tubes advise that 1 tablespoon is equivalent to 1 tablespoon of fresh chopped herbs or aromatics.

^ SAVORY APPLE TARTS

chapter

>ONE<

BREAKFAST

I ALWAYS TELL MY CHILDREN TO POWER UP IN THE MORNING!

My husband pulls together breakfast for our family, but I like to help out by having some savory mini meals ready for him to reheat in the oven or bake fresh for the children come morning so that when they wake up, they have a warm, sometimes sweet, sometimes savory meal to start the day on an upbeat note.

The savory breakfast bites that follow are so convenient, you can have them ready within an hour, or even sooner if you bake them the night before and reheat them in the A.M. It beats pulling out the cereal box every morning and gives your family a chance to sit down together before dashing off in different directions. Most of the meals in this book can be prepped the day before and placed in the refrigerator, unbaked, until you are ready to bake them the following day. (I've specified if a meal should not be prepped the night before—some ingredients can get soggy!)

My children love the Apple Sausage Breakfast Cakes (page 18) and the Egg Mini Muffins (page 39) because they are filled with their favorite flavors. I love them because I wanted to find a simpler way to make breakfast using ingredients already in my pantry and freezer, staples that make meals better, faster, smarter, and tastier.

Many of these dishes can be eaten out of hand, so a good breakfast is still possible on the busiest of days. And you have the benefit of starting your morning with something that doesn't come from a drive-through window. These mini breakfasts are a portable feast! Don't limit these recipes to just breakfast, either. An assortment of these mini meals makes a great brunch for a large gathering of people.

Apple Sausage
BREAKFAST
>CANES<

OVEN: 350°F (175°C) > PREP TIME: 1 hour >
BAKING TIME: 20 to 25 minutes > YIELD: 12 cakes

FOR THE MAPLE-GLAZED APPLES

⅓ cup (75 ml) pure maple syrup

1 tablespoon brandy

½ teaspoon cinnamon

⅛ teaspoon ground cloves

⅛ teaspoon freshly grated nutmeg

Pinch of kosher salt

8 large Granny Smith or other favorite tart apples, peeled, cored, and cut into ¼-inch (6-mm) dice

FOR THE CORNMEAL AND CURRANT CAKE

1 cup (125 g) all-purpose flour

½ cup (80 g) yellow cornmeal

3 tablespoons sugar

2 teaspoons baking powder

1 teaspoon baking soda

⅛ teaspoon kosher salt

⅓ cup (50 g) dried currants

1¼ cups (300 ml) whole-milk yogurt

2 large eggs

½ cup (1 stick / 115 g) unsalted butter, melted and cooled

FOR THE ASSEMBLY

Nonstick cooking spray, for the pan

3 tablespoons unsalted butter, softened

¼ cup (55 g) packed light brown sugar

12 ounces (340 g) fully cooked chicken apple sausage, cut into ¼-inch (6-mm) dice

4 teaspoons maple sugar or brown sugar, plus more for serving

¾ cup (180 ml) pure maple syrup, warmed, for serving

APPLES AND CHICKEN SAUSAGE in cornmeal cake look so elegant. This mini meal resembles pineapple upside-down cake or apple tarte tatin, but the variety of tastes and textures make it something completely different. Everyone has a favorite apple, but I suggest using Granny Smith because of its firm texture, which is retained after it cooks. As alternatives, use Pink Lady or Honeycrisp apples. The recipe for Maple-Glazed Apples makes about twice as much as you need, so you can bathe the Cornmeal and Currant Cake in as much of it as you like. I also love to use the apples as a topping for waffles or oatmeal, on toast, mixed with yogurt, or even just as a yummy dessert.

Make Ahead **This recipe can be assembled in the pan the night before, refrigerated, and then popped into the oven in the morning for a freshly baked, hassle-free breakfast.**

> **MAKE THE MAPLE-GLAZED APPLES**

In a 12-quart (12-L) stockpot, combine 2 cups (480 ml) of water, the maple syrup, brandy, cinnamon, cloves, nutmeg, and salt, and bring to a boil. Boil for 3 minutes, then add the apples. Lower the heat to medium and simmer, stirring occasionally, until thickened, about 30 minutes. The mixture should be chunky and the apples should hold their shape. Transfer to a medium bowl and let cool slightly, about 20 minutes.

> **MAKE THE CORNMEAL AND CURRANT CAKE**

In a large bowl, whisk together the flour, cornmeal, sugar, baking powder, baking soda, salt, and currants.

In a separate bowl, stir together the yogurt and eggs. Add the yogurt mixture and the cooled, melted butter to the dry ingredients and mix until just incorporated.

> ASSEMBLE AND BAKE THE CAKES

Preheat the oven to 350°F (175°C). Spray a 12-well classic cupcake pan generously with nonstick cooking spray.

In a small bowl, mix the butter with the brown sugar. Spread the butter-sugar mixture evenly in the bottom of each well of the pan. Place 1 tablespoon of the glazed apples on top, then add a layer of sausage, distributing it evenly among the 12 wells. Mound ¼ cup (60 ml) of the cornmeal batter in each well and sprinkle with ¼ teaspoon of the maple sugar. Bake until cooked through and golden brown around the edges, 20 to 25 minutes.

Let the cakes cool in the pan for 10 minutes, then loosen the sides of each cake with a table knife and invert the cakes onto a sheet pan. Some of the apples may stick to the pan, but they are easily removed with a small spoon. Plate the cakes individually, drizzled with warm maple syrup and garnished with more maple sugar.

Store the cakes in an airtight container in the refrigerator for up to 5 days. Reheat, wrapped in tin foil, for 15 minutes at 350°F (175°C).

VARIATION For a muffinlike dish, mix ¾ cup (170 g) of the maple-glazed apples and sausage into the batter. Pour the batter into each well of the pan, then top with ¼ teaspoon of maple sugar. Bake at 350°F (175°C) until golden brown and a toothpick inserted in the top comes out with a few moist crumbs, 25 to 30 minutes. Serve with a dollop of maple butter: ¼ cup (½ stick / 60 g) salted butter, softened, beaten with ¼ cup (60 ml) of maple syrup.

> MEXICAN <
Breakfast
ROLLS

OVEN: 350°F (175°C) > **PREP TIME:** 40 minutes >
BAKING TIME: 45 minutes > **YIELD:** 24 rolls

- 1 pound (455 g) spicy pork sausage, or turkey sausage, casings removed
- 1 tablespoon extra-virgin olive oil
- 1 pound (455 g) frozen hash browns
- ½ teaspoon chili powder
- Pinch each of kosher salt and freshly ground black pepper
- 1 (15-ounce / 430-g) package ready-made pie dough (2 rounds), at room temperature

- ¼ cup (20 g) fresh cilantro leaves, chopped, or ¼ cup (60 ml) cilantro from a tube
- 1 cup (225 g) refried beans
- ⅔ cup (150 ml) ready-made salsa
- 1 cup (225 g) grated pepper Jack cheese
- Nonstick cooking spray, for the pan

VARIATIONS Filling and rolling up breakfast rolls is a great project for children. You and the children can try these filling variations or make your own signature rolls.

- SAGE BREAKFAST SAUSAGE, sautéed onion with diced apples, and cheddar
- CRISPY BACON, sautéed mushrooms and peppers, tomato sauce, and provolone
- THIN SLICES OF SERRANO HAM, pesto, mozzarella, and sun-dried tomatoes
- NUTELLA with a layer of your favorite granola, some raisins, and a sprinkling of cinnamon-sugar

MY SAVORY BREAKFAST ROLLS evolved from a childhood love of making cinnamon rolls. My mother had her own special recipe for sweet rolls, and she almost always included me in the process. She'd let me help roll the yeast dough, then sprinkle it with cinnamon and sugar. I never have time to make yeast dough now, but I like how well savory ingredients rolled into dough works with the cupcake pan. At my home, this savory roll recipe is a child-friendly adventure in baking, especially since it calls for several store-bought items. Present the ingredients in individual bowls—or in the wells of an extra cupcake pan—to make layering fun and easy for your children.

Make Ahead **These rolls should not be prepared the night before and baked the next day—the liquid in the salsa will prevent the pie dough from baking correctly. They can, however, be baked the night before and reheated, wrapped in tin foil, for 15 minutes at 350°F (175°C).**

Cook the sausage in a 12-inch (30-cm) nonstick skillet over medium heat, using a wooden spoon to break up the sausage, until it is well browned and crumbled, about 15 minutes. Drain the meat in a fine-mesh colander over a bowl, continuing to break up the sausage in the colander to release additional grease. Transfer to a medium bowl. Wipe the skillet out with a paper towel when cool enough to handle.

Add the oil to the skillet, then add the hash browns in an even layer. Press down firmly with a heatproof spatula, then let the potatoes cook undisturbed over medium heat until they begin to brown on the bottom, about 8 minutes. Sprinkle the top of the hash browns with the chili powder and salt and pepper. Cook for about 15 minutes longer, using the spatula to occasionally scrape the bottom of the pan and turn over the hash browns, until they are browned on all sides. Transfer to another medium bowl.

Preheat the oven to 350°F (175°C). Spray a 12-well classic cupcake pan with nonstick cooking spray.

RECIPE CONTINUES

Unroll one of the rounds of pie dough onto a cutting board large enough to fit the entire round. Leaving a ½-inch (1-cm) border, sprinkle the dough with 2 tablespoons fresh cilantro, or using a table knife, evenly spread the cilantro paste onto the dough. Top with half of each of the following: refried beans, browned sausage, salsa, hash browns, and grated cheese.

Roll the pie dough into a log, starting on one side and rolling tightly to keep all the filling inside. With a serrated knife, gently slice the log into six 2-inch-thick (5-cm) pieces, making sure not to lose any of the filling as you cut.

Arrange the pieces of filled dough, cut-sides up, in the wells of the pan and press down gently to fill each hole. Repeat the process with the second round of dough and remaining ingredients.

Bake until cooked through and golden brown around the edges, 35 to 45 minutes. Let the rolls cool in the pan for 5 minutes, then loosen the sides of each roll with a table knife and pop them out of the pan. These breakfast rolls can be eaten out of hand, plated with a side of guacamole, sour cream, and additional salsa, or served as a brunch alongside your favorite morning eggs and sliced fruit or a yogurt parfait. My children enjoy them as a meal with a side of beans, guacamole, and a salad of fresh corn, tomatoes, and cucumbers.

Store the rolls in an airtight container in the refrigerator for up to 5 days. Reheat, wrapped in tin foil, for 15 minutes at 350°F (175°C).

MUSHROOM & POTATO
CHARLOTTES
Topped with a Fried Egg

OVEN: 350°F (175°C) > PREP TIME: 1 hour 25 minutes >
BAKING TIME: 25 minutes > YIELD: 12 charlottes

FOR THE MUSHROOM AND POTATO HASH

3 tablespoons unsalted butter

2 leeks, washed, light green and white parts thinly sliced

2 medium russet potatoes, peeled and cut into ¼-inch (6-mm) dice

14 ounces (400 g) mixed fresh mushrooms, such as portobello, shiitake, morel, porcini, oyster, baby bello, or button, roughly chopped

2 tablespoons snipped fresh Italian parsley or parsley from a tube

1 tablespoon snipped fresh tarragon

¼ teaspoon kosher salt

¼ teaspoon freshly ground black pepper

1½ cups (360 ml) whole milk

3 large eggs, lightly beaten

FOR THE ASSEMBLY

½ cup (1 stick / 115 g) salted butter, softened

15 thin slices white bread, such as Pepperidge Farm's Very Thin White Bread

Nonstick cooking spray, for the pan

FOR THE MORNAY SAUCE

¾ teaspoon kosher salt

1 small shallot, chopped

1 large clove garlic, peeled, or 1 tablespoon garlic from a tube

2 tablespoons chopped fresh flat-leaf parsley

5 fresh basil leaves

1 tablespoon fresh thyme leaves

2 tablespoons unsalted butter

1½ tablespoons all-purpose flour

1 cup (240 ml) whole milk

1 cup (240 ml) half-and-half

1 bay leaf

Pinch of white pepper

1 tablespoon dry sherry

1 teaspoon Worcestershire sauce

½ cup (60 g) grated cheddar

FOR THE PRESENTATION

12 eggs, cooked sunny-side up

LEGEND CLAIMS these traditional baked puddings were named for Queen Charlotte, an eighteenth-century British ruler famous for her love of apples. I love apple charlottes, too, but using savory ingredients instead of sweet is a fun way to update the traditional version. Whichever flavors you choose, it's always a surprise to see the finished creations when they come out of the oven. In this savory rendition, I used fresh shiitake, oyster, and baby bello mushrooms, but a mixture of your favorites would work equally well.

Make Ahead These charlottes should not be prepared the night before and baked the next day; the bread will get soggy. The mushroom and potato hash, however, can be prepared the night before, refrigerated, and used in the assembly the next day.

> MAKE THE MUSHROOM AND POTATO HASH

In a large skillet, melt 2 tablespoons of the butter over medium heat; add the leeks and cook until wilted, about 2 minutes. Add the potatoes and cook until tender, using a metal spatula to turn them over when they turn golden brown, about 30 minutes. Transfer to a large bowl.

Wipe out the skillet and melt the remaining 1 tablespoon of butter over medium heat. Add the mushrooms and cook until tender, stirring occasionally, about 20 minutes. Remove from the heat and stir in the parsley, tarragon, salt, and pepper. Mix well to combine. Add half of the mushroom mixture to the cooled potato mixture; reserve the remaining mushrooms in the skillet. Stir the milk and eggs into the mushroom and potato mixture in the bowl.

> ASSEMBLE AND BAKE THE CHARLOTTES

Preheat the oven to 350°F (175°C). Spray a 12-well classic cupcake pan with nonstick cooking spray.

Butter the bread slices on one side with the salted butter, using the entire stick. Cut 3 of the slices into quarters and place one quarter, buttered side down, in each well. Cut the 12 remaining slices in half lengthwise.

RECIPE CONTINUES

Line the sides of each well with 2 halves of bread in cross formation to form a shell. Tuck in the bread to fill the gaps between the bottom and sides of the wells. There may be small spaces where the pan shows through and the edges of the bread may peek over the top of the pan.

Divide the hash evenly among the wells. Place one of the reserved mushrooms on top of each charlotte as a garnish. Bake until cooked through and golden brown on the edges, about 25 minutes.

> MAKE THE MORNAY SAUCE

In the bowl of a small food processor, combine the salt, shallot, garlic, parsley, basil, and thyme; pulse until coarse. Set aside.

In a medium saucepan, melt the butter over medium heat, then add the flour and whisk until a thick paste forms, about 2 minutes. Add the milk, half-and-half, and bay leaf and continue whisking until the sauce thickens, about 10 minutes. Stir in the reserved shallot and herb mixture, white pepper, sherry, Worcestershire, and cheese, whisking until smooth. Remove and discard the bay leaf. Cover and keep warm.

Let the charlottes cool in the pan for 5 to 10 minutes, then loosen the sides of each charlotte with a table knife and insert the tines of a fork between the pan and each charlotte to lift it out. Gorgeous! Just before serving, fry the eggs and reheat the reserved mushrooms; set the mushrooms aside in a serving dish. Serve the charlottes individually, with Mornay sauce spooned over each. Top each savory bite with a fried egg and serve the mushrooms alongside.

Savory PUDDING

> CHARLOTTES <

OVEN: 350°F (175°C) > PREP TIME: 30 minutes >
BAKING TIME: 25 to 30 minutes > YIELD: 12 charlottes

1 tablespoon unsalted butter

1 small onion, finely chopped

1¼ cups (125 g) fresh
mushrooms, any type,
chopped into medium
pieces

½ bunch thin asparagus,
ends trimmed, sliced
crosswise into ½-inch
(1-cm) pieces

1 teaspoon chopped fresh
oregano

2 teaspoons fresh thyme
leaves, or ¾ teaspoon
dried thyme, crumbled

½ teaspoon kosher salt

¼ teaspoon freshly ground
black pepper

¼ cup (½ stick / 60 g) salted
butter

12 thin slices white bread,
such as Pepperidge Farm's
Very Thin White Bread

½ cup (50 g) grated
Parmesan

2 cups (225 g) mixed grated
cheese, such as any
combination of provolone,
Swiss, Jack, Parmesan, or
Gouda

4 large eggs, beaten

1 cup (240 ml) half-and-half
or whole milk

3 tablespoons snipped chives

I'VE ADDED SAVORY NOTES to these puddings by incorporating vegetables—onions, asparagus, and mushrooms—instead of fruit. One thing I love about creating savory meals in a cupcake pan is it offers you a beginning and end to the meal in one perfect bundle. At that last bite, you'll be asking yourself when you can have another.

Preheat the oven to 350°F (175°C). In a 10-inch (25-cm) sauté pan, melt the butter over low heat. Add the onion and mushrooms and sauté until the onions are softened and moisture has been released, about 10 minutes. Add the asparagus and sauté until bright green, about 3 minutes more. Stir in the oregano, thyme, salt, and pepper; turn off the heat.

Butter each of the bread slices on one side with the salted butter, using the entire ½ stick. Sprinkle the grated Parmesan onto the slices and gently press the cheese so it sticks to the butter. Line the wells of a 12-well classic cupcake pan with the slices of bread, buttered side down. Firmly press the bread into the wells and tuck in any edges that still poke up, so that when you fill the wells with the egg mixture, all of the bread will be soaked.

Top the bread in each well with 1 heaping tablespoon of the mixed cheese. Evenly distribute the vegetable mixture among the wells, and then add another heaping tablespoon of cheese. Whisk the half-and-half into the beaten eggs, then pour about ¼ cup (60 ml) of the egg mixture into each well, pushing the bread down a bit as you go to make room. Sprinkle the tops of the charlottes with the chives.

Bake until puffed on the top and golden brown around the edges, 25 to 30 minutes.

Let the charlottes cool in the pan for 5 to 10 minutes, then loosen the sides of each charlotte with a table knife and insert the tines of a fork between the pan and each charlotte to lift it out. The bottoms will be soft like pudding and the tops will be golden and crispy.

FRENCH *Toasters*

OVEN: 325°F (165°C) > PREP TIME: 15 minutes >
BAKING TIME: 35 minutes > YIELD: 12 toasters

Nonstick cooking spray, for the pan

1 cup (220 g) packed light brown sugar

6 tablespoons (¾ stick / 90 g) salted butter

½ teaspoon cinnamon, plus extra for dusting

9 thin slices white, wheat, or cinnamon-raisin bread, such as Pepperidge Farm's Very Thin Bread

8 large eggs

1½ cups (360 ml) whole milk

2 teaspoons pure vanilla extract

VARIATIONS Top the toasters with maple syrup or smother them with hazelnut-chocolate spread. Better yet, add these goodies to the layers before you bake! Or top the toasters with sliced bananas sautéed in butter until browned and omit the caramel sauce topping.

THE GENIUS OF THESE MINI MEALS is in their simplicity. The classic French toast flavor survives, but the cupcake pan offers a twist: toasted bread on top with a custard center and caramel base. But that's just the beginning! There are so many flavor options: Use cinnamon-raisin or whole wheat bread, or top the toasters with fresh fruit or another delicious topping, such as hazelnut-chocolate spread or flavored cream cheese. I like to prepare these toasters the night before and refrigerate them so my husband can toss them in the oven come morning, just in time for the children's appearance at the breakfast table.

Preheat the oven to 325°F (165°C) if baking immediately. Spray a 12-well classic cupcake pan generously with nonstick cooking spray.

In a small saucepan, combine the brown sugar, 3 tablespoons of the butter, and the cinnamon. Cook over medium heat, stirring occasionally, until the mixture reaches a caramel-like consistency, about 8 minutes. Pour 1 tablespoon of the caramel sauce into each well of the prepared pan. Reserve the remaining caramel.

Butter the bread on one side only with the remaining 3 tablespoons of butter. Cut each slice of bread into quarters.

In a medium bowl, beat the eggs and milk with the vanilla. Working in batches, soak the bread in the egg and milk mixture until soft, making sure it is fully soaked but not to the point of falling apart. Layer 3 pieces of bread on top of the caramel in each well. Using a large spoon, evenly fill each well with the egg mixture remaining in the bowl.

Bake until golden brown, 35 minutes. Loosen the sides of each toaster with a table knife and pop them out of the pan. Place them on serving plates and drizzle about 1 tablespoon of the remaining caramel sauce on top, then dust with the cinnamon.

Store the French toasters in an airtight container in the refrigerator for up to 5 days. Reheat, wrapped in tin foil, for 15 minutes at 350°F (175°C).

Spanish
TORTILLAS

OVEN: 350°F (175°C) > PREP TIME: 25 minutes >
BAKING TIME: 20 to 25 minutes > YIELD: 12 tortillas

Nonstick cooking spray, for the pan

6 frozen hash brown potato patties, from a 16-ounce (455-g) package

6 large eggs

¼ cup (60 ml) ready-made pesto

Freshly ground black pepper

1 cup (100 g) button mushrooms, finely chopped

1 (6-ounce / 170-g) jar roasted red peppers, finely chopped, or 1 small red bell pepper, finely chopped and sautéed to soften

1 medium zucchini, cut into ¼-inch (6-mm) dice

6 ounces (170 g) fontina, cut into ¼-inch (6-mm) dice

10 fresh basil leaves, cut into ribbons

1 small bunch fresh chives, snipped into ⅛-inch (3-mm) pieces

¾ cup (75 g) grated Parmesan

VARIATION For a beautiful presentation, serve each tortilla on top of creamy tomato sauce with a crostini on the side. To prepare the crostini, toast or grill 12 slices of Italian bread, rub with fresh garlic, drizzle with olive oil, and sprinkle with coarse salt.

THE MIXTURE OF FLAVORS in this breakfast— peppers, zucchini, mushrooms, potatoes, and basil—gives it a truly Spanish flair. While many Americans think of flatbread when they hear "tortilla," in Spain, the word also refers to a potato-based omelet. My version, designed for the cupcake pan, is equally as delicious as the original, with the Parmesan forming a flavorful crusty topping. Olé!

Make Ahead These tortillas can be assembled the night before, refrigerated, and baked the next day.

Preheat the oven to 350°F (175°C). Spray a 12-well classic cupcake pan with nonstick cooking spray.

Cut the hash brown patties in half and place 1 half in each well of the pan, trimming them to fit as needed.

In a medium bowl, beat the eggs with a fork and stir in the pesto along with a few grinds of black pepper. Add the mushrooms, roasted peppers, zucchini, and fontina to the eggs and mix well. Divide the egg mixture evenly among the wells of the pan.

Sprinkle the basil and chives over each well and top with the Parmesan. Bake until golden on top, 20 to 25 minutes. The eggs will be a bit jiggly when you remove them from the oven; don't worry—they will continue to cook while they cool in the pan.

Let the tortillas cool in the pan for 5 minutes. (Do not let them rest longer that that, as the eggs will begin to sweat.) Then loosen the sides of each tortilla with a table knife and insert the tines of a fork between the pan and each tortilla to lift it out. Serve the tortillas with your favorite toast and preserves and a variety of sausages and crispy bacon alongside.

Store the tortillas in an airtight container in the refrigerator for up to 5 days. Reheat, wrapped in tin foil, for 15 minutes at 350ºF (175ºC).

Savory Tidbit When I visited Spain, my hosts always made me a tortilla in the morning. We would all gather in the kitchen to watch as the cook flipped the tortillas: First, he gently—and then briskly—shook the pan to loosen the egg mixture. Then, he dramatically flipped the contents of the pan. The tortilla would shoot up into the air and he would catch it in the pan on its way back down. What was once the top became the bottom, so all of the tortilla was browned to a delicious finish.

Tomato-Basil
CHARLOTTES

OVEN: 300°F and 350°F (150°C and 175°C) > **PREP TIME:** 20 minutes > **BAKING TIME:** 2 hours > **YIELD:** 12 charlottes

FOR THE TOMATO CONFIT

6 plum tomatoes, halved lengthwise

2 cloves garlic, sliced

½ cup (120 ml) extra-virgin olive oil

Kosher salt

3 sprigs fresh thyme

FOR THE CUSTARD

4 large eggs

1 cup (240 ml) whole milk

½ teaspoon kosher salt

¼ teaspoon freshly ground black pepper

FOR THE ASSEMBLY

1 tablespoon unsalted butter

1 medium yellow onion, cut into ¼-inch (6-mm) dice

Nonstick cooking spray, for the pan

1 tube (4 ounces / 115 g) basil, or ½ cup (120 ml) ready-made pesto

15 thin slices white bread, such as Pepperidge Farm's Very Thin White Bread

1½ cups (170 g) shredded mozzarella

¼ cup (25 g) grated Parmesan

THIS IS A MULTIPURPOSE DISH: The custard makes it suitable for breakfast, while the tomato confit makes it a meal for any time of day. From the sweetness of the onions to the richness of the tomatoes, the flavors in these charlottes are outrageously good. They're sure to become a family favorite.

When preparing these mini meals, make sure to use cow's-milk mozzarella; buffalo mozzarella has too much moisture. As for the roasted tomatoes, you might find some already packed in oil at the better gourmet markets. If you do purchase them from a store, the tomatoes will be in quarter slices, so make sure to buy twenty-four pieces.

Make Ahead The tomato confit can be prepared in advance and stored, covered in a layer of olive oil, in an airtight container in the refrigerator until needed. It will last for up to 2 weeks.

> MAKE THE TOMATO CONFIT

Preheat the oven to 300°F (150°C). In a medium bowl, toss the tomatoes and garlic with the oil to coat and season with salt. Line a rimmed baking sheet with a Silpat mat or aluminum foil for easy cleanup. Transfer the tomato mixture to the lined baking sheet, spreading out the tomatoes so they do not overlap. Tuck the thyme sprigs underneath the tomatoes.

Roast the tomatoes until they have caramelized and are just beginning to dehydrate, about 1½ hours. If they begin to caramelize too quickly, lower your oven temperature to 275°F (135°C). Remove the confit from the oven and set it aside.

> MAKE THE CUSTARD

Raise the oven temperature to 350°F (175°C). In a medium bowl, beat the eggs with the milk, salt, and pepper. Set aside.

> ASSEMBLE AND BAKE THE CHARLOTTES

In a medium skillet over medium heat, melt the butter. Add the onion and cook, stirring occasionally, until translucent, about 3 minutes. Remove from the heat.

Spray a 12-well classic cupcake pan with nonstick cooking spray. Spread 1½ teaspoons basil paste or pesto on each slice of bread. Cut 3 of the slices into quarters and place one quarter, basil side up, in each well. Cut the 12 remaining slices in half lengthwise. Line the sides of each well with 2 halves of bread in cross formation to form a shell. Tuck in the bread to fill the gaps between the bottom and sides of the wells. There may be small spaces where the pan shows through, and the edges of the bread may peek over the top of the pan.

Divide the mozzarella evenly among the wells of the pan. Top the cheese in each well with 1 tablespoon of the sautéed onions. Divide the custard evenly among the wells. Top each charlotte with a tomato half from the confit and sprinkle each with 1 teaspoon of Parmesan. Bake until cooked through and golden brown on the edges, 25 to 30 minutes.

Let the charlottes cool in the pan for 10 minutes, then loosen the sides of each charlotte with a table knife and insert the tines of a fork between the pan and each charlotte to lift it out.

SAVORY
Apple Tarts

OVEN: 350°F (175°C) › **PREP TIME:** 35 minutes ›
BAKING TIME: 40 to 45 minutes › **YIELD:** 12 tarts

SAVORY, SLIGHTLY SWEET, and a little tangy, these tarts combine the best of fall's bounty. They're like a dream-come-true version of the classic American apple pie, but transformed into a savory tart that is baked in an all-American kitchen tool: the cupcake pan. Don't worry if your tarts don't look perfect; that's one of the charms of these bites. We are not trying to create perfectly filled little pies here. The asymmetrical nature of the dough placement in this recipe gives a one-of-a-kind feel to each of the tarts. Invite your children to lend a hand with these: I let mine peel the apples and layer them in the wells of the pan.

Make Ahead **The apple filling can be prepared up to 2 days in advance and stored in an airtight container in the refrigerator until needed. It will last for up to 1 week. The tarts can also be assembled 1 day in advance and baked the following day.**

FOR THE APPLE FILLING

4 Granny Smith apples, peeled, halved, and cored

2 tablespoons walnut oil (see Notes)

½ large shallot, finely chopped

Kosher salt and freshly ground black pepper

⅓ cup (75 g) packed light brown sugar

¼ teaspoon freshly grated nutmeg

FOR THE CHEDDAR WALNUT TOPPING

1½ cups (175 g) grated sharp white cheddar

¼ cup (65 g) turbinado sugar (or substitute granulated or brown sugar)

½ cup (60 g) finely chopped walnuts (see Notes)

2 tablespoons unsalted butter

¼ cup (30 g) whole wheat flour

FOR THE ASSEMBLY

Nonstick cooking spray, for the pan

1 (15-ounce / 430-g) package ready-made pie dough (2 rounds), at room temperature

2 tablespoons fresh rosemary, finely chopped, or 1 scant tablespoon dried rosemary, finely ground (but not powdered) in a spice mill

› **MAKE THE APPLE FILLING**

Cut each apple half into 6 wedges, then cut crosswise into ½-inch (1-cm) pieces. Heat the walnut oil in a 10-inch (25-cm) skillet over medium heat. Add the apples and shallot and season with a pinch of salt and a few grinds of black pepper. Cook the apple mixture, stirring occasionally, until tender, about 5 minutes. Turn off the heat and add the brown sugar and nutmeg, stirring to coat. Let the mixture cool, allowing time for the juices in the pan to macerate the filling, about 20 minutes.

› **MAKE THE CHEDDAR WALNUT TOPPING**

In a small bowl, combine the cheddar, sugar, and walnuts. Mix in the butter, then incorporate the flour just until combined.

Notes Walnut oil adds a nutty flavor to the filling that complements the cheddar walnut topping. If you prefer, you can use another oil that you have on hand (I like using nut oils).

Chop the walnuts by hand. When a fine texture is needed, it's too easy to overprocess nuts in a food processor, turning finely chopped nuts into flour.

> ASSEMBLE AND BAKE THE TARTS

Preheat the oven to 350°F (175°C). Spray a 12-well classic cupcake pan with nonstick cooking spray.

Unroll the pie dough onto a flat work surface; no need to flour it first. Evenly sprinkle half of the rosemary onto each of the rounds, pressing the rosemary gently into the dough. Cut each round of dough in half, and then cut each half into even thirds for a total of 12 pieces. Working quickly, place one piece of dough, rosemary side down, in each well of the prepared pan, letting the edges of the dough overhang the pan.

Fill each well with a heaping ¼ cup (55 g) of the apple mixture. If you have any left over, go back and add it to the wells. (Do not press down.) Top each tart with ¼ cup (55 g) of the walnut topping, then gently fold in the excess dough; don't press down to seal—just keep this loose. You will now see why the rosemary was sprinkled on the outside of the dough: It is revealed here on the fold over and will add *another* dimension—the scent of rosemary—when you unpan the tarts.

Bake until the crust is golden brown and the juices are bubbling, 40 to 45 minutes, then loosen the sides of each tart with a table knife and insert the tines of a fork between the pan and each tart to lift it out. Serve the tarts warm.

Store the tarts in an airtight container in the refrigerator for up to 5 days. Reheat, wrapped in tin foil, for 15 minutes at 350°F (175°C).

Savory Tidbit **Select your favorite apple-and-herb combination to create a one-of-a-kind taste your family will love. I like to use sharp white Grafton cheddar in the topping, as it reminds me of fall foliage in Vermont. Some of the flavors in this book are inspired by my experiences with food there.**

Three-Cheese TARTS
WITH PEAR & FIG COMPOTE

OVEN: 350°F (175°C) > **PREP TIME:** 30 minutes >
BAKING TIME: 30 to 35 minutes > **YIELD:** 12 tarts

FOR THE PEAR & FIG COMPOTE

5 ripe Bosc pears

2 tablespoons unsalted butter

12 pitted Kalamata or Niçoise olives, sliced lengthwise (optional)

2 tablespoons honey

2 tablespoons balsamic vinegar

8 fresh figs, cut into ¼-inch (6-mm) dice, or ¼ cup (60 ml) fig preserves

FOR THE THREE-CHEESE CUSTARD

1 cup (225 g) fresh goat cheese

¾ cup (115 g) mascarpone

½ cup (75 g) whole-milk ricotta

⅓ cup (75 ml) honey

Zest of 1 lemon (about 1 tablespoon)

2 large eggs

1 large egg white

¾ cup (180 ml) heavy cream

FOR THE ASSEMBLY

1 (15-ounce / 430-g) package ready-made pie dough (2 rounds), at room temperature

Nonstick cooking spray, for the pan

THOUGH THESE TARTS ARE ELEGANT IN presentation and flavor, little ones still love them. My children have no idea they are made with goat cheese. (They like goats at the farm, not in their food.) The flavor of the cheeses blends perfectly with the sweetness of the honey-and-balsamic-glazed fruit. The firmness of Bosc pears means they stand on their own in this compote without becoming mushy. Step beyond breakfast and serve them at a luncheon with a salad of greens and fresh herbs.

Make Ahead The pear & fig compote can be prepared up to 2 days in advance and stored in an airtight container in the refrigerator until needed. It will last for up to 2 weeks.

> MAKE THE COMPOTE

Leaving the skin on, cut the pears in half and core them, then cut them into ½-inch (1-cm) pieces. Melt the butter in a medium sauté pan over medium heat. Add the pears, turn the heat to high, and sauté until the pears are golden, about 3 minutes, making sure to toss them in the butter as they cook so they brown evenly. Add the olives, honey, and vinegar, stirring to coat. Cook until the vinegar and honey begin to thicken, about 5 minutes. Turn off the heat, add the figs, and toss to coat. Let the compote cool, then transfer it to a serving dish.

> MAKE THE THREE-CHEESE CUSTARD

In a large mixing bowl, whisk the three cheeses, honey, and lemon zest by hand until smooth. (Whisking with an electric mixer will incorporate too much air into the custard.) Add the eggs, egg white, and cream and whisk again, making sure to get all of the lumps out of the custard. Set aside.

> ASSEMBLE AND BAKE THE TARTS

Preheat the oven to 350°F (175°C). Spray a 12-well classic cupcake pan with nonstick cooking spray.

Unroll the pie dough onto a flat work surface (no need to flour it first). Cut each round of dough in half, and then cut each half into even thirds for a total of 12 pieces. Place one piece of dough in each well of the prepared pan, pulling the dough up to the top edge and manipulating it as needed for full coverage. Using kitchen scissors, trim any excess dough hanging over the edges of the wells. Using a ⅓-cup (75-ml) measure, fill each well with the custard, then top off each one until you have used all of the custard.

Bake until the tarts are golden brown around the edges and puffed, 30 to 35 minutes. (The custard will deflate slightly after the tarts come out of the oven.) Let the tarts cool in the pan for 3 minutes, then loosen the sides of each tart with a table knife and insert the tines of a fork between the pan and each tart to lift it out. Serve the tarts individually with a ramekin of the compote on the side, or arrange them on a serving platter with the compote in a bowl in the center.

Store the tarts in an airtight container in the refrigerator for up to 5 days. Reheat, wrapped in tin foil, for 15 minutes at 350ºF (175ºC).

PINEAPPLE *Upside-Down* CAKES

OVEN: 350°F (175°C) > PREP TIME: 35 minutes >
BAKING TIME: 20 to 25 minutes > YIELD: 12 cakes

FOR THE PINEAPPLE AND GLAZE

1 pineapple, peeled, halved, and cored

2 tablespoons unsalted butter, softened

½ cup (110 g) packed light brown sugar

¼ cup (45 g) packed dried cherries

FOR THE HAM AND ONIONS

2 teaspoons extra-virgin olive oil

10 ounces (280 g) ham steak, cut into ¼-inch (6-mm) dice

2 tablespoons pure maple syrup

½ cup finely chopped red onion

FOR THE VANILLA CAKE

½ cup (1 stick / 115 g) unsalted butter

¾ cup (150 g) granulated sugar

1 teaspoon pure vanilla extract

3 large eggs

½ cup (120 ml) whole milk

2 cups (250 g) all-purpose flour

2½ teaspoons baking powder

MY SAVORY TAKE on this classic includes a salty element in the form of maple-glazed ham. Add the caramelized red onion, and you get a buttery meal overlaid with caramelly goodness.

> ### MAKE THE PINEAPPLE AND GLAZE

Preheat the oven to 350°F (175°C). Cut one half of the pineapple into 4 long wedges, then cut each wedge into ¼-inch (6-mm) slices to create 36 pieces. In a small bowl, mix the softened butter and brown sugar together to form a paste. Divide the mixture evenly among the wells of a 12-well classic cupcake pan. Top each well with 1 teaspoon of dried cherries and 3 slices of pineapple. Set aside.

> ### MAKE THE HAM AND ONIONS

In a medium skillet, heat 1 teaspoon of the oil over medium heat. Add the ham and cook, stirring occasionally, until browned, about 5 minutes. Stir in the maple syrup, then transfer to a small bowl.

Add the remaining oil to the skillet. Add the red onion and cook, stirring occasionally, until browned, about 8 minutes. Set aside to cool.

> ### MAKE THE VANILLA CAKE

Place the butter and sugar in the bowl of an electric mixer fitted with a paddle and beat until fluffy, about 3 minutes. Add the vanilla, eggs, and milk, and beat until just combined. Sift the flour and baking powder together. Add the flour mixture to the wet ingredients and beat until smooth. Add half of the browned onions and beat until just combined. Using a large spatula, fold in half of the ham.

> ### ASSEMBLE AND BAKE THE CAKES

Divide the batter equally among the 12 wells, then dot the top of the batter with the remaining onion and ham. Bake until golden on top and cooked through, 20 to 25 minutes. Let the cakes cool in the pan for 2 minutes, then insert the tines of a fork between the pan and each cake to lift it out. Invert the cake so the pineapple is on top. Serve immediately.

Store the cakes in an airtight container in the refrigerator for up to 5 days. Reheat, wrapped in tin foil, for 15 minutes at 350°F (175°C).

WAFFLINIS

OVEN: 350°F (175°C) > PREP TIME: 25 minutes >
BAKING TIME: 20 to 25 minutes > YIELD: 12 wafflinis

Nonstick cooking spray, for the pan

24 frozen mini waffles, from one 10.9-ounce (310-g) package

6 slices pepper Jack cheese, from one 8-ounce (225-g) package presliced cheese

8 ready-made turkey sausage patties from one 10-ounce (280-g) package, defrosted if frozen

1 (12-ounce / 340 g) jar roasted red peppers, drained and chopped

8 large eggs

Salt and freshly ground black pepper

1 teaspoon chili powder

VARIATIONS **Use sun-dried tomatoes in place of the roasted red peppers. Or, for a nonspicy take, replace the roasted peppers, pepper Jack cheese, and chili powder with provolone cheese, an additional waffle, and a slice of ham or bacon and serve with your favorite preserves or pure maple syrup on the side.**

THESE BREAKFAST STACKS are just plain goodness—and so easy to create! My children have fun layering them with their favorite breakfast combinations. Mini waffles are perfect for the cupcake pan as they fit inside the wells so nicely. Be adventurous in your choice of waffle. Why not try blueberry, whole grain, or chocolate chip? I also like to eat these for lunch with a salad of field greens, avocado, and red onion tossed with a citrus vinaigrette.

Preheat the oven to 350°F (175°C). Spray a 12-well classic cupcake pan with nonstick cooking spray and place one mini waffle in the bottom of each well. Reserve the remaining 12 waffles.

Cut the 6 slices of cheese into quarters to make 24 slices total, then layer 1 slice on top of each waffle. Trim the 8 sausage patties, removing an even sliver around the edge of each patty to create 2-inch (5-cm) rounds. Reserve the trimmings.

Place the trimmed sausage patties in 8 wells. Evenly distribute the trimmings among the remaining 4 wells, gathering them together in each well to form a solid layer of sausage. Evenly distribute the peppers among the wells, followed by the remaining 12 slices of cheese.

In a medium bowl, beat the eggs until light and fluffy, then season with salt, a few grinds of black pepper, and the chili powder and mix well.

Drop the remaining 12 mini waffles into the egg mixture and let them soak for 3 minutes. Place one soaked waffle on top of each mini meal, then divide the remaining egg mixture between the wells, filling them almost to the top. Bake until cooked through and puffed, 20 to 25 minutes.

Let the wafflinis cool in the pan for 3 minutes, then loosen the sides of each wafflini with a table knife and pop them out of the pan. Get out your collection of hot sauces and serve. Yum!

Store the wafflinis in an airtight container in the refrigerator for up to 5 days. Reheat, wrapped in tin foil, for 15 minutes at 350°F (175°C).

APPLE CURRANT *Spoon* BREADS

OVEN: 350°F (175°C) > **PREP TIME:** 20 minutes >
BAKING TIME: 25 to 30 minutes > **YIELD:** 12 spoon breads

Nonstick cooking spray, for the pan

12 frozen mini breakfast pork or turkey sausage patties, from one 12-ounce (340-g) package

1 cup (125 g) all-purpose flour

½ cup (80 g) yellow cornmeal

3 tablespoons sugar

2 teaspoons baking powder

1 teaspoon baking soda

⅛ teaspoon kosher salt

⅓ cup (50 g) dried currants

1¼ cups (300 ml) plain whole-milk yogurt

2 large eggs

½ cup (1 stick / 115 g) unsalted butter, melted and cooled

Maple syrup, for serving

Thyme sprigs or fresh sage leaves, for serving (optional)

SWEET CURRANTS SERVE as the perfect comple-ment to the cornmeal spoon bread. My children love how the sweetness of the maple syrup mixes with the savory sausage. You can sprinkle some maple sugar crystals on top of the finished spoon bread to give it more texture. These are so yummy you'll have a hard time not digging in with a spoon before the rest of the family gets to the table!

Preheat the oven to 350°F (175°C). Spray a 12-well classic cupcake pan with nonstick cooking spray. Place one sau-sage patty in each well of the pan.

In a large bowl, whisk together the flour, cornmeal, sugar, baking powder, baking soda, and salt. Stir in the currants.

In a medium bowl, whisk the yogurt and eggs until well combined. Add the yogurt mixture and the melted and cooled butter to the dry ingredients; mix until just incorporated.

Mound the cornmeal batter in each well; they will be filled up to the top. Bake for 25 to 30 minutes, until a wooden toothpick inserted in the center comes out clean.

Let the spoon breads cool in the pan for 10 minutes, then loosen the sides of each spoon bread with a table knife and insert the tines of a fork between the pan and each spoon bread to lift it out. Serve each of the spoon breads individually, sausage-side up, with a drizzle of maple syrup and, if desired, a sprig of thyme or a sage leaf.

Store the spoon breads in an airtight container in the refrigerator for up to 5 days. Reheat, wrapped in tin foil, for 15 minutes at 350ºF (175ºC).

EGG
Mini Muffins

OVEN: 350°F (175°C) > PREP TIME: 20 minutes >
BAKING TIME: 18 to 20 minutes > YIELD: 12 muffins

● ● ●

Nonstick cooking spray, for
the pan

1 pound (455 g) turkey or
pork bacon, finely chopped

10 large eggs

2 cups (230 g) grated
cheddar

12 thin slices white bread,
such as Pepperidge Farms
Very Thin White Bread

VARIATION If you prefer, these mini muffins can be
made with biscuits instead of bread. Keep it simple! Buy
ready-made biscuits from the grocery store and slice
them in half crosswise, placing one half in the bottom of
a cupcake well, topping it with the egg and cheese mixture, and then topping the whole thing off with the other
biscuit half.

THE CLASSIC FLAVORS of breakfast come to life
when tucked together in this tasty little bite. I always have
to tell my son to sit down when he eats, but this is one dish
he can take with him on the go. Once you've tasted these
scrumptious—and simple!—egg muffins, drive-through
versions will leave you unsatisfied and longing for the ones
you make at home.

Preheat the oven to 350°F (175°C). Spray a 12-well classic
cupcake pan with nonstick cooking spray.

In a 10-inch (25-cm) skillet, cook the bacon over
medium-high heat, stirring occasionally, until crisp, 12 to
15 minutes. If using turkey bacon, turn off the heat and
leave the bacon in the pan. If using pork bacon, drain it on
paper towels.

In a medium bowl, beat the eggs until fluffy. Stir in
the grated cheese, then add the cooked bacon and mix
thoroughly.

Nestle a slice of bread in each of the wells, pressing
down to make sure the bread fits snugly in the bottom of
the pan. (The bread will not fill the entire well and it may
even poke up above the lip of the pan.) Using a ½-cup
(120-ml) measure, divide the egg mixture among the
wells, filling them to the top.

Bake until cooked through, 18 to 20 minutes. For a
creamy texture, remove these muffins from the oven when
the eggs are still a bit jiggly. They will continue to cook
after they come out. There's no need to let them cool,
though: Just loosen the sides of each muffin with a table
knife and pop them out of the pan. Serve with a side of
seasonal fruit or as part of a larger breakfast buffet.

Biscuits

> & <

GRAVY

OVEN: 350°F (175°C) > PREP TIME: 25 minutes >
BAKING TIME: 18 to 22 minutes > YIELD: 12 biscuits

Nonstick cooking spray, for
the pan

1 pound (455 g) ground
breakfast sausage or
ground turkey sausage
(see Note)

1 tablespoon unsalted butter

1 small yellow onion, finely
chopped

¼ cup (30 g) all-purpose
flour

2 teaspoons concentrated
chicken broth base, such

as Better Than Bouillon
brand

Freshly ground black pepper

1 cup (240 ml) whole milk

1 cup (240 ml) heavy cream

2 (12-ounce / 340-g) cans
buttermilk biscuits
(refrigerate until ready to
use), or 12 (2-inch / 6-cm
diameter) homemade
biscuits

Notes I like to use classic breakfast sausage with
sage seasoning in this recipe. It's available in most
supermarkets, but if you can't locate it, stir 1 teaspoon
finely chopped fresh sage or ½ teaspoon crumbled dried
sage leaves into any type of sausage meat that you can
purchase by the pound.

There's no need to add salt to the gravy, as the
salt in the chicken broth base will suffice. In any case,
it's always better to use less salt, then add more later
if needed, to keep from oversalting. Wait until you've
added the sausage to the gravy, then taste and adjust
the seasoning if necessary.

HERE, I'VE ADAPTED a classic to accommodate your
desire for a good Southern breakfast without the guilt associated with traditional Southern serving sizes. As the gravy
melts into the biscuit while baking, it creates a portable item
that is great for breakfast on the run. You can have it all in
this mini meal. The drippings and browned tidbits left in the
pan from cooking the sausage make the gravy so flavorful.
(If you're a true Southerner, use your own gravy recipe!)

Make Ahead You can assemble these savory
cupcakes the night before, then pop them in a 350°F
(175°C) oven for a quick breakfast before school.

Preheat the oven to 350°F (175°C). Spray a 12-well classic
cupcake pan with nonstick cooking spray.

In a 10-inch (25-cm) nonstick skillet, cook the sausage
over medium heat, breaking the meat up with a wooden
spoon, until browned throughout, 10 to 12 minutes.
Drain the sausage in a fine-mesh colander over a paper
towel–lined plate. Continue to break up the sausage in the
colander with the back of a wooded spoon until no large
clumps of meat remain. Transfer the sausage to a medium
bowl and set aside.

In the same nonstick skillet, melt the butter over
medium heat, add the onion, and sauté until translucent,
about 3 minutes. Add the flour and chicken base to the
skillet, stirring until a paste forms, no longer than 1 minute.
Add a few grinds of black pepper, then slowly pour in
the milk and cream, whisking constantly until the gravy
thickens, about 3 minutes. Turn off the heat and stir in
the cooked sausage. Adjust the seasoning if necessary
(see Notes).

Remove 12 biscuits from the cans (see "Savory
Tidbits" at right for ideas on how to use extras). Using
a serrated knife, slice each biscuit in half crosswise to
create 24 halves. Place half a biscuit in each of the wells
of the prepared cupcake pan and top with the sausage
gravy, about 3 heaping tablespoons per well. Top with the
remaining biscuit halves, pressing down firmly. Bake until
the tops of the biscuits are golden, 18 to 22 minutes.

Let the biscuits cool in the pan for 3 minutes, then loosen the sides of each biscuit with a table knife and pop them out of the pan. Serve them hot.

Store the leftover biscuits in an airtight container in the refrigerator for up to 5 days. The gravy can be stored in a separate container in the refrigerator for up to 5 days. These leftovers taste great at room temperature, but, if you prefer,the biscuits can be reheated, wrapped in tin foil, for 15 minutes at 350°F (175°C), and the gravy can be warmed in a small saucepan on the stovetop.

Savory Tidbits **If you have any leftover canned biscuits, your children can simply dust the tops of the biscuits with cinnamon and sugar. Or, make jam biscuits by stretching the biscuit dough slightly and placing 1 tablespoon of jam in the middle of each. Fold the dough over like a taco and dust with cinnamon and sugar. Bake at 350°F (175°C) for 8 to 10 minutes.**

SOUTHERN
Breakfasts

After years of living in southern California, I made my way east. When we arrived, in Raleigh, North Carolina, it was freezing cold and the house we'd bought had a crack in the foundation. It was too late to do anything but stay in North Carolina, so we got out of the bad purchase, rented a house, and tolerated the cold for four months.

While we were freezing there, we frequently visited a local diner in the morning. They always had sausage or fried chicken with biscuits and cream gravy on the breakfast menu. I died with pleasure at every sinful mouthful!

Breakfast down south is a sumptuous affair that includes a broad variety of foods not usually associated with breakfast in other parts of the country, such as fried apple rings, citrus marmalade, and creamy eggs with creamed corn, red peppers, and bacon. What a way to start the day! Despite the amazing diner fare, after enduring that cold North Carolina winter, I finally said, "Florida is close." So we packed up our cars and drove straight to Orlando with our two babies.

< FIG & BLUE CHEESE TARTS

chapter

>TWO<

EGG & CHEESE

ONE MORNING WHEN I WAS FIVE YEARS OLD, I PULLED A STEP
stool up to the stove. My mission: to make a poached egg for my father, as this was my favorite breakfast to have with him.

I grew up watching Julia Child and had seen her swirl the boiling water for the egg with a spoon. Even though I did it on my own without an adult nearby, in two tries I got it right without making a big mess. My father was blown away when I presented him with the egg and toast on a silver tray, complete with an ironed linen placemat.

Ever since then, I have been experimenting with eggs and cheese, using them in many different dishes and combining them with a wide variety of ingredients. Because they frequently play a supporting role in dishes, these two essentials are often ignored in the larger scope of meal making. Without cheese or eggs, though, eating would be drab. In this chapter, they're the stars.

Eggs form the unnoticed essence of custards and give these puddinglike meals their rich, creamy texture. Cheese joins with eggs to form the base for omelets, quiches, and huevos rancheros—and there are countless savory meals that benefit from the addition of one or two cheeses.

So, test out your new skills with the cupcake pan by creating some of the simple yet heavenly delights in this chapter. Your mouth will thank you.

FIG
& BLUE CHEESE
Tarts

OVEN: 400°F (205°C) > **PREP TIME:** 20 minutes >
BAKING TIME: 15 to 20 minutes > **YIELD:** 12 tarts

● ● ●

Nonstick cooking spray, for the pan

1 (17.3-ounce / 485-g) box puff pastry (2 sheets), at room temperature

4 ounces (115 g) blue cheese, crumbled

1 cup (240 ml) fig jam, or 16 fresh figs, stemmed and cut into ¼-inch (6-mm) dice

5 tablespoons (75 ml) honey

¾ cup (75 g) walnuts or black walnuts, finely chopped

6 tablespoons (95 g) turbinado sugar (if using fresh figs rather than jam; see Note)

Note When I use fresh figs, I sprinkle them with some turbinado sugar before baking. The sugar keeps its texture, giving the figs a delightful crunch. If you want to expand your horizons, turbinado sugar is available infused with different flavors, including ginger, lemon, or cinnamon.

Savory Tidbit With the extra puff pastry, why not make your children a little treat? Sprinkle cinnamon and sugar on top of each piece of pastry and bake at 400°F (205°C) for 15 minutes. Break up a bar of chocolate into small squares and serve one square on top of each warm, puffy treat.

FRESH FIGS are heavenly, though it can sometimes be a problem finding them in season. Fig jam is available in most specialty shops, but if figs are in season in your area, I forbid you to use anything other than fresh figs. Even though I've lived in Florida for eight years now, I still miss the fig trees that grew in my garden in California. Once, while browsing the Middle Eastern foods section at the grocery store, I discovered the most amazing jar of fig jam: pure fig seasoned with sesame seeds and anise. I was blown away by the flavor! The addition of blue cheese to the figs keeps this tart from being too sweet. I adore Maytag, Gorgonzola, Danish blue . . . there are so many blues to choose from!

Preheat the oven to 400°F (205°C). Spray a 12-well classic cupcake pan with nonstick cooking spray.

Cut each piece of puff pastry dough into thirds lengthwise, then crosswise, for a total of 18 pieces. (You will have 6 extra pieces of dough; see "Savory Tidbit," below, for ideas on how to use them.) Stretch 12 pieces of dough gently in both directions (do not use a rolling pin, as rolling will keep the dough from puffing properly during baking), then place one piece of dough in each well of the prepared cupcake pan.

Sprinkle the puff pastry with 1 tablespoon blue cheese crumbles per well. If using fresh figs, place them in a small bowl and stir in 2 tablespoons honey to coat. Divide the fig jam, or fresh figs mixed with honey, evenly among the 12 wells. In a small bowl, mix the walnuts with 3 tablespoons of honey to coat, then top the figs with 1 tablespoon of honeyed walnuts per well. If using fresh figs, sprinkle ½ tablespoon turbinado sugar on top of each tart.

Bake until the edges are golden brown and crispy and the filling is bubbling, 15 to 20 minutes. Do not let these tarts cool in the pan, as they will sweat and the pastry will get soggy: use your hands to lift them from the pan using the puff pastry wrappers as handles. Serve hot.

CHEESE & NUT *Loaves*

OVEN: 350°F (175°C) > **PREP TIME:** 45 minutes >
BAKING TIME: 20 to 25 minutes > **YIELD:** 12 loaves

2 cups (200 g) raw, unsalted mixed nuts

2 tablespoons salted butter

1 medium yellow onion, finely chopped

Pinch each of kosher salt and freshly ground black pepper

2 cloves garlic, finely chopped, or 1 tablespoon garlic from a tube

½ cup (50 g) white mushrooms, wiped clean and chopped

1 ounce (30 g) dried porcini or shiitake mushrooms, reconstituted (see page 97), then finely chopped

2 tablespoons chopped fresh parsley or parsley from a tube

2 teaspoons fresh thyme leaves, or ½ teaspoon dried

1 tablespoon chopped fresh marjoram, or 1 teaspoon dried

1 teaspoon chopped fresh sage, or ½ teaspoon dried sage, crumbled

1½ cups (300 g) cooked brown rice

4 large eggs, beaten

1 cup (250 g) whole-milk ricotta

1½ cups (175 g) grated cheese, any type

Nonstick cooking spray, for the pan

THIS IS A TERRINE I CREATED for some clients who (prior to their vegetarian days) used to love my duck liver terrine—and the creamy texture that only duck liver can create. While there isn't any liver in these loaves, they're just as enjoyable, which my clients discovered once I finally convinced them to try this vegetarian alternative.

Make Ahead **These loaves can be assembled up to 2 days in advance.**

Preheat the oven to 350°F (175°C).

On a rimmed baking sheet, toast the nuts until golden, 10 to 12 minutes. Cool slightly, then finely chop by hand or in a food processor.

Melt the butter in a 10-inch (25-cm) skillet over medium heat. Add the onion and cook until translucent, about 4 minutes, then season with the salt and pepper. Stir in the garlic, fresh and dried mushrooms, and parsley, thyme, marjoram, and sage, then transfer the vegetable mixture to a large bowl. Add the cooked rice, chopped nuts, eggs, ricotta, and grated cheese and mix to combine thoroughly.

Spray a 12-well classic cupcake pan with nonstick cooking spray. Using an ice cream scoop, fill each of the wells with the cheese and nut mixture. Bake until golden and firm to the touch, 20 to 25 minutes. Do not overbake.

Let the loaves cool for 5 minutes in the pan, then loosen the sides of each loaf with a table knife and pop them out of the pan.

Serve the loaves paired with a mixed greens and herb salad or, for a more filling meal, a simple mélange of sautéed vegetables, roasted or mashed potatoes, and a vegetarian gravy.

Store the loaves in an airtight container in the refrigerator for up to 5 days. Reheat, wrapped in tin foil, for 15 minutes at 350ºF (175ºC).

VARIATIONS Personalization here is key. You can use any combination of nuts and cheeses you like, so have fun! Walnuts, almonds, and pecans are fairly standard, but don't forget about cashews and pistachios. For the mixed cheese, consider fontina, Gruyère, Jack, Muenster, and Gouda.

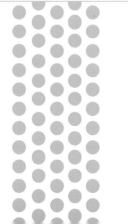

OVEN-ROASTED
TOMATO & GRUYÈRE
Tarts

OVEN: 375°F to 400°F (190°C to 205°C) > **PREP TIME:** 45 minutes >
BAKING TIME: 50 minutes > **YIELD:** 12 tarts

● ● ●

FOR THE TOMATOES AND GARLIC

1 pint (300 g) cherry tomatoes (red, yellow, or orange, preferably heirloom, if in season), cut in half lengthwise

6 cloves garlic

2 tablespoons extra-virgin olive oil

½ teaspoon kosher salt

¼ teaspoon freshly ground black pepper

FOR THE CUSTARD

4 large eggs

¼ teaspoon kosher salt

¼ teaspoon freshly ground black pepper

2 tablespoons finely snipped fresh basil or basil from a tube

¼ teaspoon freshly grated nutmeg

½ cup (120 ml) whole milk

½ cup (120 ml) half-and-half

FOR THE ASSEMBLY

Nonstick cooking spray, for the pan

1 (15-ounce / 430-g) package ready-made pie dough (2 rounds), at room temperature

1 cup (115 g) grated Gruyère

4 slices bacon, cooked until crispy then cut crosswise into 2-inch (5-cm) strips

Savory Tidbit **These tarts can be eaten as soon as they come out of the pan, but the custard is creamier the cooler they are: Try them at room temperature.**

THESE TARTS hit about every note on the savory scale: Rich, salty bacon and Gruyère are offset by the natural sweetness of caramelized tomato and roasted garlic. Bake that up in a creamy custard, and you have a handheld bite of bliss. When they're in season, I like to use heirloom tomatoes to intensify the flavor.

> ### MAKE THE TOMATOES AND GARLIC

Preheat the oven to 400°F (205°C). Line a rimmed baking sheet with foil or a Silpat mat for easy cleanup.

In a small bowl, combine the tomatoes, garlic, oil, salt, and pepper. Mix well and turn onto the prepared baking sheet. Roast until the tomatoes are dehydrated and golden, about 25 minutes. Set aside.

> ### MAKE THE CUSTARD

In a small bowl bowl, beat the eggs with the salt, pepper, basil, nutmeg, whole milk, and half-and-half until thoroughly combined.

> ### ASSEMBLE AND BAKE THE TARTS

Preheat the oven to 375°F (190°C). Spray a 12-well classic cupcake pan with nonstick cooking spray.

Unroll the pie dough onto a flat work surface; no need to flour it first. Cut each round of dough in half, and then cut each half into thirds for a total of 12 pieces. Place one piece of dough in each well of the prepared pan. (The fit will be asymmetrical.) Using kitchen scissors, trim any excess dough to ½ inch (1 cm) at most.

Finely chop the roasted garlic cloves, then distribute them in the bottom of each well. Top each with 1 heaping tablespoon cheese.

Fill each well three-quarters full with the custard. Evenly distribute the tomato halves among the wells. Top each tart with several strips of bacon. Bake until golden and puffed like a soufflé, about 25 minutes. Let cool in the pan for 5 minutes. (The custard will deflate slightly after the tarts come out of the oven.) Loosen the sides of each tart with a table knife and insert the tines of a fork between the pan and each tart to lift it out.

If you would like to make these ahead of time, refrigerate the tarts overnight (or for up to 5 days), then reheat, wrapped in tin foil, in a 350°F (175°C) oven for 15 minutes.

WELSH RAREBITS

> WITH <

Apple Ketchup

OVEN: 350°F (175°C) > **PREP TIME:** 30 minutes >
BAKING TIME: 40 minutes > **YIELD:** 12 rarebits

• • •

FOR THE BREAD WRAPPERS

Nonstick cooking spray, for the pan

12 thin slices white bread, such as Pepperidge Farm's Very Thin White Bread

¼ cup (½ stick / 60 g) butter, softened

2 tablespoons fresh thyme leaves or other fresh herb, chopped (optional)

FOR THE CHEESE SAUCE

2 tablespoons butter

2 tablespoons all-purpose flour

¼ cup (60 ml) beer

3 cups (345 g) grated cheddar

1 teaspoon Worcestershire sauce

1 teaspoon dry mustard

⅛ teaspoon cayenne

1 large egg, beaten

FOR THE APPLE KETCHUP

2 tablespoons butter

¼ cup (60 ml) ketchup

¼ cup (60 ml) sherry vinegar (see Note)

1 large tomato, seeded and finely chopped

2 large tart apples, such as Honeycrisp, peeled, cored, and cut into ¼-inch (6-mm) dice

Note If you don't have any sherry vinegar on hand, mix 2 tablespoons of white vinegar (or white wine, white balsamic, or seasoned rice wine vinegar) with 2 tablespoons of dry sherry borrowed from the liquor cabinet.

THIS DISH MIGHT SOUND FANCY, but it's really just a grown-up version of a grilled cheese and tomato sandwich. In this gourmet treatment of a childhood favorite, the sandwich filling is lightened to a soufflé consistency and then toasted. My children love this served with a bowl of tomato soup. The apple ketchup acts as the perfect accompaniment to the richness of the rarebit. I love Honeycrisp apples for the ketchup, but any apple you have on hand will do.

Make Ahead The apple ketchup can be prepared up to 2 days in advance and stored in an airtight container in the refrigerator until needed. It will last for up to 1 week.

> MAKE THE BREAD WRAPPERS

Preheat the oven to 350°F (175°C). Spray a 12-well classic cupcake pan with nonstick cooking spray. Butter one side of each slice of bread. For added flavor, sprinkle the thyme on each buttered slice. Line the wells of the prepared cupcake pan with the slices of bread, buttered side down. Firmly press the bread into the pan and tuck in any edges that poke up, so that when you fill the wells with the cheese sauce, all of the bread will be soaked. Toast the bread wrappers in the oven for 20 minutes, then remove the pan and set aside.

> MAKE THE CHEESE SAUCE

In the top of a double boiler, whisk together the butter and flour. Let it cook for 2 to 3 minutes to form a paste, stirring occasionally. Add the beer slowly, whisking to make sure no lumps remain, then stir in the cheese, Worcestershire, mustard, and cayenne.

Continue to stir until the cheese mixture is melted and smooth, about 4 minutes. Remove the top pan from the double boiler and quickly whisk the beaten egg into the cheese mixture to create a very smooth, creamy sauce.

› ASSEMBLE AND BAKE THE RAREBITS

Working quickly, use an ice cream scoop to fill each of the bread wrappers with the cheese sauce, then top off each one until you have used all of the sauce. Bake until firm to the touch, about 20 minutes.

› MAKE THE APPLE KETCHUP

In a medium sauté pan over medium heat, brown the butter—it will sizzle—until golden brown, about 2 minutes. Reduce the heat to medium-low and stir in the ketchup and sherry vinegar, then add the tomato and apples. Cook, stirring occasionally, until the apples have softened, about 8 minutes. Place the ketchup in a serving bowl and set aside.

When the rarebits are done, remove the pan from the oven and use your hands to lift the rarebits from the pan using the toasted bread wrappers as handles. Eat these savory bites with the apple ketchup on the side as soon as your mouth will allow, but be careful—the cheese sauce is hot! Or serve them at room temperature—the flavor is still amazing.

Store the rarebits in an airtight container in the refrigerator for up to 1 week. Enjoy the leftovers at room temperature or reheat, wrapped in tin foil, for 15 minutes at 350°F (175°C).

VARIATIONS The cheese sauce in Welsh rarebit is traditionally topped with tomato slices and broiled in the oven. To make these mini meals more authentic, thinly slice 1 or 2 tomatoes to make 12 slices, place 1 slice on top of the cheese sauce in each well of the cupcake pan, and season with salt and pepper. Bake as directed in the recipe above.

For a fresh twist on a classic grilled cheese and tomato sandwich, macerate 2 cups (360 g) diced cherry tomatoes in their own juices for 20 minutes. Top the baked Welsh rarebit with the cherry tomatoes, sprinkle with fresh herbs and a pinch of salt, and serve with a simple green salad tossed with an olive oil and vinegar dressing on the side.

HERB GOAT CHEESE & HONEY CAKES

OVEN: 325°F (165°C) > **PREP TIME:** 20 minutes > **BAKING TIME:** 18 to 25 minutes > **YIELD:** 12 cakes

• • •

FOR THE HONEY CAKES

Nonstick cooking spray, for the pan

12 edible leaves (scented geranium or other fresh herb, such as lavender, thyme, or rosemary; see Note)

3 cups (375 g) sifted all-purpose flour

2 teaspoons baking powder

¾ cup (1½ sticks / 175 g) salted butter, softened

1 cup (200 g) sugar

6 tablespoons (90 ml) honey

4 large eggs

1 tablespoon fresh lemon zest (from 1 lemon)

1 tablespoon fresh thyme leaves, finely chopped

FOR THE GOAT CHEESE–HONEY BUTTER

½ cup (1 stick / 115 g) unsalted butter, softened

⅓ cup (75 ml) honey

2 cups (225 g) goat cheese, at room temperature

Sprigs of fresh thyme, for serving

Note There are twenty-one varieties of scented geranium, including apricot, rose, pineapple, lemon, cinnamon, mint, and ginger. The term "scented" is used for all edible geraniums. When developing this recipe, I used rose geranium. Please do not confuse edible geranium with the inedible type that you plant in your flower boxes!

In addition, there are many varieties of edible thyme, including silver, English, Pennsylvania Dutch, orange, Hi-Ho Silver, and lemon.

IT'S IMPOSSIBLE TO KEEP my mouth from watering at the delicious scents wafting from the oven as these cakes bake. The secret is a fresh herb leaf placed at the bottom of each well. I'm in love with edible flowering herbs—edible geranium is my favorite, but other herbs will do. Several varieties of thyme and edible scented geranium surround my garden, which is how they found their way into this recipe. I've been infusing oil and sugar with herbs, as well as baking them into cakes to create a range of delightful natural flavors, for as long as I have been baking. Top the cakes with a dollop of goat cheese–honey butter, and you'll wonder why you never tried baking with flowers before.

Make Ahead The goat cheese–honey butter can be prepared up to 2 days in advance and stored in an airtight container in the refrigerator until needed. It will last for up to 1 week.

> ### MAKE THE HONEY CAKES

Preheat the oven to 325°F (165°C).

Spray a 12-well classic cupcake pan with nonstick cooking spray and place 1 edible leaf in the bottom of each well.

In a medium bowl, combine the flour and baking powder. Set aside.

Place the butter, sugar, and honey in the bowl of a stand mixer fitted with a whisk attachment. Whisk on medium-high speed until creamy, about 3 minutes. Add the eggs, one at a time, and beat well after each addition. Adjust the speed to low and add the zest, thyme, and flour mixture and beat until just combined.

Using an ice cream scoop, fill each well with the batter. Bake until cooked through and a toothpick inserted in the center comes out clean, 18 to 25 minutes. Let the cakes rest in the pan for 5 minutes, then loosen the sides of each cake with a table knife and insert the tines of a fork between the pan and each cake to lift it out. Transfer the cakes to a wire rack to cool completely.

› MAKE THE GOAT CHEESE–HONEY BUTTER

In the bowl of a stand mixer fitted with a whisk attachment, beat the butter, honey, and goat cheese until fluffy, occasionally scraping the sides of the bowl.

To serve, invert the honey cakes so that the geranium is visible. Serve them individually with a dollop of the goat cheese–honey butter on the side, topped off with a flowering sprig of thyme.

Store the cakes in an airtight container in the refrigerator for up to 1 week.

EDIBLE
Flowers

My love for herbs and edible flowers began when I was a little girl and my mother taught me about edible violets. My interest in them grew with my childhood garden. I learned from an early age that many items in our flower garden were edible. So many tastes and aromas await if you take a moment to ponder your garden and the limitless possibilities it offers for enhancing your meals.

> SPINACH & <
Mushroom
QUICHES

OVEN: 350°F (175°C) > **PREP TIME:** 25 minutes >
BAKING TIME: 20 to 25 minutes > **YIELD:** 12 quiches

• • •

5 large eggs

½ cup (120 ml) whole milk

½ cup (120 ml) half-and-half

Pinch of kosher salt and freshly ground black pepper

3 cups (300 g) button mushrooms, wiped clean and finely chopped

2 teaspoons extra-virgin olive oil

1 (8-ounce / 230-g) package turkey bacon or ham, chopped

Nonstick cooking spray, for the pan

1½ cups (150 g) grated Parmesan

12 thin slices white bread, such as Pepperidge Farm's Very Thin White Bread

1 cup (115 g) grated Gruyère, Swiss, provolone, or mozzarella

1 (10-ounce / 280-g) package frozen spinach, thawed and chopped

1 bunch chives, snipped with scissors

THIS UNCONVENTIONAL "Real Man" quiche is a meal in itself that offers hearty, robust flavors. My husband doesn't like quiche. As a matter of fact, none of my male clients ever really did—too much crust and not enough gusto! This recipe solves that problem because the wells of a cupcake pan are deeper than a pie pan, so you can really fill it to the brim with lots of good-tasting ingredients. Save time by prepping the ingredients the night before you plan to bake these.

In a medium bowl, beat the eggs with the milk, half-and-half, salt, and pepper until thoroughly combined. Set aside.

In a medium sauté pan over medium heat, sauté the mushrooms in 1 teaspoon oil until all the liquid has cooked down, about 5 minutes. Transfer the mushrooms to a medium bowl and set aside.

Using the same sauté pan, heat the remaining 1 teaspoon oil. Add the bacon and cook over medium heat until crispy, about 6 minutes. Set aside.

Preheat the oven to 350°F (175°C).

Spray a 12-well classic cupcake pan with nonstick cooking spray. Sprinkle 1 tablespoon Parmesan in the bottom of each well. Top with 1 slice of bread, pushing down to fill the well. Sprinkle each well with 1 heaping tablespoon Gruyère, then divide the mushrooms and bacon among the wells, using up all of each ingredient. Top with equal portions of spinach, then sprinkle with chives.

Using a ¼-cup (60-ml) measure, fill each well with the egg mixture, then sprinkle with an additional tablespoon of Parmesan. Bake until the center is slightly jiggly, 20 to 25 minutes. Let the quiches rest in the pan for 5 minutes, then loosen the sides of each quiche with a table knife and insert the tines of a fork between the pan and each quiche to lift it out. Serve right away or at room temperature.

Store the quiches in an airtight container in the refrigerator for up to 5 days. Enjoy the leftovers at room temperature or reheat, wrapped in tin foil, for 15 minutes at 350°F (175°C).

BUTTERMILK CORNBREAD
Corn Puddings

OVEN: 350°F (175°C) > **PREP TIME:** 20 minutes > **BAKING TIME:** 45 to 50 minutes > **YIELD:** 24 puddings

• • •

FOR THE BUTTERMILK CORNBREAD

Nonstick cooking spray, for the pan

1 cup (125 g) all-purpose flour

1 cup (160 g) cornmeal

¼ cup (50 g) sugar

2 teaspoons baking powder

1 teaspoon baking soda

1 teaspoon kosher salt

1 cup (140 g) packed grated cheddar

1 cup (240 ml) buttermilk

2 large eggs

¼ cup (½ stick / 60 g) salted butter, melted and cooled

FOR THE CORN PUDDING

Nonstick cooking spray, for the pan

2 cups fresh corn cut off the cob (about 4 ears), or 1 (16-ounce / 455-g) bag frozen corn, thawed

2 cups (230 g) grated cheddar, plus 1 cup (115 g) more for the top, if desired

1 red bell pepper, seeded and cut into ¼-inch (6-mm) dice

1 dried Anaheim or pasilla chile, torn into small bits

1 bunch scallions, chopped

1¾ cups (420 ml) buttermilk

1 cup (240 ml) canned enchilada sauce

4 large eggs

1 teaspoon kosher salt

VARIATION For a simpler version without the cornbread, spray a 12-well classic cupcake pan with nonstick cooking spray, then place 1 (6-inch / 16-cm) flour tortilla in each well. Make the corn pudding, but use only 1 cup (240 ml) buttermilk and omit the crumbled cornbread. Fill the tortillas with the corn pudding and top with 1 cup (115 g) shredded cheddar. Bake until golden on top and cooked through, 35 minutes. Let the puddings rest in the pan for 10 minutes before popping them out with a table knife. Makes 12 puddings.

THIS NEW TAKE ON A CLASSIC southern staple adds southwest flavors, creating a tender, moist mini meal with a touch of sweetness and bit of bite. The Anaheim and pasilla chiles aren't very spicy, so feel free to use another chile of your choice if you'd like more heat.

> MAKE THE BUTTERMILK CORNBREAD

Preheat the oven to 350°F (175°C) degrees. Spray an 8-by-8-inch (20-by-20-cm) square baking pan with nonstick cooking spray.

In a large bowl, whisk together the flour, cornmeal, sugar, baking powder and soda, and salt, then stir in the cheese. In another bowl, combine the buttermilk, eggs, and melted butter. Add the wet ingredients to the dry; do not overmix. Pour into the prepared baking pan and bake until golden, about 25 minutes. Remove the cornbread from the oven and leave the oven on.

> MAKE THE CORN PUDDING

Spray two 12-well classic cupcake pans with nonstick cooking spray. In a medium bowl, mix together the corn, 2 cups (230 g) of the cheese, the bell pepper, dried chile, scallions, buttermilk, enchilada sauce, eggs, and salt. Break the cornbread into chunks and stir it in.

Fill each well with batter, then distribute the remaining 1 cup (115 g) cheese evenly over the tops, if desired. Bake in the upper and lower thirds of the oven, rotating the pans halfway through, until golden on top, 20 to 25 minutes. Let the puddings cool in the pan for 10 minutes, then loosen the sides of each pudding with a table knife and pop them out of the pan.

Store the puddings in an airtight container in the refrigerator for up to 5 days. Reheat, wrapped in tin foil, for 15 minutes at 350°F (175°C).

HAM & CHEESE
in a Basket

OVEN: 350°F (175°C) > **PREP TIME:** 15 minutes >
BAKING TIME: 20 to 25 minutes > **YIELD:** 12 puddings

● ● ●

Nonstick cooking spray, for
the pan

1 (12-ounce / 350-g) ham
steak, cut into ¼-inch
(6-mm) dice

12 slices thin white bread,
such as Pepperidge Farm's
Very Thin White Bread

2 cups (230 g) grated
Gruyère, cheddar, Swiss,
Muenster, provolone, or
mozzarella

8 large eggs

¼ teaspoon kosher salt

¼ teaspoon freshly ground
black pepper

2 tablespoons half-and-half

HAM ADDS just the right saltiness to this bread pudding–like dish. The bread base surrounds a custard center and the cheese melts beautifully on top. It tastes amazing drizzled with maple syrup. A great breakfast treat!

Make Ahead These bread puddings can be assembled one day in advance and refrigerated wrapped in plastic wrap until baking. When ready to bake, preheat the oven to 350°F (175°C) and proceed as directed.

Preheat the oven to 350°F (175°C).

Spray a medium sauté pan with nonstick cooking spray and sauté the ham steak over medium-high heat until browned, about 5 minutes. Set aside.

Spray a 12-well classic cupcake pan with nonstick cooking spray and line the wells with the slices of bread. Firmly press the bread into the wells but do not trim the bread; it will peek up above the pan's edge and become crispy during baking. Top each slice of bread with about 2½ tablespoons cheese, using all of it. Divide the sautéed ham among the wells.

In a medium bowl, beat the eggs, salt, pepper, and half-and-half. Using a ⅓-cup (75-ml) measure, top each well with the egg mixture. Let the first pour settle, and then go back and fill to the rim.

Bake until the egg is set and the bread is golden brown, 20 to 25 minutes. It's okay if the tops are slightly jiggly, as the puddings will continue to bake after you've removed them from the oven. Use your hands to lift the puddings from the pan. Serve them immediately with a favorite breakfast side: fresh berries, sliced tomatoes, or ambrosia (supremes of grapefruit and orange with their juices, tossed with coconut).

Store the bread puddings in an airtight container in the refrigerator for up to 5 days. Reheat, wrapped in tin foil, for 15 minutes at 350ºF (175ºC).

Ricotta
AL FORNO
CHARLOTTES

OVEN: 375°F (190°C) > **PREP TIME:** 20 minutes > **BAKING TIME:** 25 to 30 minutes > **YIELD:** 12 charlottes

• • •

12 thin slices white bread, such as Pepperidge Farm's Very Thin White Bread

1 (6-ounce / 175-g) can tomato paste, or ½ cup (120 ml) tomato paste from a tube

Nonstick cooking spray, for the pan

1¼ cups (50 g) fresh basil leaves

¾ cup (30 g) fresh mint leaves

¾ cup (30 g) fresh parsley leaves

2 cups (500 g) whole-milk ricotta

½ cup (120 ml) heavy cream

2 large eggs

Freshly ground black pepper

1¼ cups (125 g) freshly grated Parmesan

12 mixed olives, such as Kalamata, Niçoise, or Gaeta, pitted and finely chopped

Savory Tidbit **Open cans of tomato paste always get lost in the back of my fridge, and I never use them up before they spoil. Tomato paste in a tube is a brilliant alternative because it lasts much longer—about 2 months—in the refrigerator.**

I LEARNED TO PREPARE this bright green ricotta soufflé in a wood-burning oven in Florence. Running my fingers through the fields of herbs to get handfuls for this dish is only a memory now. Things have changed since then, as has this recipe, which I adapted for the cupcake pan. I would eat this for breakfast or lunch with a platter of vine-ripened tomatoes in all colors, shapes, and stages of perfection. There's no need to add any salt—the Parmesan takes care of that.

Preheat the oven to 375°F (190°C).

Spread one side of each slice of bread with 2 teaspoons tomato paste. Spray a 12-well classic cupcake pan with nonstick cooking spray. Line the wells of the prepared pan with the slices of bread, tomato paste side up. Firmly press the bread into the wells but do not trim the bread; it will peek up above the pan's edge and become crispy during baking.

In the bowl of a food processor fitted with the blade attachment, puree the basil, mint, and parsley with 1 cup (250 g) of the ricotta, and ¼ cup (60 ml) of the cream until smooth. Add the remaining 1 cup (250 g) ricotta and ¼ cup (60 ml) cream and the eggs, one at a time, and pulse to combine. Add a few grinds of black pepper.

Remove the bowl and blade from the food processor and, using a rubber spatula, fold in the Parmesan in batches. Divide the cheese and egg mixture evenly among the wells and sprinkle the olives on top. Bake until puffed up like a soufflé, 25 to 30 minutes.

Let the charlottes cool in the pan for about 5 minutes, then loosen the sides of each charlotte with a table knife and pop them out of the pan. Serve immediately.

CROQUE MADAMES

OVEN: 350°F (175°C) > **PREP TIME:** 10 minutes >
BAKING TIME: 25 to 28 minutes > **YIELD:** 12 mini meals

● ● ●

Nonstick cooking spray, for the pan

3 tablespoons unsalted butter, softened

12 thin slices white bread, such as Pepperidge Farm's Very Thin White Bread

2 tablespoons Dijon mustard

12 ounces (340 g) thinly sliced cooked ham, cut in half if too large to fit in the wells

1 cup (115 g) grated Gruyère

12 large eggs

Kosher salt and freshly ground black pepper

THE FRENCH ARE MASTERS at creating simple dishes with extraordinary taste, and Croque Madames are no exception. The gooey yolk and melted cheese complement the crisp edges of the ham and golden brown toasted bread. Sometimes you just need a meal that feels extra special, and these Croque Madames make comfort food into something fabulous. They're perfect served as part of a brunch or with a green salad at lunch.

Preheat the oven to 350°F (175°C).

Butter one side of each slice of bread. Flip the bread over and spread mustard on the other side. Spray a 12-well classic cupcake pan with nonstick cooking spray. Line the wells of the prepared pan with the slices of bread, mustard side up. Firmly press the bread into the wells but do not trim the bread; it will peek up above the pan's edge and become crispy during baking. Place 1 slice of ham in each well, pressing down to shape it to the well. Sprinkle each with about 1 tablespoon of cheese, using it all.

Crack an egg into each well and season with salt and pepper. Bake until the egg is set, 25 minutes for a soft yolk and 28 minutes for a firm yolk. Use your hands to lift the puddings from the pan. Serve them immediately.

SAUSAGE, CHEDDAR & POACHED EGG
WAFFLINIS

OVEN: 350°F (175°C) > **PREP TIME:** 20 minutes >
BAKING TIME: 13 to 15 minutes > **YIELD:** 12 wafflinis

● ● ● ●

Nonstick cooking spray, for the pan

3 frozen multigrain waffles, from 1 (10-ounce / 290-g) box, or 12 frozen mini waffles

1 pound (455 g) mildly spicy ground Italian turkey or pork sausage, or 5 mildly spicy Italian sausages, casings removed (see Note)

1½ cups (175 g) grated sharp cheddar

12 large eggs

Note I prefer sausage links because, in most markets, you can get a variety of flavors from the deli: andouille, apple, pork, chicken, chorizo, duck, Italian, Polish, smoked Hungarian, and so on!

YOU HAVE TO TRY THIS to believe it! That's all I can say. The egg on top creates a creamy blanket for the melted pile of heaven beneath, while juices from the sausage seep into the sweetness of the multigrain-waffle base. What an amazing way to start the day! These wafflinis can be eaten with a fork and knife or, if you're on the run, they're a great replacement for the fast-food version. (If you plan to eat this out of hand, be sure to hard cook the egg so the yolk doesn't make a mess.)

Preheat the oven to 350°F (175°C). Spray a 12-well classic cupcake pan and a large nonstick skillet with nonstick cooking spray.

If using regular-size waffles, cut them diagonally into quarters for a total of 12 triangles. (If using mini waffles, there is no need to cut them.) Place 1 piece of waffle (or 1 mini waffle) into each well of the pan. Sauté the sausage in the skillet over medium heat, breaking it up with a wooden spoon, until browned, about 10 minutes. Drain, if necessary, over a colander lined with a paper towel. Set aside.

Divide 1 cup (115 g) of the cheese among the wells. Evenly divide the sausage among the wells, pressing down on the sausage layer to make room for the eggs. Finally, crack 1 egg onto each mini meal and sprinkle with the remaining ½ cup (60 g) cheese.

For a perfectly poached egg with a runny yolk, bake for 13 minutes. For a hard-cooked egg, bake for 15 minutes. To unpan, loosen the sides of each wafflini with a table knife and insert the tines of a fork between the pan and each wafflini to lift it out. Serve them immediately.

VARIATIONS Try a blueberry waffle with provolone cheese or a cinnamon waffle with Muenster and serve them with a little maple syrup.

HUEVOS
Rancheros

OVEN: 350°F (175°C) › **PREP TIME:** 20 minutes ›
BAKING TIME: 25 to 28 minutes › **YIELD:** 12 cupcakes

● ● ●

Nonstick cooking spray, for the pan

12 (6-inch / 15-cm) flour tortillas

1 teaspoon extra-virgin olive oil

1 pound (455 grams) ground turkey

1 (1.25-ounce) package taco seasoning, or 3 tablespoons homemade taco seasoning (see Notes)

1 (16-ounce / 455-g) can refried or black beans, drained (see Notes)

1 (16-ounce / 455-g) jar mild salsa, any flavor you prefer, plus more for serving if desired

2 cups (230 g) grated sharp cheddar, plus more for serving if desired

12 large eggs

OPTIONAL TOPPINGS

Guacamole

Jalapeños, sliced

Olives, black or California, pitted and sliced crosswise

Scallions, sliced

Green chiles, chopped

Queso fresco cheese

Crema or sour cream

Notes If you'd like to make your own taco seasoning, combine the following spices in a small bowl: 1 tablespoon chili powder, 1½ teaspoons ground cumin, ¼ teaspoon dried oregano, ¼ teaspoon garlic powder, ¼ teaspoon onion powder, ½ teaspoon paprika, ¼ teaspoon crushed red pepper flakes, 2 teaspoons salt, and 1 teaspoon freshly ground black pepper. Store in an airtight container for up to 3 months.

Using refried beans will give you a smooth texture; using whole black beans will give you a chunkier texture. If you prefer your black beans smashed, you can mash them against the side of the pan with a wooden spoon.

I LOVE HUEVOS RANCHEROS because all of my favorite flavors are wrapped up into one dapper little package. Dapper might not sound like the right word to describe these, but they look truly chic when served. The bean-and-meat filling is spectacular when it mixes with the creamy yolk of the egg. My children like scooping the filling out of the flour tortilla with corn chips. They think I'm crazy because I let them eat these for breakfast, but I say meals are more fun with a little craziness.

Preheat the oven to 350°F (175°C). Spray a 12-well classic cupcake pan with nonstick cooking spray. Line each well with a flour tortilla; the edges will peek over the top.

Heat the oil in a medium nonstick skillet over medium heat, then sauté the turkey, breaking it up with the back of a wooden spoon until the pieces are crumbled. Stir in the taco seasoning and continue cooking until the turkey is browned, about 12 minutes total. Add the refried beans and stir to combine. If the mixture is soupy, continue to cook until all of the liquid evaporates. Adjust the seasoning, if necessary, and remove from the heat.

Divide the meat and bean filling among the tortillas, then top each with 2 tablespoons salsa (you will use the whole jar), followed by 2 tablespoons cheese (you will use 1 cup / 115 g), pressing down firmly to make room for the eggs. Crack one egg into each well and sprinkle them with the remaining 1 cup (115 g) of cheese.

Bake until the eggs are cooked through and the tortillas are golden brown, 25 minutes for a soft yolk or 28 minutes for a firm yolk. Use a table knife to pop the huevos rancheros out of the pan. Serve them immediately with your choice of one or more of the suggested toppings. Garnish with additional salsa and cheese, if desired. Serve any leftover meat and bean filling on the side as a dip for tortilla chips.

OMELETS

OVEN: 350°F (175°C) > **PREP TIME:** 35 minutes >
BAKING TIME: 25 minutes > **YIELD:** 12 omelets

● ● ●

2 tablespoons olive oil

1 cup (150 g) chopped red or yellow onion

1 large clove garlic, finely chopped, or 1 tablespoon garlic from a tube

1 cup (150 g) chopped red, yellow, and/or orange peppers

10 large eggs

2 teaspoons hot sauce or chile paste

½ teaspoon kosher salt

Freshly ground black pepper

1 (9-ounce / 255-g) ham steak, cut into ¼-inch (6-mm) dice

1 (16-ounce / 455-g) jar salsa

2 cups (230 g) grated extra-sharp cheddar

Nonstick cooking spray, for the pan

12 (6-inch / 15-cm) flour tortillas

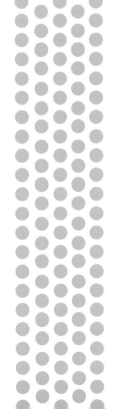

AN OMELET CAN BE GOOD, great, or grandiose; this is the latter. Here, individual flavors are lovingly seasoned and then layered to create memories on your tongue. But keep it simple! Leave the order of layering ingredients as is; they are arranged that way for a reason. You'll see why once you make these the first time and sample the perfect balance of rich and salty, tangy and creamy. And don't mix all of the ingredients together and pour them into the shell. This little package packs a powerful punch when done right.

In a medium skillet, heat the oil over medium heat. Add the onion and cook, stirring occasionally, until it begins to brown, about 5 minutes. Stir in the garlic and pepper and cook until softened, about 5 minutes. Set aside.

In a medium bowl, whisk together the eggs, hot sauce, salt, and a few grinds of black pepper.

In a medium nonstick skillet over medium heat, scramble the eggs until loosely scrambled, using a wooden spoon to stir and break up the pieces, about 8 minutes. Remove from the heat.

In a medium bowl, toss the ham with the reserved pepper and onion mixture. In another medium bowl, mix together the salsa and 1½ cups (175 g) of the cheese. Set both bowls aside.

Preheat the oven to 350°F (175°C).

Spray a 12-well classic cupcake pan with nonstick cooking spray. Line each well with a flour tortilla (the edges will peek over the top). Fill each tortilla with 2 heaping tablespoons scrambled eggs. Evenly distribute the ham and pepper mixture among the wells, on top of the eggs, then evenly distribute the salsa and cheese mixture over the ham and peppers. Evenly divide the remaining ½ cup (60 g) cheese among the wells.

Bake until the egg mixture is cooked through and the cheese has melted, about 25 minutes. Loosen the sides of each omelet with a table knife and pop them out of the pan. Eat the omelets immediately on their own or as part of a breakfast buffet that includes spicy flank steak and home fries.

CORNBREAD
Chili Cheese
BAKES

OVEN: 350°F (175°C) > **PREP TIME:** 30 minutes >
BAKING TIME: 18 to 20 minutes > **YIELD:** 12 mini meals

FOR THE CHILI

1 teaspoon olive oil

½ pound (225 g) ground beef
or ground turkey

1 (12-ounce / 340-g) package
frozen vegetarian chili (see
Note), thawed

1 cup (115 g) grated Monterey
Jack

FOR THE CORNBREAD

1 cup (160 g) cornmeal

1 cup (125 g) all-purpose flour

1 tablespoon chili powder

½ teaspoon kosher salt

2 teaspoons baking powder

2 large eggs, lightly beaten

¼ cup (½ stick / 60 g) butter,
melted and cooled

⅓ cup (75 ml) honey

1 cup (240 ml) buttermilk

8 slices bacon

Nonstick cooking spray,
for the pan

OPTIONAL TOPPINGS

Sour cream

Scallions, sliced

Hot sauce

Cheddar, grated

Black olives, sliced

Lettuce, shredded

Tomatoes, diced

Note Very good vegetarian chili can be found in
most supermarkets. Look for it in the refrigerated or
frozen section. If using a can of vegetarian chili, add
1 teaspoon each of cumin and chili powder, and diced
fire-roasted red peppers from a 3.5-ounce (100-g) jar.

THESE HEARTY CORNBREAD hand pies could
easily become a Super Bowl staple. They are a little sweet,
but also salty and tangy. Even better, they can be eaten out
of hand, cutting down on much of the mess, and make a
fast and hearty meal for the crowd gathered around the TV.
Serve with the same sides you would enjoy with chili, including sour cream, hot sauce, scallions, and chiles.

Make Ahead The chili can be prepared up to 2 days
in advance and stored in an airtight container in the
refrigerator until needed. It will last for up to 1 week.

> MAKE THE CHILI

Heat the oil in a medium nonstick skillet over medium
heat, then add the ground meat and cook, breaking it up
with a wooden spoon until browned, about 10 minutes.
Drain the meat well in a colander, then place it in a large
bowl and stir in the chili and the cheese. Set aside.

> MAKE THE CORNBREAD

Preheat the oven to 350°F (175°C).

In the bowl of a stand mixer fitted with the paddle
attachment, mix the cornmeal, flour, chili powder, salt,
and baking powder. In a small bowl, mix the eggs, butter,
honey, and buttermilk. Add the wet ingredients to the dry
ingredients, mixing on low until combined. Set aside.

In a large skillet over medium heat, cook the bacon
until crisp. Drain the bacon on paper towels, then break it
into small pieces.

Spray a 12-well classic cupcake pan with nonstick
cooking spray. Add 2 heaping tablespoons of cornbread
batter to each well (you will have leftover batter). Divide
the chili evenly among the wells, using it all. Add another
layer of cornbread batter, evenly distributing all of the
remaining batter, and then top with the bacon pieces.

Bake until golden on top, 18 to 20 minutes. Let the hand pies rest in the pan for 1 to 2 minutes, then loosen the sides of each mini meal with a table knife and pop them out of the pan. Serve them with the optional toppings on the side.

Store the hand pies in an airtight container in the refrigerator for up to 5 days. Reheat, wrapped in tin foil, for 15 minutes at 350°F (175°C).

VARIATION If you want to offer a vegetarian hand pie, omit the meat from the chili and add ½ cup (240 g) drained canned pinto, black, or kidney beans instead. Or create a salad: In a serving bowl, toss the suggested toppings (minus the sour cream) with buttermilk dressing, and serve the warm chili-cheese bake on top.

**BUCATINI PASTA &
PUMPKIN CUSTARD TARTS >**

chapter

>THREE<

PASTA & RICE

PASTA AND RICE MAKE AMAZING MINI MEALS WITHOUT THE overindulgence typical at a large family dinner. Instead of getting stuck with a big heaping bowl of pasta or rice, you'll get just the right serving size and amount of carbs when you make your meal in a cupcake pan.

Have fun with these recipes. Make your own homemade sauces for the pasta: tomato, vegetable, pesto, béchamel, and more. Switch up the cheese called for in the recipes with your favorites. Open the fridge and see what you can find. Some of these recipes will work with just about any pasta you want to toss in, while others take to last night's rice just fine.

Perhaps my favorite thing about these recipes is the ease with which children can be part of creating the family's meal. There are plenty of small hands wanting to help out in the kitchen, and I've discovered some great ways to include them in the process, while teaching them to cook at the same time. Some recipes, like Pasta Pies (page 67), are perfect for young helpers. Your children can assemble dinner themselves if you have everything waiting for them when they arrive home from school!

AUBERGINE
Pasta Timbales
WITH BEEF RAGU

OVEN: 350°F (175°C) > **PREP TIME:** 40 minutes >
BAKING TIME: 20 minutes > **YIELD:** 12 timbales

FOR THE EGGPLANT

2 large globe eggplants

1 tablespoon olive oil

½ teaspoon kosher salt

¼ teaspoon freshly ground
   black pepper

FOR THE BEEF RAGU

¼ cup (½ stick / 60 g) salted
   butter

4 cloves garlic, finely
   chopped, or 2 tablespoons
   garlic from a tube

10 ounces (280 g) beef
   tenderloin, cut into ¼-inch
   (6-mm) dice

1 (14.5-ounce / 415-g) can
   plum tomatoes with their
   juice

1½ cups (360 ml) Chianti or
   other dry red wine

½ teaspoon kosher salt

¼ teaspoon freshly ground
   black pepper

FOR THE ASSEMBLY

6 ounces (170 g) rigatoni

½ cup (50 g) grated
   Parmesan

Nonstick cooking spray, for
   the pan

1 cup (115 g) shredded
   mozzarella

1 (24-ounce / 680-g) jar
   ready-made tomato sauce,
   for plating

Note Alternatively, bake the eggplant slices at 450°F
(230°C) until golden and softened, 6 to 8 minutes.

Make Ahead The beef ragu can be prepared
up to 2 days in advance and stored in an airtight
container in the refrigerator until needed. It will
last for up to 1 week.

HERE, TOMATO SAUCE brings together the flavors
of the eggplant shell, beef ragu, and rigatoni filling. When
plated in a pool of sauce, the final creation is gorgeous. Use
a store-bought sauce as a time-saver, but keep a homemade sauce recipe in mind for your next special occasion.

> ### MAKE THE EGGPLANT

Preheat the broiler to high with the oven rack set as near
to the broiler as possible.

   Cut 12 horizontal slices, each about ¼-inch (6-mm)
thick, from the widest parts of the eggplants. (These will
form the wrappers for your timbales.) Chop ½ cup (40 g)
from the remaining eggplant and set it aside. Arrange the
slices of eggplant on 2 rimmed baking sheets lined with
foil and brush each slice with the oil, then season with the
salt and pepper. Broil for 2 to 3 minutes, until browned on
one side (see Note).

> ### MAKE THE BEEF RAGU

Heat the butter in a large saucepan over high heat; add the
garlic and brown it lightly, about 1 minute. Stir in the beef
and the tomatoes and their juice; let the mixture boil for
4 minutes. Add the reserved ½ cup (40 g) chopped
eggplant and the red wine, and continue to cook until the
sauce has thickened, 10 to 12 minutes more. Season with
the salt and pepper and set aside.

> ### ASSEMBLE AND BAKE THE TIMBALES

Preheat the oven to 350°F (175°C). Boil the pasta in salted
water until al dente, about 7 minutes. Drain the pasta and add
it to the beef ragu, mixing to combine. Stir in the Parmesan.

   Spray a 12-well classic cupcake pan with nonstick
cooking spray, then line each well of the pan with a full
slice of eggplant. Fill each well with the pasta and ragu
mixture, then sprinkle the mozzarella on top, using it all.

   Bake until the tops are lightly browned, about
20 minutes. Let the timbales cool in the pan for 5 minutes,
then loosen the sides of each timbale with a table knife
and invert them onto a sheet pan. Serve the timbales
individually, in a pool of warm tomato sauce.

   Store the timbales in an airtight container in the
refrigerator for up to 5 days. Reheat, wrapped in tin foil, for
15 minutes at 350°F (175°C).

Pasta PIES

OVEN: 350°F (175°C) > PREP TIME: 15 minutes >
BAKING TIME: 25 to 30 minutes > YIELD: 12 pies

1 cup (240 ml) milk

4 large eggs

FOR THE ADD-INS

2 tablespoons rinsed and chopped capers

3 tablespoons olive tapenade

3 tablespoons ready-made pesto

8 ounces (225 g) any cooked meat of your choice, such as Italian sausage, bacon, Canadian bacon, or ground beef

¼ cup (10 g) chopped fresh flat-leaf parsley

2 cups (230 g) mixed grated cheese (use odd pieces of cheese from the fridge, such as Gouda, mozzarella, provolone, or asiago)

1½ cups (400 g) store-bought tomato sauce, plus additional for serving (optional)

5 cups (450 g) leftover cooked pasta, any kind (from 8 ounces / 225 g dried pasta)

Nonstick cooking spray, for the pan

Homemade white sauce, for serving (optional; page 88)

DON'T TOSS OUT that extra pasta from last night's dinner! No one will recognize it in this new, remarkably fresh meal. I like how this recipe allows you to use up odds and ends found in the kitchen. It's a great way to make the most of your ingredients and your time.

Preheat the oven to 350°F (175°C).

In a medium bowl, whisk together the milk and eggs until blended; stir in one or more of the add-ins with the parsley, 1½ cups (175 g) of the cheese, and the tomato sauce. Add the pasta. (If you are using small pasta, there is no need to chop it; if you are using spaghetti, you will need to give it a few chops to break it up.) Mix to combine.

Spray a 12-well classic cupcake pan with nonstick cooking spray. Fill each well to the top with the pasta mixture and evenly distribute the remaining ½ cup (60 g) cheese over top. Bake until golden, 25 to 30 minutes.

Cool in the pan for 1 minute, then insert the tines of a fork between the pan and each pie to lift it out. Serve the pies individually in a pool of red or white sauce with a fresh salad and a piece of grilled fish on the side.

Store the pies in an airtight container in the refrigerator for up to 5 days. To reheat, fill the bottom of an ovenproof dish with ½ inch (1 cm) of tomato sauce and place the pies in the sauce. Cover with tin foil and reheat at 350ºF (175ºC) for 15 minutes.

Pasta Bolognese
AL FORNO
WITH CANADIAN BACON & PROVOLONE

OVEN: 350°F (175°C) › PREP TIME: 4 hours 40 minutes ›
BAKING TIME: 25 minutes › YIELD: 12 mini meals

FOR THE BOLOGNESE SAUCE

2 tablespoons olive oil

6 tablespoons (90 g) unsalted butter

1 cup (160 g) chopped yellow onion

1½ cups (150 g) chopped celery

1½ cups (195 g) chopped carrots

2 pounds (910 g) ground beef sirloin or a combination of ground meats, such as turkey, veal, and chicken

1 teaspoon kosher salt

Freshly ground black pepper

2 cups (480 ml) whole milk

¼ teaspoon freshly grated nutmeg

2 cups (480 ml) dry white wine

1 (28-ounce / 675-g) can Italian plum tomatoes with their juice

FOR THE ASSEMBLY

10 ounces (280 g) mini fusilli or penne

Nonstick cooking spray, for the pan

12 slices Canadian bacon

12 slices presliced provolone

½ cup (60 g) grated Parmesan

Savory Tidbit **Pasta is a personal food, as each individual has a certain way they like to eat it. My children like to eat these pasta al forno bites out of hand. My husband likes his with extra sauce and a crusty wedge of bread. I like mine with a side salad. No matter which way, you can't go wrong!**

BOLOGNESE IS THE CELEBRATED meat sauce of the Bologna. It is characterized by a mellow, comfortable flavor that is the result of using great milk and meat. This sauce requires your time, but you will certainly be rewarded! What makes it so successful is that it takes full advantage of the sweetness from the fat of the meat, as well as the milk, carrots, and onions. While learning how to make this sauce in Italy, I used ingredients such as veal, rabbit, and chicken, and so can you, if you like.

A large cast-iron, heavy-gauge pot with a fitted lid works nicely. If you can't watch the sauce for three hours, turn off the heat and cover it with the lid; be sure to complete the sauce the same day. Go ahead and use high-quality sauce from a jar if you're looking for a quick dinner and don't have time to create sauce from scratch. Just make sure to leave out the milk (it'll only thin out the jarred sauce).

› MAKE THE BOLOGNESE SAUCE

In a heavy-bottomed 12-quart (11-L) stockpot, heat the oil and butter over medium heat. When the butter is melted, add the onion and cook, stirring occasionally, until translucent, about 6 minutes. Add the celery and carrots and cook for 2 minutes more, stirring the vegetables to coat them well with the butter.

Add the ground beef, salt, and pepper to the vegetables and use a wooden spoon to break up the meat. Cook until the beef has lost its raw red color (but do not let it brown throughout), about 8 minutes. Turn the heat down to medium-low, add the milk, and let it simmer gently, stirring frequently, until it has bubbled away completely, about 30 minutes. Stir in the nutmeg.

Add the wine and simmer until it is evaporated, about 30 minutes. Cut up the tomatoes and stir them into the sauce, along with their juice. When the tomatoes begin to bubble, turn the heat down to low so that the sauce cooks at the lowest possible simmer. Continue to simmer, uncovered, for 3 hours, stirring from time to time. If you notice that the pot begins to dry out and the sauce is sticking to the bottom, stir in ½ cup (120 ml) water. By the end of the cooking time, no liquid should be present. Taste and adjust the seasoning.

› ASSEMBLE AND BAKE THE MINI MEALS

Preheat the oven to 350°F (175°C). Bring a large pot of salted water to a boil. Add the pasta and cook until it is al dente, 3 to 4 minutes. Drain and return the pasta to the pot. Mix 4 cups (960 ml) of the Bolognese sauce with the pasta. Set aside. (There will be about 2½ cups of extra Bolognese sauce that can be served on the side or stored in an airtight container in the refrigerator for up to 5 days.)

Spray a 12-well classic cupcake pan with nonstick cooking spray. Line each well with 1 slice Canadian bacon, no need to cut to fit. Place 1 slice provolone on top of each bacon slice. Using a ⅓-cup (75-ml) measure, mound each well to the top with the pasta mixture, pressing down to fit as much of the mixture as possible. Sprinkle each mini meal with ½ tablespoon grated Parmesan.

Bake until the tops are browned (see Note), about 25 minutes. Let the mini meals cool for 15 minutes in the pan, then loosen the sides of each with a table knife and pop them out of the pan. Serve them hot.

Store the mini meals in an airtight container in the refrigerator for up to 5 days. Reheat, wrapped in tin foil, for 15 minutes at 350°F (175°C).

Note **As these mini meals bake, they will bubble up and the Parmesan will brown. Don't be alarmed: They're not burning—they're becoming masterpieces. The cheese is forming a crust that will help hold this yummy package together. When you remove these from the pan, you'll see all the layers: Canadian bacon, golden cheese, and the pasta and meat sauce.**

PENNE PASTA
Gratins

OVEN: 350°F (175°C) > PREP TIME: 20 minutes >
BAKING TIME: 20 minutes > YIELD: 12 gratins

FOR THE PASTA

1 (16-ounce / 455-g) package mezze penne or other short pasta of your choice, such as bowtie or macaroni

1 quart (1 L) chicken broth, chilled

1½ cups (360 ml) half-and-half

⅓ cup (50 g) crumbled feta

1 cup (115 g) grated Gruyère

¾ cup (75 g) grated Parmesan, plus more for serving

½ cup (60 g) grated smoked Gouda

½ cup (60 g) grated provolone

Freshly ground black pepper

FOR THE BREAD CRUMB TOPPING

2 tablespoons salted butter

2 cups (220 g) panko bread crumbs

3 tablespoons finely chopped fresh sage

FOR THE FRIED SAGE

2 tablespoons olive oil

12 whole sage leaves

FOR THE TOMATO SAUCE

1 tablespoon salted butter

2 tablespoons olive oil

3 pints (900 g) cherry tomatoes

1 small clove garlic, finely chopped, or 1 teaspoon garlic from a tube

1 teaspoon sugar

2 teaspoons balsamic vinegar

Nonstick cooking spray, for the pan

THIS PERFECTLY PORTIONED pasta treat features five different cheeses and a sage butter–bread crumb topping that cannot be beat! Thyme would make a lovely alternative to sage for the bread crumbs. These mini meals offer just enough richness without going overboard. I serve this in a pool of tomato sauce. You can choose one from your pantry, or use the simple and fresh recipe below, which is very quick to make. I make it when I have a basket full of summer cherry tomatoes from the garden. Serve it with some homemade meatballs, salad, and a sautéed assortment of your favorite peppers and you've got yourself a yummy meal!

Make Ahead The tomato sauce can be prepared up to 2 days in advance and stored in an airtight container in the refrigerator until needed. It will last for up to 5 days in the refrigerator or 2 months in the freezer.

> ### MAKE THE PASTA

In a medium stockpot over medium heat, combine the pasta and the cold chicken broth and cook slowly for about 12 minutes, until half of the liquid has cooked down. Turn off the heat. Add the half-and-half; feta, Gruyère, Parmesan, Gouda, provolone, and a few grinds of black pepper. Stir to combine; taste and adjust the seasoning, if needed. Set aside.

Preheat the oven to 350°F (175°C).

> ### MAKE THE BREAD CRUMB TOPPING

Melt the butter in a small skillet over low heat. Add the bread crumbs and sage. Cook for about 3 minutes, stirring until the butter has combined with the crumbs. (Do not brown.) Turn off the heat.

> ### MAKE THE FRIED SAGE

Heat the oil in a small skillet over medium heat. To test the temperature, drop a bread crumb into the oil; if it sizzles, then the oil is hot enough. Add the sage leaves, a couple at a time. Fry for about 20 seconds, until they are crisp but still green. Use a slotted spoon to transfer the leaves to a paper towel–lined plate to drain. Set aside.

RECIPE CONTINUES

> MAKE THE TOMATO SAUCE

In a large skillet over medium heat, heat the butter and olive oil. When the butter is melted, add the tomatoes and garlic and cook until soft, about 5 minutes. Sprinkle with the sugar and the vinegar. Cook 2 to 3 minutes more and set aside. (You can serve this sauce chunky or puree it in a food processor until smooth.)

> ASSEMBLE AND BAKE THE GRATINS

Spray a 12-well classic cupcake pan with nonstick cooking spray. Sprinkle 1 tablespoon of the bread crumb topping in the base of each well, then divide the pasta and cheese mixture among the wells. Add the remainder of the crumbs to the wells and top with more Parmesan.

Bake until the tops are golden brown, about 20 minutes. Loosen the sides of each gratin using a table knife and insert the tines of a fork between the pan and each gratin to lift it out. Serve the gratins individually in a pool of the tomato sauce. Garnish each with a fried sage leaf.

Store the gratins in an airtight container in the refrigerator for up to 5 days. Reheat, wrapped in tin foil, for 15 minutes at 350°F (175°C).

BUCATINI PASTA &
Pumpkin Custard
TARTS

OVEN: 350°F (175°C) > **PREP TIME:** 30 minutes > **BAKING TIME:** 35 to 40 minutes > **YIELD:** 12 tarts

FOR THE PUMPKIN CUSTARD

¼ cup (60 ml) olive oil

1 onion, chopped

3 cloves garlic, minced, or 2 tablespoons garlic from a tube

1 (15-ounce / 430-g) can pumpkin puree

1 tablespoon fresh marjoram leaves, chopped, or ½ teaspoon dried marjoram

1 teaspoon freshly grated nutmeg

1 cup (240 ml) half-and-half

3 large eggs

1 cup (100 g) grated Parmesan

4 ounces (115 g) bucatini or spaghetti, broken into thirds

FOR THE ASSEMBLY

1 (15-ounce / 430-g) package ready-made pie dough (2 rounds), at room temperature

Nonstick cooking spray, for the pan

½ cup (50 g) grated Parmesan, plus more for garnish (optional)

2 tablespoons cinnamon (optional)

¼ cup (50 g) sugar (optional)

BUCATINI NOODLES are hollow, so they fill with the custard in this dish, but you can use spaghetti and still get incredible results. Swirly, spiky noodles poke out of the custard, and as the tarts bake, the Parmesan becomes golden brown and crusty on top. Delicious! And plenty of fun to look at, too. I like to serve these during the holidays (or "Hollydays," as they are called in my shops) as part of a larger, traditional feast.

> ### MAKE THE PUMPKIN CUSTARD

In a medium skillet, heat the olive oil over medium heat. Add the onion and garlic and cook, stirring occasionally, until soft but not browned, about 5 minutes. Turn off the heat and let rest until cool to the touch.

In a large bowl, combine the pumpkin puree, marjoram, nutmeg, half-and-half, eggs, and cheese. Mix until fully blended, then stir in the onion and garlic mixture.

Meanwhile, bring a large pot of salted water to a boil. Add the pasta, and cook until it is al dente, about 8 minutes. Drain the pasta, run it under cold water, and drain it again. Add the pasta to the pumpkin custard and stir to combine.

> ### ASSEMBLE AND BAKE THE TARTS

Preheat the oven to 350°F (175°C).

Unroll the pie dough onto a flat work surface; no need to flour it first. Cut each round in half, and then cut each half into thirds, for a total of 12 pieces. Spray a 12-well classic cupcake pan with nonstick cooking spray. Place 1 piece of dough in each well of the pan. Some pieces of dough will overlap and some areas will be bare; the asymmetrical quality of the dough will add a unique flair to each tart. Fill each well to the top with the pumpkin custard–pasta mixture. Sprinkle the tops with the cheese and loosely fold in the excess dough. Sprinkle with cinnamon and sugar or with additional Parmesan.

Bake until the crust is golden brown, 35 to 40 minutes. Let the tarts rest in the pan for 5 minutes, then loosen the sides of each tart with a table knife and pop them out of the pan.

Pasta Tarts
WITH SMOKED CHEESE & PRIMAVERA SAUCE

OVEN: 350°F (175°C) > PREP TIME: 30 minutes > BAKING TIME: 25 to 30 minutes > YIELD: 12 tarts

FOR THE PASTA

1 (16-ounce / 455-g) package bucatini pasta or spaghetti

1 tablespoon unsalted butter

1 cup (240 ml) whole milk, half-and-half, or heavy cream

1½ cups (175 g) grated smoked provolone or smoked Gouda

¾ cup (75 g) grated Parmesan

Kosher salt and freshly ground black pepper

FOR THE BREAD CRUMB TOPPING

½ cup (55 g) fresh bread crumbs (from 3 slices bread)

1 tablespoon finely chopped fresh sage leaves

2 tablespoons unsalted butter, melted

FOR THE ASSEMBLY

1 (17.3-ounce / 485-g) package puff pastry (2 sheets per package)

Nonstick cooking spray, for the pan

¼ cup (½ stick / 60 g) melted butter, for brushing the top (optional)

½ cup (60 g) grated smoked provolone or smoked Gouda

FOR THE PRIMAVERA SAUCE

2 tablespoons unsalted butter

2 tablespoons olive oil

1 small zucchini, cut into ¼-inch (6-mm) dice

1 carrot, peeled and cut into ¼-inch (6-mm) dice

4 asparagus stalks, tough ends snapped off and stalks thinly sliced on the bias

1 cup (100 g) green beans, thinly sliced on the bias

2 large tomatoes, seeded and cut into ¼-inch (6-mm) dice

2 tablespoons chopped fresh flat-leaf parsley or parsley from a tube

½ cup (75 g) frozen peas, thawed

1 teaspoon kosher salt

½ teaspoon freshly ground black pepper

THIS RECIPE IS Mini Meal Creativity 101, demonstrating the flexibility of the mini meal wrapper. No matter what type of wrapper you use, these tarts will taste great. You can get creative with the filling, too. The variations at the end of the recipe will give you some ideas about how to deliciously change things up for your family.

> MAKE THE PASTA

Bring a pot of salted water to a boil. Break the noodles into 3 pieces, then add them to the water and cook until the pasta is al dente, about 7 minutes. Drain well, then return the pasta to the pot and toss with the butter; set aside.

In a medium saucepan over medium heat, bring the milk almost to a boil, about 4 minutes. Turn off the heat. Stir in the provolone and Parmesan, then season with salt and pepper. Add the sauce to the cooked pasta and toss to combine. (If you want to include any of the add-ins in the Variations, this is when you should add them.)

> MAKE THE BREAD CRUMB TOPPING

In a small bowl, mix the bread crumbs, sage, and melted butter until combined.

> ASSEMBLE AND BAKE THE TARTS

Preheat the oven to 350°F (175°C). Unroll the puff pastry and cut each sheet crosswise into 3 equal strips, and then cut each strip into 3 pieces, for a total of 18 pieces. Set aside 12 pieces to use for the pan (see "Savory Tidbit" on page 44 for ideas on how to use the extra pastry).

Spray a 12-well classic cupcake pan with nonstick cooking spray. Line each well with 1 piece of puff pastry (or wrapper of your choice; see Variations), stretching each piece slightly in both directions and letting it over-hang the edges of the well slightly. (Make sure any pastry overhanging the well doesn't touch any other pastry or the pieces will fuse together when baking.) Fill each well with the pasta mixture. Keep the tarts open-faced or loosely fold the overhanging dough toward the center of each tart. Brush the dough with the melted butter.

Bake until the tops are golden brown, 25 to 30 minutes. During the last 5 minutes of baking, sprinkle the tops with the bread crumb topping.

> MAKE THE PRIMAVERA SAUCE

While the tarts are baking, melt the butter and oil in a large sauté pan over medium heat. Add the zucchini, carrot, asparagus, and green beans and cook until the colors brighten and the vegetables are al dente, about 5 minutes; add the tomato and cook until heated through, about 2 minutes more. Remove from the heat and add the parsley and thawed peas. Season with the salt and pepper, then set aside.

Let the tarts cool in the pan for 3 to 5 minutes, then loosen the sides of each tart with a table knife and pop them out of the pan. Serve the tarts individually on a pool of the primavera sauce.

Store the leftover tarts in an airtight container in the refrigerator for up to 3 days. The primavera sauce can be stored in a separate airtight container in the refrigerator for up to 3 days. To reheat the tarts, plate them on a pool of the primavera sauce and microwave for 1 minute.

Note Bucatini is a good choice for this recipe because it won't lose its shape after it's been boiled and baked.

VARIATIONS Add-ins! To make room for these additions, use 3 cups (420 g) cooked pasta instead of the 4 cups (560 g) called for in the recipe. Mix in these additions when you add the sauce to the pasta.

- Mix 1 cup (145 g) frozen peas, thawed, with the pasta.
- In a medium skillet over medium heat, cook 8 ounces (225 g) pancetta or bacon with 2 tablespoons olive oil, stirring occasionally, until the pancetta is golden and the fat renders, about 15 minutes. Transfer to a paper towel–lined plate to drain, then crumble and mix with the pasta.
- Mix 1 cup (225 g) chopped roasted or grilled vegetables and ¼ cup (60 ml) pesto or olive paste with the pasta.
- Stir 1 cup (225 g) roasted pumpkin with 2 teaspoons finely chopped fresh sage leaves into the pasta.

> CLASSIC <
Lasagnas

OVEN: 350°F (175°C) > PREP TIME: 35 minutes >
BAKING TIME: 35 minutes > YIELD: 24 lasagnas

FOR THE SAUSAGE

12 ounces (340 g) sweet Italian sausage, casings removed

7 ounces (200 g) provolone, cut into ¼-inch (6-mm) dice

1½ cups (175 g) shredded mozzarella

FOR THE RICOTTA FILLING

3 cups (450 g) whole-milk ricotta

2 large eggs, slightly beaten

1 to 2 tablespoons dried Italian herb blend, or a combination of oregano, thyme, savory, chervil, and rosemary

2 tablespoons chopped fresh basil leaves or 2 tablespoons basil paste from a tube

3 medium cloves garlic, crushed to a fine paste, or 2 tablespoons garlic from a tube

Pinch each kosher salt and freshly ground black pepper

FOR THE ASSEMBLY

3 cups (800 g) store-bought tomato sauce

Nonstick cooking spray, for the pan

24 lasagna noodles

3 cups (300 g) grated Parmesan

THIS BEAUTIFULLY proportioned take on a home-made classic is so simple and easy to make. Just line the wells of the pan with pasta and fill it with sweet Italian sausage, a variety of cheeses, and tomato sauce. The portability of these mini lasagnas makes them perfect for neighborhood potlucks.

> MAKE THE SAUSAGE

In a medium nonstick skillet over medium heat, cook the sausage, breaking it up with a wooden spoon, until it is browned and crumbled, about 12 minutes. Transfer the sausage to a large bowl to cool slightly, then add the provolone and mozzarella and toss to combine. Set aside.

> MAKE THE RICOTTA FILLING

In a large bowl, combine the ricotta, eggs, herb blend, basil, garlic, and salt and pepper. Set aside.

> ASSEMBLE AND BAKE THE LASAGNAS

Preheat the oven to 350°F (175°C) degrees.

Bring a large pot of salted water to a boil. Add the lasagna noodles and cook until al dente, about 10 minutes. Drain the noodles, rinse them under cold water, and drain them again.

Spray the wells of two 12-well classic cupcake pans with nonstick cooking spray. Lay one lasagna noodle evenly over each well and press down to form a cup for the fillings. Layer 2 tablespoons of the sausage mixture, 2 tablespoons tomato sauce, and 2 tablespoons ricotta filling in each well. Fold one end of each noodle over to seal in the fillings and top it with 2 more tablespoons of sauce. Fold the other end of the noodle over to seal, and sprinkle 2 tablespoons of Parmesan over each lasagna. Bake until golden and bubbling, about 35 minutes.

Let the lasagnas cool in the pan for 10 minutes, then loosen the sides of each lasagna with a table knife and invert the lasagnas onto a sheet pan. Serve the lasagnas individually, right side up.

Store the lasagnas in an airtight container in the refrigerator for up to 5 days. To reheat, fill the bottom of an ovenproof dish with ½ inch (1 cm) of tomato sauce and place the pies in the sauce. Cover with tin foil and reheat at 350°F (175°C) for 15 minutes.

POBLANO, SPINACH & BLACK BEAN
LASAGNAS
with Goat Cheese

OVEN: 350°F (175°C) > **PREP TIME:** 30 minutes >
BAKING TIME: 20 to 25 minutes > **YIELDS:** 12 lasagnas

FOR THE ROASTED CHILES

2 poblano chiles

1 teaspoon kosher salt

FOR THE BEANS

1 (15-ounce / 430 g) can black beans

2 teaspoons cumin

2 teaspoons chili powder

¼ cup (35 g) raisins

½ teaspoon kosher salt

¼ teaspoon freshly ground black pepper

FOR THE GOAT CHEESE SAUCE

½ cup (120 ml) whole milk or heavy cream

8 ounces (225 g) goat cheese

1 tablespoon chopped fresh cilantro leaves

¼ teaspoon kosher salt

FOR THE SPINACH

1 (10-ounce / 280-g) box frozen chopped spinach, thawed and all liquid squeezed out

1 cup (115 g) grated mozzarella or crumbled queso fresco

FOR THE ASSEMBLY

1 (16-ounce / 455-g) jar salsa

½ cup (60 g) grated queso fresco, mozzarella, or pepper Jack

Nonstick cooking spray, for the pan

12 (6-inch / 15-cm) flour tortillas

THIS IS A delicious combination of Mexican flavors, fresh spinach, and tart goat cheese. I use poblano chiles, which are dark green and glossy with a medium heat. Using flour tortillas as the wrapper for the lasagna makes this package especially easy to present at a buffet or as a single serving. They would be excellent served alongside jalapeño-glazed chicken breasts and a green salad with oranges and avocado.

> ### MAKE THE ROASTED CHILES

Roast the poblano chiles over a high flame on your stovetop, turning them with tongs to make sure you blacken all sides, about 4 minutes. Or, roast the chiles under a broiler set to high, flipping the chiles occasionally to blacken all sides, 8 to 10 minutes. Transfer the chiles to a zip-top plastic bag and sprinkle them with the salt, then close the bag to let them steam and cool for about 15 minutes. When the chiles are cool enough to handle, peel off the skin, then cut the chiles open and remove and discard the spines and the seeds. Finely chop the chiles and set them aside.

> ### MAKE THE BEANS

Drain off half the liquid from the can of black beans. Place the beans and the remaining liquid in a blender or the bowl of a food processor fitted with a blade. Add the cumin, chili powder, raisins, salt, and pepper. Puree until smooth and set aside.

> ### MAKE THE GOAT CHEESE SAUCE

In a small saucepan over medium heat, warm the milk for about 2 minutes, then stir in the goat cheese and heat until it is melted and smooth, about 3 minutes. Turn off the heat, then stir in the cilantro and salt.

› MAKE THE SPINACH

In a medium bowl, combine the spinach with the mozzarella, the goat cheese sauce, and the roasted chiles. Mix well.

› ASSEMBLE AND BAKE THE LASAGNAS

Preheat the oven to 350°F (175°C). In a medium bowl, mix the salsa with the queso fresco.

Spray a 12-well classic cupcake pan with nonstick cooking spray. Fill each well with a flour tortilla, making sure it fits snugly into the bottom of the pan. The tops will poke up above the wells.

Divide the black bean mixture evenly among the tortilla "shells." Top with the spinach and goat cheese mixture, and then the salsa mixture.

Bake until the tortillas are golden brown around the edges and the filling is heated through, 20 to 25 minutes. Let the lasagnas rest in the pan for 5 minutes, then lift them out using your fingers.

> PUMPKIN <
RISOTTOS

OVEN: 400°F (205°C) > PREP TIME: 40 minutes >
BAKING TIME: 20 minutes > YIELD: 12 risottos

FOR THE RISOTTO

1 quart (1 L) chicken broth

3 tablespoons unsalted butter

2 cloves garlic, finely chopped, or 1 tablespoon garlic from a tube

½ cup (80 g) diced red onion

¾ cup (150 g) Arborio rice

3 tablespoons dry vermouth

1 (15-ounce / 430-g) can pumpkin puree (see Note)

½ teaspoon cinnamon

¼ teaspoon freshly grated nutmeg

1 tablespoon sugar

½ cup (120 ml) heavy cream

¾ cup (75 g) grated Parmesan

1 teaspoon dried crumbled sage

1 tablespoon finely chopped fresh oregano leaves

1 tablespoon finely chopped fresh mint leaves

FOR THE PUMPKIN CRUMB TOPPING

2 tablespoons unsalted butter

1½ cups (165 g) panko bread crumbs or fresh crumbs taken from the center of a loaf of plain Italian bread

½ cup (65 g) pumpkin seeds, finely chopped

FOR THE ASSEMBLY

Nonstick cooking spray, for the pan

1 (17.3-ounce / 485-g) package puff pastry (2 sheets), at room temperature

THESE RISOTTOS COULD almost be a dessert, though the crunchy pumpkin seed and crumb topping offers up a nutty flavor. I've never been one to turn down a little sweetness with my meals, but with a dollop of cinnamon whipped cream or vanilla bean ice cream, this becomes a savory dessert. This version is wonderful served alongside roast pork loin with roasted apples and pears, and autumn vegetables, while the richness of the spices and herbs make the dessert version an excellent treat for a fall evening.

> MAKE THE RISOTTO

In a small saucepan over low heat, bring the broth to a simmer.

In a medium saucepan, melt the butter over medium heat. Add the garlic and onion and cook, stirring occasionally, until softened, about 4 minutes. Add the rice, tossing it in the pan to coat it with the butter, about 1 minute.

Add ½ cup (120 ml) of the broth and cook at a simmer, stirring constantly, until the broth is absorbed. Add the remaining 3½ cups (840 ml) broth, ½ cup (120 ml) at a time, stirring constantly and letting each addition be absorbed before adding the next, until the rice is al dente, about 25 minutes. Turn off the heat and stir in the vermouth, pumpkin, cinnamon, nutmeg, sugar, cream, and Parmesan. Stir in the sage, oregano, and mint. Set aside.

> MAKE THE PUMPKIN CRUMB TOPPING

In a small sauté pan over medium heat, melt the butter, then add the crumbs and pumpkin seeds and stir to combine. Cook until the butter evenly coats the crumbs, about 1 minute. Remove from the heat.

> ASSEMBLE AND BAKE THE RISOTTOS

Preheat the oven to 400°F (205°C).

Spray a 12-well classic cupcake pan with nonstick cooking spray. Unroll the puff pastry and cut each sheet crosswise into 3 equal strips, and then cut each strip into thirds, for a total of 18 pieces. Set aside 12 pieces to use for the pan (see "Savory Tidbit" on page 44 for ideas on how to use the extra pastry). Line each well with 1 piece of puff pastry, stretching each piece slightly in both directions and letting it overhang the edges of the well slightly. (Make sure any pastry overhanging the well doesn't touch any other pastry or the pieces will fuse together when baking.) Fill each well to the top with the pumpkin risotto mixture, then top off each well with the risotto mixture, using all of it. Evenly distribute the pumpkin crumb topping among the wells, using all of it.

Bake until golden brown and puffed around the edges, about 20 minutes. Do not allow the risottos to cool in the pan, as they will get soggy. To unpan, loosen the sides of each risotto with a table knife, then lift the risottos out of the pan with your fingers, using the wrappers as handles.

Store the risottos in an airtight container in the refrigerator for up to 3 days. Reheat, wrapped in tin foil, for 15 minutes at 350°F (175°C).

Note To save time, I used canned pumpkin in this dish—not to be confused with pumpkin pie filling, which has sugar and spices included. Homemade pumpkin puree is great, however, because it can be made ahead and even frozen to be used when pumpkin is out of season. Roasting your own pumpkin will make this dish even better!

Preheat the oven to 425°F (220°C). Cut a 6½-pound (3-kg) pumpkin in half and remove and discard the seeds and fibers. Cut the flesh into large chunks and place them, skin side down, on a foil-lined rimmed baking sheet. Drizzle with ½ cup (120 ml) olive oil and season with salt and pepper. Add 3 whole cloves of garlic to the pan. Cover with foil and roast until the flesh is tender, about 50 minutes. Scrape the flesh from the skin and puree. (Makes about 3 cups / 735 g, depending on the size of your pumpkin.)

Risotto CAKES
WITH PORCINI MUSHROOM RAGU

OVEN: 350°F (175°C) > **PREP TIME:** 1 hour 5 minutes >
BAKING TIME: 18 to 20 minutes > **YIELD:** 12 cakes

FOR THE RISOTTO CAKES

1 quart (1 L) chicken or
  vegetable broth

1 tablespoon extra-virgin
  olive oil

1 small onion, finely chopped

1½ cups (300 g) Arborio rice

¼ cup (60 ml) dry white wine

½ cup (50 g) grated
  Parmesan

1 tablespoon fresh thyme
  leaves

FOR THE PORCINI MUSHROOM RAGU

1½ pounds (680 g) fresh
  mushrooms, preferably
  wild porcini, or 7 ounces
  (200 g) dried porcini,
  reconstituted (see Note
  page 97)

2 tablespoons extra-virgin
  olive oil

1 large onion, cut into ¼-inch
  (6-mm) dice

1 medium carrot, peeled and
  cut into ¼-inch (6-mm)
  dice

Kosher salt

1 cup (240 ml) dry white wine

¼ cup dry sherry

¼ cup (½ stick / 60 g)
  unsalted butter

Freshly ground black pepper

2 cloves garlic, minced, or
  1 tablespoon garlic from a
  tube

2 tablespoons all-purpose
  flour

3 cups (720 ml) vegetable or
  chicken broth

FOR THE ASSEMBLY

Nonstick cooking spray, for
  the pan

24 slices prosciutto (about
  1 pound / 455 grams)

½ cup (40 g) chopped fresh
  flat-leaf parsley

CUPCAKE WELLS are very similar in shape to timbale pans, so this, and any other savory meals in this book, could be called timbales. This meal is especially delicious because of the porcini mushroom ragu. I learned how to make this and to eat porcini five hundred ways in Florence in September, when porcini are in abundance. You can find dried porcini at most markets. If they are in a mélange of mushrooms, go ahead and use the mix. Porcini are my first choice because of their incredible flavor, but if you can't find them, don't let that keep you from making this amazing dish. You can use any combination of fresh portobello, button, and cremini mushrooms instead.

Serve these cakes as part of a buffet with Cornish game hens or duck, or a tenderloin of beef. They would also be great for lunch with a thick slice of fresh bread with melted cheese and tomatoes, and a big salad with nuts, herbs, and artichokes.

Make Ahead **The porcini mushroom ragu can be prepared up to 2 days in advance and stored in an airtight container in the refrigerator until needed. It will last for up to 1 week in the refrigerator or 2 months in the freezer.**

> MAKE THE RISOTTO CAKES

In a small saucepan over low heat, bring the broth to a simmer.

In a medium saucepan, heat the oil over medium heat. Add the onion and cook, stirring occasionally until softened. Add the rice and stir to coat. Add the wine and stir constantly until all the wine is absorbed, about 8 minutes. Add 1 cup (240 ml) of the broth and cook at a simmer, stirring constantly, until the broth is absorbed. Add broth ½ cup (120 ml) at a time, letting each addition be absorbed before adding the next, until the rice is al dente, about 25 minutes. Remove from the heat; stir in the Parmesan and thyme.

> MAKE THE PORCINI MUSHROOM RAGU

If using fresh mushrooms, clean and slice them ¼ inch (6 mm) thick. If using dried mushrooms, finely chop them.

In a large skillet, heat the oil over medium heat. Add the onion, stirring occasionally, until softened and beginning to brown, about 8 minutes. Add the carrot and continue to cook until the onions are browned, about 15 minutes. Add ½ teaspoon of salt, the wine, and sherry; raise the heat to high and reduce the liquid by half, about 5 minutes.

In another large skillet, melt the butter over medium heat. Add the mushrooms and cook until they begin to lose their juice, about 7 minutes. Season with salt and pepper and stir in the garlic and the onion mixture. Sprinkle the mushrooms with the flour, stirring to fully incorporate. Turn the heat to low, add the broth, and cook, stirring occasionally, until thickened, about 20 minutes. The sauce should be silky and creamy, not brothy.

> ASSEMBLE AND BAKE THE CAKES

Preheat the oven to 350°F (175°C).

Spray a 12-well classic cupcake pan with nonstick cooking spray. Line each well with 2 slices of prosciutto, making a cross pattern in the bottom of the well. Fill each well with the risotto mixture using a ⅓-cup (75-ml) measure. Fold the ends of the prosciutto into the center to form a package and bake until the tops are firm to the touch and golden, 18 to 20 minutes.

Let the cakes rest in the pan for 1 minute, then loosen the sides of each cake with a table knife and pop them out of the pan. Serve the cakes individually. Ladle the mushroom ragu over the risotto cakes, about ½ cup (120 ml) of sauce per serving, and garnish with the parsley.

Store the leftover risotto cakes in an airtight container in the refrigerator for up to 5 days. The porcini mushroom ragu can be stored in a separate airtight container in the refrigerator for up to 1 week. To reheat the risotto cakes, plate them on a pool of the ragu and microwave for 1 minute.

Savory Tidbit **The broth base I prefer and use most is Better Than Bouillon by Superior Touch. This concentrated paste is economical, with 38 servings per 8-ounce jar. It has a long expiration date and takes up very little room in the fridge. I keep six different flavors on hand, including chicken, beef, mushroom, and lobster. I don't often have time to make my own stock, and I'm sure you don't either!**

RISOTTOS
with Green Vegetables

OVEN: 350°F (175°C) or 400°F (205°C) > **PREP TIME:** 45 minutes >
BAKING TIME: 15 to 45 minutes, depending on choice of crust > **YIELD:** 12 risottos

● ● ●

FOR THE VEGETABLES

1½ cups (190 g) assorted chopped green vegetables, such as zucchini, asparagus, green beans, and frozen peas (thawed)

FOR THE RISOTTO

1 quart (1 L) chicken broth

1 tablespoon unsalted butter

1 tablespoon extra-virgin olive oil

1 small onion, cut into ¼-inch (6-mm) dice

1½ cups (300 g) Arborio rice

5 tablespoons (75 ml) extra-dry vermouth

2 tablespoons unsalted butter

¾ cup (75 g) grated Parmesan

Zest and juice of 1 lemon

2 tablespoons chopped fresh flat-leaf parsley or parsley from a tube

Kosher salt and freshly ground black pepper

FOR THE ASSEMBLY

Nonstick cooking spray, for the pan

1 (15-ounce / 430-g) package ready-made pie dough (2 rounds), at room temperature, or 1 (17.3-ounce / 485-g) package puff pastry (2 sheets), at room temperature

FRESH GREEN VEGETABLES of nearly every variety add the flavor of a warm summer day to this heavenly risotto. Experiment with the three wrapper options, and you'll have a completely different taste for the same meal each time. Chicken cutlets—one of the wrapper options—are wonderful for this recipe.

Pair the risotto with a variety of sauces and serve for lunch with a salad or for dinner with roasted pork loin and sautéed vegetables.

> MAKE THE VEGETABLES

If using zucchini, slice the zucchini lengthwise into 4 long planks, then cut the planks crosswise into thin strips.

If using asparagus, cut off the tips of the asparagus and slice the stalks into ¼-inch (6-mm) slices on the bias, removing the tough end.

If using peas, add the thawed peas directly from the bag.

If using green beans, trim the ends and slice the beans into ¼-inch (6-mm) slices on the bias. Blanch the beans in boiling salted water until slightly tender but still bright green, about 2 minutes. Transfer to a colander and immediately rinse in cold water; drain well.

> MAKE THE RISOTTO

In a small saucepan over low heat, bring the broth to a simmer.

In a medium saucepan, heat the butter and oil over medium heat. Add the onion and cook, stirring occasionally, until softened, about 4 minutes. Add the rice and stir to coat. Add 1 cup (240 ml) of the broth and cook at a simmer, stirring constantly, until the broth is absorbed. Add the remaining 3½ cups (840 ml) broth, ½ cup (120 ml) at a time, stirring constantly and letting each addition be absorbed before adding the next, until the rice is al dente, about 25 minutes. Remove from the heat and add the vermouth, butter, Parmesan, all of the vegetables, the lemon zest and juice, salt and pepper, and the chopped parsley. Stir to combine.

RECIPE CONTINUES

> ASSEMBLE AND BAKE THE RISOTTOS

Preheat the oven to 350°F (175°C) if using pie dough, or to 400°F (205°C) if using puff pastry.

Spray a 12-well classic cupcake pan with nonstick cooking spray.

If using pie dough, unroll the dough onto a flat work surface; no need to flour it first. Cut each round of dough in half, and then cut each half into thirds, for a total of 12 pieces. Place 1 piece of dough in each well of the pan. The dough can be draped loosely in the well; no need to press it in perfectly. Fill the dough to the top with the risotto mixture, using it all. Bake until golden brown at the edges, 40 to 45 minutes. Let the risottos cool in the pan for 10 minutes (no longer, or they will become soggy), then loosen the sides of each risotto with a table knife and pop them out of the pan.

If using puff pastry, unroll the puff pastry and cut each sheet crosswise into 3 equal strips, and then cut each strip into thirds, for a total of 18 pieces. Set aside 12 pieces to use for the pan (see "Savory Tidbit" on page 44 for ideas on how to use the extra pastry). Line each well with 1 piece of puff pastry, stretching each piece slightly in both directions and letting it overhang the edges of the well slightly. (Make sure any pastry overhanging the well doesn't touch any other pastry or the pieces will fuse together when baking.) Using a ⅓-cup (75-ml) measure, fill each well with the risotto mixture, using it all. Bake until the pastry has puffed and turned golden brown, 15 minutes. Loosen the sides of each risotto with a table knife and pop them out of the pan.

Store the risottos in an airtight container in the refrigerator for up to 3 days. Reheat, wrapped in tin foil, for 15 minutes at 350°F (175°C).

Note **To pound the chicken cutlets or breasts, place them in a large zip-top bag. Cover the bag with a tea towel and gently pound with a mallet or the bottom of a heavy saucepan. Leave the chicken in the bag—you can use it to toss the chicken with the rest of the ingredients.**

The cutlets should be ¼ inch (6 mm) thick. Some markets sell chicken cutlets ready to go in 1½- to 2-pound (680- to 910-g) packages. Make sure there are six pieces that can be cut in half lengthwise, each half about 3½ to 4 inches (9 to 10 cm) long, to fill the wells.

CHICKEN CUTLET VARIATION

One seemingly odd choice is to use a chicken cutlet as the wrapper. I thought it was crazy as well; then I made it, and wow! Now I know how to get that yummy risotto filling inside that thin, juicy, flavorful chicken wrapper without drying out the chicken. The whole dish reminds me of a Greek avgolemono soup with chicken, rice, and lemon.

> Nonstick cooking spray, for the pan
>
> 6 chicken cutlets or breasts (2 pounds / 680 g), pounded to ¼-inch (6-mm) thickness and cut in half lengthwise (see Note)
>
> Pinch kosher salt and freshly ground black pepper
>
> 2 tablespoons chopped fresh parsley or parsley from a tube
>
> 3 tablespoons lemon juice
>
> Pinch of cayenne

Preheat the oven to 350°F (175°C). Spray a 12-well classic cupcake pan with nonstick cooking spray.

Prepare the vegetables and risotto following the instructions on page 85.

In a large bowl, toss the breasts with the salt and pepper, parsley, lemon juice, and cayenne, until well coated.

Lay a piece of raw chicken into each well, overhanging the edge. Fill each well with the risotto mixture using a ⅓-cup (75-ml) measure.

Fold the chicken over onto the filling, forming a package, and bake until firm to the touch but not dry or browned, 20 to 25 minutes.

Let the risottos rest in the pan for 5 minutes, then loosen the sides of each risotto with a table knife, and pop them out of the pan, keeping them upright. Pour the juices in the bottom of each well over the risottos prior to serving.

PARSLIED VELOUTÉS

OVEN: 350°F (175°C) > PREP TIME: 25 minutes >
BAKING TIME: 35 minutes > YIELD: 12 mini meals

FOR THE CHICKEN WRAPPERS

4 large boneless, skinless chicken breasts (about 2¼ pounds / 1 kg), trimmed of excess fat

Pinch of kosher salt and freshly ground black pepper

2 tablespoons finely chopped parsley

2 tablespoons Dijon mustard

1 tablespoon olive oil

FOR THE RICE

2 cups (370 g) uncooked basmati rice, or 4½ cups (720 g) ready-made, precooked basmati rice (see Note)

1 tablespoon Better Than Bouillon mushroom base

½ cup (120 ml) half-and-half

½ cup (75 g) frozen peas, thawed

Nonstick cooking spray, for the pan

FOR THE PARSLIED CREAM SAUCE

2 tablespoons unsalted butter, melted

2 tablespoons all-purpose flour

1 cup (240 ml) milk

1 cup (240 ml) chicken broth

2 cups (160 g) finely chopped fresh parsley

Pinch of kosher salt and ground white pepper

VARIATION Try tucking in ½ cup (115 g) of any of the following before the mini meals are popped in the oven: diced ham, sun-dried tomato, roasted red pepper, or pesto. Then fold in the ends of the chicken to form a neat package.

THIS DISH IS SO SIMPLE and delicious and full of flavor. I make it for my children when they need something cozy for dinner. The ingredients are simple and likely to be in your pantry! The best part is that you can create your own flavors based on your mood. If you like curried rice, try adding a bit of your favorite curry powder and some cashews, golden raisins, and finely diced red pepper. If Italian flavors better fit your mood, add a bit of tomato paste, diced provolone, and some fresh oregano to the rice, and then top the chicken with some pepperoni and grated Parmesan. Finish it off by adding a bit of tomato to the sauce instead of parsley, to create a creamy tomato flavor.

Make Ahead These can be made a day in advance or cooked and served as a chilled lunch option with a salad. I make mine at 2:00 P.M. and then pop them into the oven at 4:00 P.M. for a family dinner. Even better, the sauce can be reheated later. It's also great served chilled on a bed of assorted lettuce leaves with your favorite combination of vegetables and a fresh vinaigrette.

> ## MAKE THE CHICKEN WRAPPERS

Cut the breasts into thirds crosswise so you have 12 pieces total, each about 4 inches (11 cm) long.

To pound the chicken breasts, place them in a large zip-top bag. Cover the bag with a tea towel and gently pound with a mallet or the bottom of a heavy saucepan. Leave the chicken in the bag—you can use it toss the chicken with the rest of the ingredients rather than dirtying a bowl.

In a shallow bowl, whisk together the salt, pepper, parsley, mustard, and oil. Transfer the mixture to the bag with the chicken, seal, and shake to coat the chicken pieces. Refrigerate until the rice is ready.

> ## MAKE THE RICE

Cook the rice, if necessary, following the directions on the back of the package. To the cooked rice, add the mushroom base, half-and-half, and peas; stir to combine.

> ASSEMBLE AND BAKE THE VELOUTÉS

Preheat the oven to 350°F (175°C).

Spray a 12-well classic cupcake pan with nonstick cooking spray. Lay a piece of raw chicken into each well. You can cut the breasts to fit so they overhang the well on both sides by ½ inch (1 cm). Some might be torn, but don't worry—they will seal up in the pan as they cook. Fill each well with ⅓ cup (75 g) of the rice mixture and any of the variation ingredients, then fold the sides of the chicken pieces over the rice mixture to create a sealed package. Bake until the chicken is firm to the touch but the tops are not browned, about 35 minutes.

> MAKE THE PARSLIED CREAM SAUCE

While the mini meals are baking, combine the butter and flour in a medium saucepan over medium-low heat, then whisk in the milk and chicken broth, making sure to get all of the bits of the paste from the corners of the pan. Bring to a boil over medium heat, and whisk until the mixture has thickened, 8 to 10 minutes. Turn off the heat.

Place the white sauce and the parsley leaves in a blender. Blend until bright green, about 30 seconds. Season with the salt and white pepper. The sauce can be served right away or reheated later. It is delicious chilled or warm.

As soon as the mini meals are done baking, loosen the sides of each with a table knife, then insert the tines of a fork between the pan and each mini meal to lift it out. Spoon any sauce remaining in the wells over each meal.

Spoon the cream sauce over the chicken, and serve the veloutés alongside peas and carrots sautéed in a little butter.

Store the leftover veloutés in an airtight container in the refrigerator for up to 3 days. The parslied cream sauce can be stored in a separate airtight container for up to 5 days. Enjoy at room temperature or reheat, wrapped in tin foil, for 15 minutes at 350°F (175°C). The parslied cream sauce can be reheated in a saucepan on the stovetop.

Note To save time, use ready-made basmati rice, which is precooked without preservatives. Alternatively, other types of raw rice, such as wild, garnet, or red rice, can be used instead of basmati.

BLENDING
Hot Liquids

Safety is important when blending a hot liquid. Remove the inner cap of the top of the blender and place a dishcloth or several paper towels over the hole so that the steam can escape but the liquid stays in the blender. Blend the sauce in two batches so you don't overfill the blender. The last thing you want is for the liquid to explode all over the place and burn whoever is blending!

^ GRAPE-LEAF PURSES WITH COUSCOUS & LAMB STUFFING

chapter
>FOUR<
VEGETABLES

IN MY MIND, VEGETABLES ARE ASSOCIATED WITH WORDS LIKE "fresh," "new," and "vibrant." When is the last time you held a vegetable fresh off the vine and carefully sliced the tender flesh for a bright addition to your meal? If it's been awhile, you're missing out! Let's introduce some freshness into your meals.

Vegetables can be so much more than frozen peas or canned corn tossed in the microwave at the last minute to cover the recommended daily servings. Besides, another night of drab veggies does nothing to entice the children. Instead, why not cook up some yellow squash, orange carrots, red tomatoes, and purple eggplant? Why, peppers alone come in four different colors! You can have a rainbow of green, yellow, orange, and red within one dish. Use the vibrant natural color of vegetables to create excitement at dinnertime.

When deciding which veggies to purchase for the evening meal, avoid the supermarket and their sometimes slim offerings. Instead, take advantage of local farmers' markets. Spring brings tender zucchini and stately asparagus, while fall is filled with meaty squash and crisp apples. Get creative!

While we're talking fresh, what could possibly be fresher and taste better than vegetables from your own garden? If you've never grown your own vegetables before, start with something simple but incredibly delicious eaten straight off the vine: tomatoes. Zucchini and squash are hardy plants that produce and produce and produce throughout the summer. Once you get going with your garden, you'll see how wonderful it is to get dinner from your backyard.

Grape-Leaf PURSES
WITH COUSCOUS & LAMB STUFFING

OVEN: 325°F (165°C) > **PREP TIME:** 1 hour >
CHILLING TIME: 3 hours or up to 3 days > **YIELD:** 12 purses

FOR THE COUSCOUS
½ cup (70 g) pine nuts

1 cup (240 ml) beef broth

⅔ cup (175 g) couscous

Zest and juice of 1 lemon

Zest and juice of 1 orange

¼ cup (20 g) chopped fresh
mint leaves

4 ounces (120 g) feta cheese,
crumbled

Kosher salt and freshly
ground black pepper

FOR THE LAMB
2 tablespoons olive oil

3 large shallots, cut into
¼-inch (6-mm) dice

2 teaspoons cinnamon

3 teaspoons allspice

3 teaspoons cumin

1¾ pounds (800 g) ground
lamb

1 teaspoon kosher salt

½ cup (25 g) snipped fresh
chives

½ cup (75 g) golden raisins,
finely chopped

FOR THE TOMATOES
1 pint (300 g) cherry
tomatoes

1 tablespoon olive oil

Kosher salt

Nonstick cooking spray, for
the pan

24 large grape leaves, rinsed

THE INGREDIENTS FOR THESE grape-leaf purses have personality on their own. Once the chilled ingredients macerate, or get acquainted with one another, they create a combined flavor sensation in such a dazzling way. I especially love the taste of these terrines after they've been chilled a few days—then, these no-bake, sensational little purses burst with flavor once they hit your taste buds.

Make Ahead The couscous can be prepared up to 2 days in advance and stored in an airtight container in the refrigerator until needed. It will last for up to 5 days.

> MAKE THE COUSCOUS
Preheat the oven to 325°F (165°C). Place the pine nuts on a sheet pan and toast in the oven until fragrant, 5 to 8 minutes.

In a small saucepan, bring the beef broth to a simmer over medium heat. Add the couscous, turn off the heat, stir, and cover for at least 10 minutes. Allow to cool, then stir in the toasted pine nuts, citrus zest and juice, mint, and feta. Season with salt and pepper and set aside.

> MAKE THE LAMB
In a large skillet over medium heat, heat the oil and sauté the shallots until browned, about 8 minutes. Add the cinnamon, allspice, and cumin and cook until fragrant, about 30 seconds. Add the lamb and the salt and cook, breaking up the lamb with a wooden spatula, until no longer pink, about 10 minutes. Drain the meat over the sink into a fine-mesh colander. Return the meat to the pan and stir briefly to mix the flavors together; remove from the heat.

> MAKE THE TOMATOES
In a 10-inch (25-cm) sauté pan over low heat, combine the tomatoes, oil, and a dash of salt, and cook, stirring occasionally, until the tomatoes are brown on all sides and fully softened, about 20 minutes. Remove the pan from the heat.

❯ ASSEMBLE THE GRAPE-LEAF PURSES

Spray a 12-well classic cupcake pan with nonstick cooking spray. Unfold the grape leaves on a flat work surface and use a knife to remove any thick center ribs. Working 3 wells at a time to avoid crowding, line the wells using 2 large leaves per well. Make sure the leaves overhang the edges of the wells so you will be able to fold them over the filling.

Add about 3 tablespoons of the lamb mixture to each well, filling them about halfway. Place 2 tomatoes on top and press the contents down firmly to make room for the couscous. Add 2 heaping tablespoons of couscous to each well and press down firmly.

Fold the overhanging edges of the leaves into the center of each well and press to seal the purses. If you need more leaves to cover the top, tear off pieces of an extra leaf to fit.

Wrap the pan in plastic wrap. Place another cupcake pan on top and press down to compress the purses. Wrap both pans in another layer of plastic wrap to hold them together and refrigerate for at least 3 hours or up to 3 days.

Use a table knife to pop each chilled purse out of the pan. Bring to room temperature before serving. Serve the purses individually, inverting them so the tidy part (bottom) of the grape-leaf liners is on top, and serve with a dollop of hummus, a lemon wedge, and a piece of pita bread.

Store the purses in an airtight container in the refrigerator for up to 3 days.

CHILLED TERRINES
with Roasted Vegetables

OVEN: 350°F (175°C) > PREP TIME: 1 hour 5 minutes for baked;
3 hours or overnight for chilled > YIELD: 12 terrines

FOR THE TOMATO ASPIC

1¼ cups boiling water

3 (¼-ounce / 7-g) packets
   unflavored gelatin (see
   page 15)

1 (8-ounce / 225-g) jar
   tomato sauce

1½ tablespoons red wine
   vinegar

½ teaspoon kosher salt

½ teaspoon hot pepper
   sauce

½ cup (120 ml) ready-made
   pesto

FOR THE TAHINI YOGURT
SAUCE

2 large cloves garlic, or
   2 tablespoons garlic
   from a tube

1 cup (240 ml) tahini

Zest and juice of 3 lemons

1 cup (240 ml) plain yogurt

1 cup (40 g) packed fresh
   cilantro leaves

2 teaspoons kosher salt

FOR THE VEGETABLES

1 medium globe eggplant

Nonstick cooking spray, for
   the pans

Kosher salt

2 tablespoons balsamic
   vinegar

2 whole roasted red peppers
   or one red and one yellow
   roasted pepper (see Note)

3 medium zucchini

FOR THE ASSEMBLY

1 large bunch fresh basil

24 sun-dried tomatoes
   packed in oil

Note Whole roasted peppers are sold in jars or deli
containers packed in olive oil and herbs.

THESE TERRINES are so full of color! Roasted eggplant, zucchini, and red and yellow peppers are layered with
tomato aspic and basil, breathing new life into this charming
savory dish. They make for an excellent summer meal and
are a great option for gluten-free dining. Serve chilled, with
the tomato aspic and tahini-yogurt sauce, or hot, with a rice
and Parmesan crust (see the variation on page 96).

> MAKE THE TOMATO ASPIC

In a medium bowl, pour the boiling water over the gelatin
and stir to dissolve. Stir in the tomato sauce, vinegar, salt, hot
pepper sauce, and pesto. Set aside at room temperature.

> MAKE THE TAHINI YOGURT SAUCE

In a blender or the bowl of a food processor fitted with
the blade attachment, blend or puree the garlic, tahini,
lemon zest and juice, yogurt, cilantro, and salt with ½ cup
(120 ml) water until smooth. Season with additional salt, if
needed.

> PREPARE THE VEGETABLES

Preheat the oven to 350°F (175°C). Using a sharp knife,
remove the stem of the eggplant and slice the eggplant
crosswise as thin as possible, between 1/16 inch and 1/8 inch
(1.5 and 3 mm) thick. Halve or quarter any large rounds to
make them easier to fit into the wells.

Line 4 baking pans with Silpat mats or foil, then spray
them with nonstick cooking spray. Arrange the eggplant
slices on the pans in a single layer. Spray the eggplant
slices with cooking spray, sprinkle with salt, and drizzle
with the balsamic vinegar. Bake for 15 minutes, or until
golden and softened. Set aside.

Drain the roasted peppers, then lay them flat on a
cutting board and cut each one lengthwise into 12 thin
slices, for a total of 24 slices. Set aside.

Using a vegetable peeler, preferably a "T" peeler or
julienne peeler, thinly peel each zucchini into ribbons; stop
when you reach the seeds. Set aside.

RECIPE CONTINUES

› ASSEMBLE THE TERRINES

Line a 12-well classic cupcake pan with plastic wrap, making sure that each well is surrounded by plastic. Use 2 long pieces that overlap in the center of the pan, and leave a 3-inch (7.5-cm) border of plastic wrap overhanging all sides of the pan.

Begin by dipping the pepper slices into the aspic in batches of 2, using one of each color if you have both yellow and red peppers. (No need to wipe off excess aspic; you will need it to hold your mold together.) Place the 2 pepper slices, side by side, in the bottom of each well. (They will not completely cover the bottom of the well.) Repeat with the remaining pepper slices, until all of the wells are filled. Next, dip the zucchini ribbons in aspic and crisscross the ribbons in the wells, positioning them to cover any empty spaces and using all of the ribbons. (Do not trim the excess; it will be folded into the package at the end.)

Top the zucchini with 2 or 3 basil leaves. Dip the eggplant slices in aspic and layer 1 or 2 slices in each terrine, then add 2 sun-dried tomatoes per well, pushing down firmly to compact the vegetables. Finish layering any remaining vegetables until the wells are full. Evenly distribute the remaining tomato aspic between the wells and fold in the overhanging pieces. Wrap the pan in plastic wrap and chill for at least 3 hours or up to 3 days.

Remove the top layer of plastic wrap, then lift up on the edges of the plastic wrap lining the wells of the pan to remove the terrines. Serve the terrines individually, garnished with a fresh basil leaf and a dollop of the tahini yogurt sauce.

Store the leftover terrines in an airtight container in the refrigerator for up to 5 days. The tahini yogurt sauce can be stored in a separate airtight container for up to 5 days.

VARIATION

With the addition of a rice and Parmesan crust, this baked version of the roasted vegetable terrine is great served alongside your favorite lamb recipe or as a gluten-free main course with a salad and your favorite gluten-free breadsticks.

FOR THE RICE AND PARMESAN CRUST

1½ cups (300 g) white rice

1 teaspoon salt

1 large egg, beaten

½ cup (50 g) grated Parmesan

Make the rice and Parmesan crust: Cook the rice, following the directions on the back of the package and using the salt in the water. When the rice is cooked, stir in the egg and cheese until well combined.

Prepare the tahini yogurt sauce and the vegetables from the recipe on page 95, but not the aspic.

Preheat the oven to 350°F (175°C). Layer the vegetables in the wells as described in the preceding recipe, omitting the plastic wrap and the aspic and pressing down as you go to make room for the rice and Parmesan crust. Form ¼ cup (55 g) of the rice mixture into a 3-inch (8-cm) patty and place it on top of a vegetable-filled well. Repeat with the remaining wells. Bake the terrines until the rice is golden, about 35 minutes. Let them rest in the pan for 15 minutes, then loosen the sides of each terrine with a table knife and invert the terrines onto a sheet pan. Plate them individually or on a serving platter garnished with chopped parsley. Serve with the tahini yogurt sauce.

MUSHROOM
TARTS

OVEN: 350°F (175°C) > PREP TIME: 25 minutes >
BAKING TIME: 40 to 45 minutes > YIELD: 12 tarts

FOR THE MUSHROOM FILLING

3 tablespoon unsalted butter

2 tablespoons extra-virgin olive oil

1 large shallot, thinly sliced

1 pound (455 grams) assorted fresh mushrooms, such as button, shiitake, portobello, cremini, or chanterelle, or 4½ ounces (130 g) dried mushrooms, reconstituted (see Note), or a mix of the two, cut into ½-inch (1-cm) dice

½ teaspoon kosher salt

¼ teaspoon freshly ground black pepper

¼ cup (60 ml) dry sherry

½ cup (120 ml) vegetable or chicken broth

½ cup (120 ml) crème fraîche

FOR THE CUSTARD

½ cup (120 ml) half-and-half

1 large egg, beaten

FOR THE ASSEMBLY

Nonstick cooking spray, for the pan

1 (15-ounce / 430-g) package ready-made pie dough (2 rounds), at room temperature

1½ cups (150 g) grated Parmesan

Note To reconstitute dried mushrooms, place them in a bowl and cover with boiling water. Let stand for 5 minutes. Strain the reconstituted mushrooms through a coffee filter or cheesecloth over a bowl, reserving the flavorful soaking liquid. Gently rinse the mushrooms under cold water and pat dry. The reserved soaking liquid may be used to flavor sauces or fillings.

THE WOMEN in my family—mother, grandmother, and aunts—all have the gift of making pie crust. Instead, I opt for the modern wonder that is prepackaged pie dough. I can achieve the great taste of homemade tarts without the hassle. The flavor of these tarts will vary depending on the mushrooms you use. Be a little adventurous!

> ### MAKE THE MUSHROOM FILLING

In a large skillet over medium heat, melt the butter with the oil. Add the shallots and cook, stirring occasionally, until golden in color, about 5 minutes. Add the mushrooms (if using reconstituted mushrooms, add the soaking liquid as well), salt, pepper, sherry, and broth. Cook until the liquid is reduced by half, 8 to 10 minutes. Stir in the crème fraîche and simmer until the liquid has thickened, about 5 minutes. Turn off the heat.

> ### MAKE THE CUSTARD

In a small bowl, whisk the egg with the half-and-half until well combined.

> ### ASSEMBLE AND BAKE THE TARTS

Preheat the oven to 350°F (175°C). Spray a 12-well classic cupcake pan with nonstick cooking spray.

Unroll the pie dough onto a flat work surface; no need to flour it first. Cut each round of dough in half and cut each half into thirds, for a total of 12 pieces. Place 1 triangle in each well of the prepared pan. No need to make the dough fit perfectly; fill the wells asymmetrically to achieve the most coverage possible. Sprinkle each piece of dough with 1 tablespoon of Parmesan.

Divide the mushroom mixture evenly among the wells, using all of it. Top each well with 1 tablespoon of the remaining Parmesan. Spoon the custard evenly over each tart, then fold any pie dough overhanging the edges of the wells over the filling.

Bake until the crust and cheese are golden brown and bubbling, 40 to 45 minutes. Let the tarts rest in the pan for 1 minute, then loosen the sides of each tart with a table knife and pop them out of the pan.

Store the tarts in an airtight container in the refrigerator for up to 3 days. Reheat, wrapped in tin foil, for 15 minutes at 350°F (175°C).

ASPARAGUS MUSHROOM
Terrines

PREP TIME: 1 hour 10 minutes > CHILLING TIME: 2 hours or overnight >
YIELD: 12 terrines

FOR THE ASPARAGUS MUSHROOM SAUCE

3 tablespoons unsalted butter

2 cloves garlic, minced, or
1½ teaspoons garlic from
a tube

2 large shallots, thinly sliced

7 ounces (200 g) fresh
mushrooms, such as
shiitake, button, portobello,
or cremini, stemmed and
sliced

⅓ cup (75 ml) heavy cream

Kosher salt and freshly
ground black pepper

1 bunch asparagus, tough
ends removed, sliced into
thin slices on the bias

FOR THE LEEK WRAPPERS

6 leeks

2 tablespoons extra-virgin
olive oil

2 tablespoons fresh thyme
leaves

Kosher salt and freshly
ground black pepper

FOR THE GOAT CHEESE CREAM

8 ounces (225 g) goat
cheese, at room
temperature

¼ cup (½ stick / 60 g)
unsalted butter, at room
temperature

2½ ounces (70 g) cream
cheese, softened

1 (14-ounce / 400-g) can
artichoke hearts, drained
and chopped

1 teaspoon grated lemon zest

1 tablespoon fresh thyme
leaves

1 tablespoon finely chopped
fresh basil leaves or basil
from a tube

2 tablespoons fresh parsley
or parsley from a tube

1 tablespoon fresh oregano or
oregano from a tube

1 large clove garlic or
1 tablespoon garlic from
a tube

Kosher salt and freshly
ground black pepper

1 (¼-ounce / 7-g) packet
unflavored gelatin

FOR THE LEMON VINAIGRETTE

2 lemons

1 tablespoon sugar

¼ cup (60 ml) olive oil

2 tablespoons white balsamic
vinegar or rice wine vinegar

Sprigs of fresh thyme, for
garnish

I LOVE THE COLOR, texture, and taste of this mini meal. Leeks gently sautéed in olive oil and fresh thyme are the real stars of this dish because they hold the packages together. Top them with goat cheese cream and lemon vinaigrette and you've created a work of art for your mouth. The light combination of flavors makes this a wonderful springtime meal.

> MAKE THE ASPARAGUS MUSHROOM SAUCE

In a medium skillet over medium-low heat, heat the butter, then add the garlic and shallots and sweat them until softened, 3 to 5 minutes. Add the mushrooms and sauté another minute, then stir in the heavy cream and season with salt and pepper to taste. Reduce the heat to low and continue to cook, stirring occasionally, until the cream thickens, about 8 minutes. Turn off the heat; add the asparagus and toss to coat. Set aside.

> MAKE THE LEEK WRAPPERS

Trim the rough dark green tops and the bottoms from the leeks, and remove the tough outer leaves. Cut each leek in half lengthwise, separate the inner leaves, and soak them in water to remove any grit. Remove the leeks from the water, making sure to rinse them well. You will need 24 leaves total; cut them in half so you have 4 pieces of leek for each well.

In a 12-inch (30-cm) sauté pan, heat the oil over medium heat. Add the fresh thyme and the leeks, season with salt and pepper, and sauté until slightly tender, 3 minutes. Add ¼ cup (60 ml) water, reduce the heat to low, cover, and steam until the leeks are tender, about 5 minutes. Remove the lid and set the leeks aside.

> MAKE THE GOAT CHEESE CREAM

In the bowl of a stand mixer fitted with the paddle attachment, beat the goat cheese, butter, and cream cheese on medium-high speed until light and fluffy, about 3 minutes. Beat in the chopped artichoke hearts, lemon zest, thyme, basil, parsley, oregano, and garlic and season with salt and pepper to taste. Sprinkle the gelatin onto the goat cheese mixture and beat to combine.

> ASSEMBLE THE TERRINES

Line a 12-well classic cupcake pan by overlapping 2 long pieces of plastic wrap along the center of the pan, leaving at least a 3-inch (7.5-cm) border of plastic wrap overhanging all sides of the pan. Line each well with 4 leek pieces, crisscrossing them on the bottom and making sure that no spaces are left uncovered. The leeks will overhang the wells. Do not trim them; they will be folded over the filling after the terrines are assembled.

Divide the asparagus mushroom sauce evenly among the wells, using all of it. Repeat with the goat cheese cream, then fold the ends of the leeks over the filling. Wrap the pan in plastic wrap and chill for 2 hours or overnight.

> MAKE THE LEMON VINAIGRETTE

Juice the lemons into a small bowl. Using a small paring knife, cut half the pulp from the lemon and add it to the bowl. Add the sugar, oil, and vinegar and whisk to combine thoroughly.

When the terrines are chilled, remove the top layer of plastic wrap, then lift up on the edges of the plastic wrap lining the wells of the pan to remove the terrines. Serve the terrines individually on a bed of lettuce and drizzle the tops with lemon vinaigrette. Garnish with sprigs of fresh thyme.

Store the leftover terrines in an airtight container in the refrigerator for up to 5 days. The lemon vinaigrette can be stored in a separate airtight container for up to 1 week.

Curried
VEGETABLE
> HAND PIES <

OVEN: 350°F (175°C) > **PREP TIME:** 45 minutes >
BAKING TIME: 20 to 25 minutes > **YIELD:** 12 hand pies

FOR THE CURRIED VEGETABLES

1 small russet potato, peeled and cut into ¼-inch (6-mm) dice, placed in a bowl of cold water to avoid discoloring

3 tablespoons olive oil

1 medium yellow onion, cut into ¼-inch (6-mm) dice

1 tablespoon grated fresh ginger or ginger from a tube

2 small cloves garlic, finely chopped, or 1½ teaspoons garlic from a tube

2 teaspoons cumin

1 teaspoon ground cardamom

½ teaspoon freshly grated nutmeg

½ teaspoon cinnamon

2 tablespoons curry powder

¼ teaspoon cayenne

Kosher salt and freshly ground black pepper

½ small head cauliflower, cored and cut into small florets

3 carrots, peeled and cut into ¼-inch (6-mm) dice

½ red pepper, seeded and cut into ¼-inch (6-mm) dice

½ yellow pepper, seeded and cut into ¼-inch (6-mm) dice

½ cup (120 ml) chicken broth

½ cup (120 ml) coconut cream or sweetened coconut milk

½ cup (75 g) frozen peas, thawed

FOR THE YOGURT SAUCE

½ cup (120 ml) plain yogurt

¼ cup (60 ml) mango chutney

FOR THE ASSEMBLY

Nonstick cooking spray, for the pan

12 (6-inch / 15-cm) tomato- or spinach-flavored tortillas

½ cup (50 g) chopped roasted almonds

½ cup (50 g) chopped pistachios

Fresh cilantro leaves, for garnish

THESE HAND PIES are beautifully crafted using either a tomato or spinach tortilla, which makes them so easy and fun to eat. The aromatic curry mixed with hearty vegetables gives it a taste reminiscent of an open-faced samosa. If you don't like spicy food, cut the amount of cayenne in half, but I think heat is the only way to go with these pies. And besides, all that spiciness is balanced by the sweet mango chutney and yogurt sauce.

Make Ahead The curried vegetables can be prepared 3 days in advance and stored in an airtight container in the refrigerator until needed. They will keep for up to 1 week. The yogurt sauce can also be assembled up to 1 week in advance and stored in a separate airtight container.

> MAKE THE CURRIED VEGETABLES

Drain the potatoes. In a large skillet over medium-high heat, combine the oil, onion, and potatoes and sauté until just tender, about 7 minutes. Stir in the ginger, garlic, cumin, cardamom, nutmeg, cinnamon, curry powder, and cayenne, and season with salt and pepper to taste. Stir in the cauliflower, carrots, both kinds of peppers, and chicken broth and reduce the heat to low. Cover and cook, tossing once halfway through, until all the veggies are tender and the mixture begins to thicken, 10 to 12 minutes.

Stir in the coconut cream and continue to cook until the curry is the consistency of a thick gravy with chunks of veggies. Turn off the heat and stir in the peas.

> MAKE THE YOGURT SAUCE

In a small bowl, mix together the yogurt and chutney. Refrigerate until serving time.

> ASSEMBLE AND BAKE THE HAND PIES

Preheat the oven to 350°F (175°C).

Spray a 12-well classic cupcake pan with nonstick cooking spray, then line the wells with the flour tortillas. Fill the wells to the top with the curried vegetables, leaving the tops of the tortillas open.

Bake until the edges of the tortillas are golden and crispy, 20 to 25 minutes. With your hands, lift the hand pies from the pan using the tortilla wrappers as handles. Drizzle yogurt sauce on top of each mini meal, then garnish with the chopped nuts and cilantro leaves.

MUSHROOM CAKES
with Mornay Sauce

OVEN: 350°F (175°C) > **PREP TIME:** 45 minutes >
BAKING TIME: 25 to 30 minutes > **YIELD:** 12 cakes

FOR THE HERB SALT

¾ teaspoon kosher salt

1 small shallot, peeled

1 large clove garlic

2 tablespoons chopped fresh
flat-leaf parsley

5 fresh basil leaves

1 tablespoon fresh thyme
leaves

FOR THE ASSEMBLY

2 tablespoons extra-virgin
olive oil

4 cups (400 g) fresh
mushrooms, such as
shiitake, button, portobello,
porcini, morel, or oyster, or
6 ounces dried
mushrooms, reconstituted
(see Note, page 97), or a
combination of the two, cut
into ½-inch (1-cm) dice

2 medium shallots, cut into
¼-inch (6-mm) dice

4 large eggs, lightly beaten

1 teaspoon Worcestershire
sauce

2 cups (220 g) fresh bread
crumbs (see Note)

2½ cups (300 g) grated
cheese, such as white
cheddar, Fontina,
provolone, mozzarella,
Gouda, or a combination

Nonstick cooking spray, for
the pan

¾ cup (75 g) grated
Parmesan

FOR THE MORNAY SAUCE

2 tablespoons unsalted
butter

1½ tablespoons all-purpose
flour

1 cup (240 ml) whole milk

1 cup (240 ml) half-and-half

1 bay leaf

Pinch of white pepper

Pinch of cayenne

2 tablespoons dry sherry

½ cup (60 g) grated cheese,
the same variety or
combination used in the
cakes

¼ cup (20 g) chopped fresh
parsley, for garnish

THESE ARE DELECTABLE! I like to make these cakes with a variety of mushrooms and cheeses, along with freshly made bread crumbs, which results in a moist and fluffy mushroom cake. You can keep it simple and use the mushrooms and cheese that you have on hand or select an interesting combination of your favorite mushrooms and cheeses.

These would be excellent served alongside a roasted chicken with pan gravy and roasted root vegetables, or as a main dish for a lunch completed by a large salad of mixed greens, herbs, dried fruit, and nuts.

Make Ahead The herb salt can be prepared up to 2 days in advance and stored in an airtight container in the refrigerator until needed. It will last for up to 1 week.

> MAKE THE HERB SALT

In the bowl of a small food processor fitted with a blade, combine the salt, shallot, garlic, parsley, basil, and thyme and pulse to combine. Set aside.

> ASSEMBLE AND BAKE THE MUSHROOM CAKES

Preheat the oven to 350°F (175°C).

In a large skillet, heat the oil over medium heat. Add the mushrooms and shallots and cook, stirring occasionally, until the mushrooms are just beginning to brown and the shallots are soft, about 10 minutes. Transfer to a large bowl to cool, about 15 minutes.

When the mushrooms are cool, stir in the eggs, half of the herb salt, the Worcestershire, and bread crumbs. Add the 2½ cups grated cheese and mix to combine.

Spray a 12-well classic cupcake pan with nonstick cooking spray. Fill each well of the prepared pan to the top with the mushroom mixture and sprinkle each with 1 tablespoon of Parmesan. Bake until the tops are golden, 25 to 30 minutes. While the cakes are baking, prepare the Mornay sauce.

> MAKE THE MORNAY SAUCE

In a medium saucepan over medium heat, melt the butter. Add the flour and cook, whisking constantly, for 2 minutes to create a paste. Reduce the heat to low; add the milk, half-and-half, and bay leaf and continue to whisk until the sauce has thickened, 8 to 10 minutes. Add the white pepper, cayenne, the remaining herb salt, sherry, and cheese and whisk until the sauce is smooth. Turn off the heat and set aside until ready to serve.

Let the cakes rest in the pan for 1 minute, then loosen the sides of each cake with a table knife and insert the tines of a fork between the pan and each cake to lift it out. Serve the cakes individually on a pool of the Mornay sauce. Garnish each cake with a little additional sauce and 1 teaspoon of the chopped parsley.

Store the leftover cakes in an airtight container in the refrigerator for up to 5 days. The Mornay sauce can be stored in a separate airtight container for up to 5 days.

Note To make bread crumbs, pulverize a loaf of day-old French or Italian bread in your food processor. (Do not use the toasty crust, only the white bread inside the loaf.) If purchasing bread crumbs at the store, select fresh crumbs, not dried, as they are not the same. Dried crumbs will give you a tough, dry result; fresh will give you a moist and fluffy outcome.

WHITE BEAN, TOMATO & SAGE
SCONES

OVEN: 350°F (175°C) > **PREP TIME:** 35 minutes >
BAKING TIME: 15 minutes > **YIELD:** 12 scones

• • •

FOR THE SCONES

2 cups (250 g) all-purpose flour

1 teaspoon baking powder

1 teaspoon baking soda

½ teaspoon kosher salt

⅓ cup (75 ml) extra-virgin olive oil

¼ cup (50 g) sugar

2 large eggs

1 cup (240 ml) plain whole-milk yogurt

2 tablespoons chopped fresh sage leaves

1 teaspoon finely chopped fresh garlic or garlic from a tube

3 tablespoons tomato paste

Nonstick cooking spray, for the pan

FOR THE CANNELLINI BEAN SPREAD

2 tablespoons olive oil

2 cloves garlic, thinly sliced

1 dried hot chile, crumbled

8 fresh sage leaves

1 (19-ounce / 545-g) can cannellini beans, drained

Kosher salt

FOR THE TOMATO FILLING

½ cup (55 g) sun-dried tomatoes packed in olive oil and herbs

Kosher salt

3 tablespoons honey

3 tablespoons water

1 tablespoon sour cream

FOR THE TOMATO VINAIGRETTE

1 small garlic clove

¼ cup (60 ml) balsamic vinegar

2 teaspoons honey

6 tablespoons (90 ml) extra-virgin olive oil

2 tablespoons chopped white onion

Kosher salt and freshly ground black pepper

1 large ripe tomato, seeded and cut into ¼-inch (6-mm) dice

3 cherry tomatoes, quartered

12 fresh sage leaves, for garnish

WITH THEIR BOLD tomato filling, creamy cannellini spread, and slight heat from the chile pepper, these scones add a punch to any mealtime.

❯ MAKE THE SCONES

Preheat the oven to 350°F (175°C). In a medium bowl, whisk together the flour, baking powder, baking soda, and salt. In the bowl of a stand mixer fitted with a paddle attachment, beat the oil, sugar, eggs, yogurt, sage, garlic, and tomato paste until smooth and creamy. Add the flour mixture and beat on low speed until smooth. Spray a 12-well classic cupcake pan with nonstick cooking spray. Fill each well three-quarters full with the batter and bake until a toothpick inserted in the center comes out clean and the tops are golden, about 15 minutes. Transfer the pan to a wire rack to cool slightly, then loosen the sides of each scone with a table knife and pop them out of the pan.

❯ MAKE THE CANNELLINI BEAN SPREAD

In a small skillet, heat the oil over low heat, then add the garlic and chile. Sauté until the garlic is just golden, about 3 minutes, then add the sage leaves. Toss to coat and transfer to the bowl of a food processor. Add the beans and pulse until combined but still chunky; do not overmix. Taste and add salt, if needed. Transfer to a small bowl.

❯ MAKE THE TOMATO FILLING

In the bowl of a small food processor, combine the sun-dried tomatoes, salt, honey, water, and sour cream and process until smooth, about 2 minutes. Transfer the tomato filling to a small zip-top plastic bag and set aside.

❯ MAKE THE TOMATO VINAIGRETTE

In a blender or the bowl of a small food processor, combine the garlic, vinegar, honey, oil, and onion. Season with salt and pepper and puree until smooth. Transfer to a small bowl and mix the tomatoes in by hand.

Using an apple corer, make a 1-inch-deep (2.5-cm) hole in the center of each scone. Cut off a corner of the plastic bag of tomato filling, then pipe filling into each hole. Spread the bean spread on top in a rustic manner. Drizzle the top of each scone with some tomato vinaigrette and garnish with a piece of cherry tomato and a sage leaf.

PARMESAN & BASIL
LOAVES
with Tomato Jam

OVEN: 350°F (175°C) > PREP TIME: 1 hour 25 minutes >
BAKING TIME: 25 to 30 minutes > YIELD: 12 loaves

FOR THE CHERRY TOMATO JAM

2 pints (600 g) cherry
tomatoes

⅓ cup (75 g) packed light
brown sugar

1 teaspoon fresh thyme
leaves

4 whole cloves

1 stick cinnamon

2 teaspoons balsamic vinegar

Juice of 2 limes

**FOR THE PARMESAN AND BASIL
LOAVES**

2 cups (250 g) all-purpose
flour

1 tablespoon sugar

3 teaspoons baking powder

½ cup (1 stick / 115 g)
unsalted butter, softened

1 large egg, beaten

1 cup (240 ml) heavy cream

½ cup (120 ml) ready-made
pesto

⅓ cup (40 g) grated
Parmesan, plus an
additional ¼ cup (25 g) for
sprinkling

Nonstick cooking spray, for
the pan

**FOR THE MASCARPONE
BASIL SPREAD**

4 ounces (115 g) cream
cheese, softened

8 ounces (230 g)
mascarpone

1 tablespoon chiffonaded
fresh basil leaves (see
Note)

12 fresh basil leaves for
garnish

Note Chiffonade is a cutting technique in which herbs
or leafy green vegetables are cut into long, thin strips.
This is generally accomplished by stacking the leaves,
rolling them tightly, then cutting across the rolled leaves
with a sharp knife, producing fine ribbons. This method
prevents the leaves from bruising.

THESE LOAVES are made with a homemade biscuit
dough mixed with pesto and Parmesan, then spread with
mascarpone and basil cream cheese before finally being
topped with fresh cherry tomato jam. I love the texture of
this syrupy, chunky jam. It is crazy good. This biscuit recipe
has been in my family for generations. This is the tried-and-
true biscuit from my childhood. It started out as just a topping for the tart cherries that grow in the area, but over the
years I have used it on potpies, cobblers, and more.

> ### MAKE THE CHERRY TOMATO JAM

In a medium saucepan, combine the tomatoes, brown
sugar, thyme, cloves, cinnamon, vinegar, and lime juice.
Simmer, uncovered, over low heat for 45 minutes to 1 hour,
stirring occasionally, until the tomatoes pop and the juices
thicken to a jam consistency. Set aside.

> ### MAKE THE PARMESAN AND BASIL LOAVES

Preheat the oven to 350°F (175°C).

In a large bowl, mix together the flour, sugar, and
baking powder. Add the butter, and using your fingertips,
a pastry cutter, or a large fork, rub the butter into the flour
mixture until coarse crumbs form. In a small bowl, whisk
together the egg and heavy cream, then mix in the pesto.
Fold the pesto cream mixture and the ⅓ cup (40 g) of
Parmesan into the batter and mix until just combined.

Spray a 12-well classic cupcake pan with nonstick
cooking spray. Divide the batter between the wells and
sprinkle with the remaining 1 teaspoon of Parmesan per
well. Bake until a toothpick inserted in the center comes
out clean, 25 to 30 minutes.

Let cool for 1 minute in the pan, then loosen the sides
of each mini loaf with a table knife and pop them out of the
pan. Let cool to room temperature before assembling.

> ### MAKE THE MASCARPONE BASIL SPREAD

In the bowl of a stand mixer fitted with the beater attachment, beat the cream cheese on medium-high speed until
light and fluffy. Fold in the mascarpone and basil with a
spatula and set aside.

Serve with a thick layer of the mascarpone spread on
each loaf and top with some of the cherry tomato jam and
garnish with a fresh basil leaf.

FENNEL &
Parmesan
GRATINS

OVEN: 400°F (205°C) > PREP TIME: 25 minutes >
BAKING TIME: 25 minutes > YIELD: 12 gratins

FOR THE SHELLS

1 (17.3-ounce / 485-g)
package puff pastry
(2 sheets), at room
temperature

Nonstick cooking spray, for
the pan

FOR THE FENNEL FILLING

3 or 4 fennel bulbs, tops and
bottoms trimmed

1 cup (240 ml) heavy cream

½ cup (50 g) grated
Parmesan

2 small cloves garlic, minced,
or 2 teaspoons garlic from
a tube

Kosher salt and freshly
ground black pepper

FOR THE BREAD CRUMBS

2 tablespoons unsalted
butter

1¼ cups (140 g) panko bread
crumbs

2 tablespoons fresh thyme
leaves, chopped

2 small cloves garlic, minced,
or 2 teaspoons garlic from
a tube

2 tablespoons chopped
fennel fronds (reserved
from the bulbs), plus more
for garnish

THIS IS ALL ABOUT being a minimalist. You don't need an elaborate presentation or fancy ingredients to make a spectacular meal, as this dish proves. The flavors in this gratin celebrate the creamy and delicate taste of fennel, which is perfectly set against the buttery crunch of the puff pastry. Be sure to look for fennel bulbs with fronds that can be used to garnish the dish.

❯ MAKE THE SHELLS

Preheat the oven to 400°F (205°C). Unroll the puff pastry and cut each sheet crosswise into 3 equal strips, and then cut each strip into 3 pieces for a total of 18 pieces. Set aside 12 pieces to use for the pan (see "Savory Tidbit" on page 44 for ideas on how to use the extra pastry).

Spray a 12-well classic cupcake pan with nonstick cooking spray. Line each well with 1 piece of puff pastry, stretching each piece slightly in both directions and letting it overhang the edges of the well slightly. (Make sure any pastry overhanging the well doesn't touch any other pastry or the pieces will fuse together when baking.)

❯ MAKE THE FENNEL FILLING

Cut the fennel in half lengthwise, remove the core, and cut the fennel lengthwise into ¼-inch-thick (6-mm) slices. Plunge the fennel into a 6- to 8-quart (6- to 8-L) pot of boiling salted water. Boil until tender, 10 to 12 minutes. Drain, rinse the fennel under cold water, and drain it again.

In a large bowl, mix together the fennel, cream, cheese, and garlic. Season with salt and black pepper.

❯ MAKE THE BREAD CRUMBS

In a small sauté pan over low heat, melt the butter. Add the bread crumbs, thyme, and garlic, stir to coat evenly with the melted butter, and sauté for 1 to 2 minutes. (Do not allow the bread crumbs to brown.) Stir in the chopped fennel fronds and remove from the heat.

Distribute the fennel and cream mixture among the wells. Top each gratin with the bread crumbs, using them all. Bake until the crust is golden brown and the filling is bubbling, about 25 minutes. Immediately loosen the sides of each gratin with a table knife and pop them out of the pan. Garnish each gratin with the reserved fresh-snipped fennel fronds.

MAYTAG BLUE, APPLE & ONION COMPOTE
CAKES

OVEN: 350°F (175°C) > **PREP TIME:** 45 minutes >
BAKING TIME: 20 minutes > **YIELD:** 12 cakes

FOR THE CAKES

Nonstick cooking spray, for
the pan

2 cups (250 g) all-purpose
flour

2 tablespoons sugar

3 teaspoons baking powder

½ teaspoon kosher salt

3 tablespoons fresh thyme
leaves or 2 tablespoons
dried

½ cup (60 g) canned
French-fried onions

½ cup (1 stick / 115 g) cold
unsalted butter

1 cup (240 ml) heavy cream

1 large egg

FOR THE APPLE & ONION COMPOTE

2 tablespoons unsalted
butter

1 large red onion, halved
crosswise and thinly sliced

6 sprigs fresh thyme, or
2 teaspoons dried thyme

4 Granny Smith apples,
peeled, cored, and cut into
⅛- to ¼-inch (3- to 6-mm)
dice

1 teaspoon minced garlic or
garlic from a tube

½ cup dry sherry

1 tablespoon frozen cranberry
juice concentrate or
balsamic vinegar

FOR THE MAYTAG BLUE SPREAD

4 ounces (115 g) Maytag blue
or other favorite blue
cheese, crumbled, at room
temperature

4 ounces (115 g) cream
cheese, at room
temperature

2 tablespoons snipped chives
(see Note), plus more for
garnish

1 tablespoon unsalted butter

12 sprigs fresh thyme, for
garnish (optional)

Fresh chives, snipped into
12 (2-inch / 5-cm) pieces,
for garnish (optional; see
Note)

I LOVE A GOOD COMPOTE! It's all about taking fresh and sometimes unripe fruit, adding in a bit of sweetener, and simmering it over low heat to create a combination of flavors that improves upon nature's bounty. Dried fruit, nuts, garlic, shallots, and onions are excellent additions to just about any compote. I really love the bitter sweetness that the cranberry contributes, but experiment with a variety of ingredients to come up with your own special flavor combination.

Here I've combined two items that marry beautifully: red onions and tart apples. The natural red of the onions gives this compote a vibrant color. Take care not to be tempted to eat half before you put together the final savory meal! I would serve this as part of a lunch with roast beef tenderloin and a spinach salad. If you have any compote left over, slather it heavily onto toast or eat it with a spoon like applesauce.

Make Ahead The apple & onion compote can be prepared up to 2 days in advance and stored in an airtight container in the refrigerator until needed. It will last for up to 1 week. The Maytag blue spread can also be prepared up to 2 days in advance, and will keep for up to 1 week in an airtight container in the refrigerator.

> MAKE THE CAKES

Preheat the oven to 350°F (175°C). Spray a 12-well classic cupcake pan with nonstick cooking spray.

In a medium bowl, using a fork, mix together the flour, sugar, baking powder, salt, thyme, and French-fried onions. Cut the butter into 5 pieces, then cut it into the flour mixture using a fork, pastry cutter, or your fingertips; the mixture should resemble coarse crumbs. In a small bowl, whisk together the cream and egg, then fold it into the flour mixture, making sure not to overmix. Divide the batter evenly among the wells of the prepared pan; each well should be about two-thirds full.

Bake until a toothpick inserted in the center comes out clean, about 20 minutes. Let the cakes cool for 1 minute in the pan, then loosen the sides of each cake with a table knife, and invert the cakes onto a cooling rack.

> ## MAKE THE APPLE & ONION COMPOTE

In a 10-inch (25-cm) sauté pan, melt the butter over low heat. Add the onion slices to the pan and toss to coat in the butter. Add the thyme, cover, and sweat the onions until soft, about 8 minutes. Add the apples and stir to coat. Cook, uncovered, stirring occasionally, until the apples have softened and most of the liquid has evaporated, about 20 minutes. Turn off the heat and stir in the cranberry concentrate. Cover and set aside to cool until needed.

> ## MAKE THE MAYTAG BLUE SPREAD

In a small bowl, using a rubber spatula or wooden spoon, mix together the blue cheese, cream cheese, chives, and butter. (Do not use an electric mixer.)

Slice the cooled cakes in half and spread with 1 to 2 tablespoons of the blue cheese spread, then a healthy slather of the compote. Sprinkle with the additional snipped chives; top with a sprig of fresh thyme or a 2-inch (5-cm) piece of chive.

Store the leftover cakes in an airtight container in the refrigerator for up to 5 days. The apple & onion compote can be stored in a separate airtight container for up to 1 week.

Note I find it's easiest to use scissors when cutting chives into very short lengths. Just take a pair of kitchen shears or a clean pair of all-purpose scissors and snip the ends of a bunch of chives into $1/8$-inch (3-mm) pieces (the size you'd use to garnish a baked potato). You can use the same method to snip longer pieces, such as those used in the garnish here.

JALAPEÑO LIME BITES
with Shrimp

OVEN: 325°F (165°C) > **PREP TIME:** 1 hour 10 minutes >
BAKING TIME: 20 to 25 minutes > **YIELD:** 12 bites

● ● ●

FOR THE LIME ALMOND BREAD

Grated zest and juice of
4 limes

½ cup (100 g) sugar

5 large egg yolks

10 tablespoons (150 g) salted
butter, at room
temperature

3 cups (420 g) almond flour

⅔ cup (90 g) self-rising flour

3 large egg whites

2 teaspoons baking powder

Nonstick cooking spray, for
the pan

FOR THE CORN PUDDING

1½ cups (385 g) canned corn,
drained; frozen corn; or
fresh corn (from about
3 ears)

⅛ teaspoon kosher salt

1½ tablespoons cornstarch

1 cup (240 ml) whole milk

½ tablespoon unsalted butter

FOR THE JALAPEÑO BUTTER

1 tablespoon honey

½ cup (1 stick / 115 g)
unsalted butter, softened

2 ounces (55 g) cream
cheese, softened

3 tablespoons chopped fresh
cilantro

1 tablespoon tomato paste

1 tablespoon fresh lime juice

¼ teaspoon kosher salt

1 fresh jalapeño chile (or
more or less to taste),
seeded and finely chopped

FOR THE SHRIMP TOPPING

2 tablespoons unsalted
butter

1 shallot, finely chopped

12 medium shrimp, peeled
and deveined

½ lime

½ teaspoon kosher salt

¼ teaspoon freshly ground
black pepper

½ cup jalapeño jelly

Cilantro sprigs, for garnish

THESE BITES HAVE IT ALL: sweet, savory, and salty. Added to that is the feel of a lazy southern BBQ. This is a pretty special meal, so purchase fresh shrimp for it. I love the density of the lime loaves made with ground almonds and the creamy corn pudding. The jalapeño butter with cilantro and lime is butter at its best! Joining in the festivities is jalapeño jelly to keep things interesting. This would be amazing with a butter lettuce salad with fresh mango and orange supremes tossed with a citrus vinaigrette.

Make Ahead You can make the loaves, corn pudding, and jalapeño butter the day prior to serving. I would not try to double the lime almond bread recipe; just make one batch and then another if you need to double the yield. If you make ahead, remember to bring all the elements to room temperature prior to assembly and service. The shrimp need to be prepared the day of the event.

> ### MAKE THE LIME ALMOND BREAD

Preheat the oven to 325°F (165°C).

In a medium saucepan over very low heat, combine the lime zest and juice, sugar, and egg yolks and cook, stirring constantly, until thick, about 15 minutes. Add the butter and stir until thoroughly combined; the mixture should look glossy. Place a fine-mesh sieve over a bowl and strain the lime curd into the lime zest–butter mixture (see Note). Let cool to room temperature, about 30 minutes.

When the lime curd is cool, whisk together the almond flour and self-rising flour in a small bowl to remove any lumps. Add the flour mixture to the lime curd and mix well with a wooden spoon.

In a medium bowl, beat the egg whites with an electric mixer until soft peaks form, about 5 minutes on medium speed. Sprinkle the baking powder over the egg whites and, with a rubber spatula, fold to combine. Fold the egg whites into the lime curd mixture to thoroughly combine.

Spray a 12-well classic cupcake pan with nonstick cooking spray. Divide the batter among the wells of the prepared cupcake pan and bake for 20 to 25 minutes, or until the breads begin to brown. Let cool in the pan for 1 minute, then loosen the sides of each mini loaf with a table knife and pop the loaves out of the pan. Set aside to cool completely.

› MAKE THE CORN PUDDING

While the bread bakes and cools, puree the corn in a blender; you should have about 1 cup (240 ml). In a medium saucepan, combine the salt and cornstarch and whisk together. Whisk in the milk and cook over medium heat, whisking constantly, until the milk mixture is boiling and has thickened, about 8 minutes. Turn off the heat and stir in the butter and corn puree. Transfer the pudding to a bowl to cool slightly.

› MAKE THE JALAPEÑO BUTTER

In a small bowl, using a rubber spatula, mix together the honey, butter, cream cheese, cilantro, tomato paste, lime juice, salt, and jalapeño. Using the spatula, transfer the lime butter to a piping bag fitted with a small tip. (Or place in a zip-top bag and snip off the tip of one of the corners with scissors.) Set aside.

› MAKE THE SHRIMP TOPPING

In a medium nonstick skillet, melt the butter over medium heat. Add the shallot and cook, stirring occasionally until soft, about 5 minutes. Add the shrimp, toss to coat, and cook until pink and cooked through, 3 to 4 minutes. Remove from the heat. When the shrimp have cooled to the touch, slice them in half lengthwise for a total of 24 pieces.

Finish the shrimp with a generous squeeze of lime juice and sprinkle with the salt and pepper. Stir, then set aside.

In a small saucepan, melt the jelly over medium heat, about 4 minutes. Set aside to cool slightly.

When the loaves have cooled to the touch, dip the top of each loaf into the jalapeño jelly. Using an apple corer, make a 1-inch-deep (2.5-cm) hole in the center of each loaf, making sure not to poke all the way through or the filling will seep out. Fill each hole to the top with the corn pudding. Pipe a small round of jalapeño butter, about 1 inch (2.5 cm) in diameter, in the center of each loaf over the corn pudding. Place 2 shrimp slices on top of each loaf and garnish with a sprig of cilantro.

Store the loaves in an airtight container in the refrigerator for up to 5 days.

Note If you don't have a fine-mesh sieve on hand, you can use a colander lined with a piece of cheesecloth to strain the lime curd.

> TANDOORI <
Carrot
SCONES

OVEN: 350°F (175°C) > **PREP TIME:** 1 hour 10 minutes >
BAKING TIME: 35 to 40 minutes > **YIELD:** 12 scones

FOR THE CARROT HALWA

¼ cup (½ stick / 60 g)
unsalted butter

3 cups (330 g) freshly grated
carrots (from 6 carrots;
see Notes)

1½ cups (360 ml) half-and-
half

¼ cup (60 ml) honey

2 tablespoons golden raisins

⅛ teaspoon ground
cardamom, or to taste

¼ cup (60 ml) cashew butter

¼ teaspoon kosher salt

FOR THE SCONES

Nonstick cooking spray, for
the pan

¾ cup (75 g) sliced almonds

1 cup (2 sticks / 230 g)
unsalted butter, at room
temperature

½ cup (100 g) granulated
sugar

½ cup (110 g) packed light
brown sugar

3 large eggs

2 cups (250 g) all-purpose
flour

1 teaspoon baking powder

1 teaspoon baking soda

1 teaspoon kosher salt

2 teaspoons cinnamon

3 teaspoons tandoori spice
(see Notes)

2 teaspoons ground ginger

3 cups (330 g) freshly grated
carrots (from 6 carrots)

FOR THE ASSEMBLY

5 tablespoons (40 g) shelled,
salted pistachios, chopped

2 tablespoons chopped
salted cashews

2 tablespoons chopped
crystallized ginger

1 (6-ounce / 170-g) bag
carrot chips or a mix of
carrot and sweet potato
chips, crushed

I WISH CARROTS had been an ingredient in the *Cupcake Wars* challenge. I would have made carrot halwa as a filling, as it's used here, or as a standalone icing. It's that good. Paired with a carrot scone, it's even better. This firm, dense scone is unlike any carrot-y baked good you have ever tasted. The flavors will be enhanced during baking by the marriage of the juicy carrots and the spices, which create the depth of flavor and color.

Halwa is a traditional Indian dessert of fresh grated carrots cooked in milk and sugar. Here, I've added tandoori flavors. In both the scone and the halwa, I reduced the sugar and added honey to allow the sweetness of the carrots and the exotic flavors of the ginger, garam masala, and toasted nuts to shine. I often serve these scones in the morning or as an afternoon snack with hot chai. They could be made on a smaller scale, using a mini cupcake pan (see Notes), and served as vegetarian hors d'oeuvres or as part of a meal with green curry vegetables or traditional curried chicken. Or twist up tradition and serve this instead of pumpkin bread at a holiday meal.

Make Ahead **If you want to serve these scones later in the day, just keep them at room temperature. If refrigerated, the butters in the halwa will harden, and you will lose the creamy texture. Plus, nobody likes a cold cupcake, and they won't want to wait for these to get to room temperature to enjoy them.**

> MAKE THE CARROT HALWA

Melt the butter in a medium nonstick skillet over medium-low heat. Add the carrots and cook for 5 minutes, stirring to coat with the butter. Stir in the half-and-half, honey, raisins, and cardamom; cook, stirring occasionally, until the carrots have softened and the mixture has thickened to the consistency of oatmeal, 25 to 30 minutes. (None of the cream should be visible.)

Remove the halwa from the heat and let it cool for about 5 minutes; transfer it to a food processor fitted with the blade attachment and process until smooth. Stir in the cashew butter and add the salt and a little more carda-mom if desired. Set the halwa aside.

> MAKE THE SCONES

Preheat the oven to 350°F (175°C). Spray a 12-well classic cupcake pan with the nonstick cooking spray. Sprinkle each well with 1 tablespoon of sliced almonds.

In the bowl of a stand mixer, cream the butter with both sugars, beating until fluffy, about 3 minutes. Add the eggs and beat well. In a medium bowl, sift together the flour, baking powder, baking soda, salt, cinnamon, tandoori spice, and ginger. Fold the carrots into the butter mixture with a spatula, and then fold in the flour mixture, making sure to mix thoroughly.

Using a 1/3-cup (75-ml) measure, fill each well of the prepared pan to the top with the batter. Bake until the scones are golden brown and a toothpick inserted in the center of a scone comes out clean, 35 to 40 minutes.

Let cool for 1 minute in the pan, then loosen the sides of each scone with a table knife and pop them out of the pan. Set them on a flat surface to cool for 5 minutes.

> ASSEMBLE THE SCONES

Using an apple corer, make two 1-inch-deep (2.5-cm) holes in the center of each scone, side by side, making sure not to cut all the way through or the filling will seep out.

Transfer the carrot halwa to a zip-top bag. Cut a 1/4-inch (6-mm) piece off one corner of the bag and pipe the halwa into the holes in the scones, filling each hole to the top and then mounding a little halwa in the center of each scone, using it all. Sprinkle the tops with the nuts, ginger, and chips.

Notes If using a mini cupcake pan, reduce the baking time to 12 to 15 minutes.

If you see a baking recipe that calls for grated carrots, never substitute the pregrated variety. They will be dry and flavorless. The moisture in fresh grated carrots is essential to the recipe.

While tandoori spice blends vary from region to region in India, several premixed varieties are available at most grocery stores. At its most basic, tandoori is a blend of ginger, cumin, coriander, paprika, turmeric, and cayenne. Garam masala, a mixture of coriander, cumin, black pepper, cloves, cinnamon, and nutmeg, is often found in tandoori spice blends. I use a premixed, store-bought tandoori spice in this recipe, and then add the sweetness of cinnamon and ginger to enhance those flavors.

CAJUN MEAT LOAF–
STUFFED
Red Peppers

OVEN: 350°F (175°C) > PREP TIME: 50 minutes >
BAKING TIME: 1 hour > YIELD: 12 mini meals

12 small red bell peppers
(4½ pounds / 2 kg)

Nonstick cooking spray, for
the pan

3 tablespoons unsalted
butter

1 medium yellow onion, finely
chopped

3 tablespoons minced fresh
garlic or garlic from a tube

1 tablespoon Worcestershire
sauce

2 to 3 tablespoons hot
pepper sauce

1 tablespoon cumin

4 bay leaves

1½ teaspoons kosher salt

1 teaspoon freshly ground
black pepper

⅛ teaspoon freshly grated
nutmeg

1¼ cups (300 ml) ketchup

¼ cup (60 ml) half-and-half

2 pounds (910 g) ground
beef, turkey, chicken, or
pork, or a combination

3 large eggs

2 Andouille sausages

Savory Tidbit **I use the slicing blade of my Cuisinart to thinly slice the onions, and then I change to the chopping blade and pulse them into medium pieces. This is the only way I can chop onions without crying!**

I HAVE BEEN MAKING this meat loaf recipe for years. I used to bake this at the studios in Hollywood, and then grill the baked slices on the barbecue behind the writers' bungalow to give it an extra kick of flavor. The red pepper, ketchup, and Andouille sausage take this mini meal to a level your grandmother never could.

The peppers will sweeten the meat loaf and help keep it from drying out and the ketchup will brown and become caramelized along with the sausage. This is a beautiful sight, and a necessary component to keep these tasting fantastic. Savor every bite!

The peppers will act as shells for the meat loaf, so they should remain whole, without cracks or tears. Slice the stem-end off the peppers about 1 inch (2.5 cm) below the base of the stem. Core the peppers, removing the seeds and membranes. Remove and discard the stems from the pepper tops and finely chop the remaining top portion into ¼-inch (6-mm) dice; set aside.

Preheat the oven to 350°F (175°C).

Spray a 12-well classic cupcake pan with nonstick cooking spray and place 1 pepper shell in each well. (The peppers should come well above the top of the pan; they will shrink as the meat loaf bakes.)

Melt the butter in a 12-inch (30-cm) skillet over medium heat. Add the onion, reserved chopped peppers, and garlic and sauté until tender, stirring occasionally, about 5 minutes. Add the Worcestershire, hot sauce, cumin, bay leaves, salt, pepper, and nutmeg. Stir for 1 minute, then adjust the heat to low. Stir in ½ cup (120 ml) of the ketchup and the half-and-half; simmer for 5 minutes, or until the vegetable mixture has thickened and heated through.

Transfer the mixture to a large bowl, and let cool completely, about 20 minutes. Remove and discard the bay leaves. Add the ground meat and the eggs to the vegetable mixture and mix by hand until all of the ingredients are fully incorporated.

Slice the sausage links on a bias into twelve ½-inch-thick (1-cm) slices. These will be used to garnish the top of the stuffed peppers. (Refrigerate or freeze any unused sausage for another meal.)

Using a spoon, fill each pepper to the top with the meat loaf mixture, making sure that the peppers are mounded but not overflowing. Dollop 1 tablespoon of the remaining ketchup on top of the filling in each pepper, and top with a slice of sausage.

Bake, uncovered, until the meat loaves are golden brown on top, about 1 hour. Let cool in the pan for 1 minute, then insert the tines of a fork between the pan and each pepper to lift it out. Serve with a side of grilled vegetables and roasted potatoes.

Store the stuffed peppers in an airtight container in the refrigerator for up to 5 days. Reheat, wrapped in tin foil, for 15 minutes at 350°F (175°C).

ZUCCHINI BREADS
with Caponata

OVEN: 350°F (175°C) > **PREP TIME:** 1 hour 25 minutes >
BAKING TIME: 35 minutes > **YIELD:** 12 loaves

FOR THE FIRE-ROASTED PEPPERS

1 yellow bell pepper, or 1 (6-ounce / 170-g) jar of roasted yellow peppers

1 red bell pepper, or 1 (6-ounce / 170-g) jar of roasted red peppers

FOR THE CAPONATA

1 (16-ounce / 455-g) globe eggplant, cut into ½-inch (1-cm) dice

2 tablespoons kosher salt

5 tablespoons (75 ml) extra-virgin olive oil

1 medium yellow onion, chopped

1 clove fresh garlic, finely chopped, or scant 1½ teaspoons garlic from a tube

¼ cup (35 g) golden raisins

¼ cup (35 g) capers

½ cup (90 g) chopped green olives (without pimentos); see Note

1 (14.5-ounce/ 430-g) can whole plum tomatoes in their juice, finely chopped

2 tablespoons pomegranate or fig balsamic vinegar, or balsamic vinegar

Freshly ground black pepper

3 tablespoons honey

2 tablespoons Dutch process cocoa powder (such as Cacao Barry Extra Brute)

Zest and juice of 1 orange

FOR THE FETA CHEESE SPREAD

1 medium orange

4 ounces (115 g) feta cheese, crumbled

4 ounces (115 g) cream cheese

2 tablespoons olive oil mayonnaise

1 teaspoon minced fresh garlic or garlic from a tube

2 tablespoons fresh basil chiffonade (see Note, page 105)

1 tablespoon honey

FOR THE ZUCCHINI BREAD

Nonstick cooking spray, for the pan

3 large eggs

¾ cup (150 g) sugar

¾ cup plus 2 tablespoons (150 g) light vegetable oil

2½ cups (290 g) grated unpeeled zucchini (from 2 to 3 medium zucchini)

3 cups (375 g) all-purpose flour

1 teaspoon kosher salt

1 teaspoon baking soda

¼ teaspoon baking powder

2 teaspoons cinnamon

2 tablespoons walnut oil

FOR THE ASSEMBLY

6 tablespoons (50 g) pine nuts

1 small bunch fresh basil leaves, cut into chiffonade (see Note, page 105)

1 large orange

Make Ahead **Keep the feta cheese spread at room temperature if assembling the same day. You may make the components of this mini meal ahead, refrigerating the caponata and feta cheese spread, but store the zucchini bread in an airtight container overnight. Before assembling, bring the feta and caponata to room temperature. Refrigerate if not assembling immediately.**

I KNOW THAT I'm mixing Middle Eastern and Sicilian flavors with Grandma's zucchini bread, but I like to combine different ethnic flavors to create a one-of-a-kind savory meal. This recipe is meant to challenge the taste buds. I love nothing more than creating savory items that pack in a ton of flavors and offer so much diversity on your table and on your palate. This bread can also be baked in a mini cupcake tin and served as exceptional hors d'oeuvres at any fête.

› MAKE THE FIRE-ROASTED PEPPERS

Roast the peppers on the stovetop, right on the flame, using tongs to flip them occasionally until they are completely blackened and charred, about 5 minutes. Transfer the peppers to a medium bowl, cover with plastic wrap, and let steam for about 15 minutes. Core the peppers and remove the skin and seeds. Finely chop them. Set aside.

› MAKE THE CAPONATA

Place the eggplant in a colander set in the sink and toss with the salt. Top the eggplant with a plate weighted down with several large cans; let drain into the sink for 1 hour. (This process removes the bitterness.) Rinse the eggplant and dry it, using a clean tea towel to pat it dry. Heat the oil in a large skillet over medium heat, then add the eggplant, tossing to coat with oil. Cook until slightly browned, about 10 minutes. Set aside.

In a medium stockpot or Dutch oven over medium heat, heat the oil, then add the onion and sauté until translucent, about 5 minutes. Reduce the heat to low and stir in the garlic, raisins, capers, olives, tomatoes and their juices, vinegar, pepper, honey, cocoa powder, and orange zest and juice. Cook at a low simmer, uncovered, until the liquid thickens, about 20 minutes. Stir in the reserved eggplant and peppers. Add the broth and keep the mixture at a low simmer, stirring occasionally, while preparing the feta cheese spread and zucchini bread.

› MAKE THE FETA CHEESE SPREAD

Zest the orange into a small bowl, then cut it in half and squeeze the juice of one half into the bowl. In the bowl of a stand mixer fitted with a whisk attachment, combine the feta and cream cheese, orange zest and juice, mayonnaise, garlic, basil, and honey. Mix on high speed until the spread is well combined but still retains a bit of texture. Transfer the mixture to a zip-top plastic bag and set aside.

› MAKE THE ZUCCHINI BREAD

Preheat the oven to 350°F (175°C). Spray a 12-well classic cupcake pan with nonstick cooking spray.

In the bowl of a stand mixer, beat the eggs on high speed until light, about 4 minutes. Add the sugar and beat to combine. Add the vegetable oil and zucchini and beat to combine.

In a medium bowl, sift together the flour, salt, baking soda, baking powder, and cinnamon. Add the dry ingredients by the cupful to the egg mixture, stirring by hand until well blended. Stir in the walnut oil, mixing well.

Using an ice cream scoop, fill each well with the zucchini batter to the top. Bake until golden brown, about 35 minutes. Let cool in the pan for 1 minute, then loosen the sides of each loaf with a table knife to remove the loaves from the pan. Place on a wire rack to cool. Do not turn off the oven.

› ASSEMBLE THE MINI MEALS

On a rimmed baking sheet, toast the pine nuts until golden, about 4 minutes. Transfer to a bowl to cool.

Using an apple corer, make a 1-inch-deep (2.5-cm) hole in the center of each loaf, making sure not to cut all the way through or the filling will seep out. Snip one corner off the zip-top bag containing the feta cheese spread. Pipe the feta cheese spread into each hole, allowing a bit to flow onto the top of the bread. Use a table knife to smooth the spread over the top of the loaf, so it will be visible when topped with the caponata. Place a heaping spoonful of the caponata on top of each loaf and dot with a few pine nuts.

Sprinkle the basil chiffonade on the caponata, then zest the orange directly over the assembled loaves, making sure to sprinkle each one. (The orange really makes all of the flavors pop, so don't skimp here!) Serve the loaves with some extra caponata on the side.

Note I like Cerignola olives because of their creamy texture. They are easily found in the "by the pound" section of the grocery store.

Roasted EGGPLANT CUPS
WITH RICOTTA & TOMATO

OVEN: 350°F (175°C) > **PREP TIME:** 1 hour >
BAKING TIME: 25 minutes > **YIELD:** 12 cups

FOR THE FRIED EGGPLANT

3 to 4 large eggplants

2 tablespoons kosher salt

¼ cup (60 ml) olive oil, plus more as needed

FOR THE TOMATO SAUCE

¼ cup (½ stick / 60 g) unsalted butter

3 cloves garlic, minced

5 anchovy fillets in oil, drained

1 (28-ounce / 795-g) can plum tomatoes in their juice, roughly chopped

¼ cup (10 g) fresh basil chiffonade (see Note, page 105)

¼ cup (60 ml) heavy cream or half-and-half (optional)

½ cup (50 g) grated Parmesan

FOR THE RICOTTA FILLING

2 cups (250 g) ricotta

1 large egg

Pinch of Kosher salt and freshly ground pepper

½ bunch fresh basil leaves

FOR THE ASSEMBLY

Nonstick cooking spray, for the pan

1 cup (110 g) fresh bread crumbs

1½ cups (150 g) grated Parmesan

1 cup (115 g) shredded mozzarella

Fresh basil leaves, for garnish

THIS PAN IS LINED WITH breaded eggplant, then filled with a ricotta mixture and a tomato anchovy sauce that accents the whole meal. Don't worry, nothing about this dish tastes fishy. Instead, you get a rich, creamy center surrounded by a delicious eggplant nest holding it all together. If you prefer, use your favorite jarred tomato sauce and doctor it up with the cream, Parmesan, and basil.

> MAKE THE FRIED EGGPLANT

Cut off the stem ends of the eggplants and slice lengthwise into ¼-inch-wide (6-mm) planks until you have 24 long slices. Lay these on paper towels on sheet pans and sprinkle with the kosher salt. Let the slices rest for about 30 minutes.

Divide the oil between 2 large skillets and heat it over medium heat. Wipe the salt off of the eggplant, then add all the pieces to the skillets in a single layer. Brown the eggplant on both sides, 2 to 3 minutes per side, adding more oil if necessary. Transfer the finished pieces to a sheet pan and set aside.

> MAKE THE TOMATO SAUCE

In a large sauté pan, melt the butter over medium heat, then add the garlic and sauté until light brown, about 1 minute. Add the anchovies and mash them against the side of the pan. Stir in the tomatoes and their juices and bring to a boil, then turn the heat to low and simmer the sauce for 20 minutes. Stir in the basil, cream, and cheese, then turn off the heat.

> MAKE THE RICOTTA FILLING

In the bowl of a food processor, combine the ricotta, egg, salt and pepper, and basil leaves and puree just until everything comes together and the mixture is flecked with the basil.

Preheat the oven to 350°F (175°C).

Spray a 12-well classic cupcake pan with nonstick cooking spray. On a rimmed sheet pan, mix the bread crumbs and 1 cup (100 g) of the Parmesan together. Dip one side of each piece of fried eggplant into the Parmesan bread crumbs. Line the sides and bottom of each well with 2 slices of fried eggplant, bread crumb side down, in a cross formation to form a shell. Depending on the width and length of the eggplant slices, you may want to cut them to better fit the wells. Leave a 2-inch (5-cm) overhang on both ends of each slice so that the eggplant can be folded into the center of the well once the other ingredients are placed inside.

Distribute the tomato sauce among the wells, then top it with the ricotta mixture, and finally with the mozzarella and remaining Parmesan. Fold the overhanging edges of the eggplant over the filling.

Bake until the tops are golden brown, about 25 minutes. Let rest in the pan for 2 minutes, then loosen the sides of each cup with a table knife and insert the tines of a fork between the pan and each cup to lift it out. Garnish with fresh basil leaves.

> EGGPLANT <
LASAGNA

OVEN: 350°F (175°C) > PREP TIME: 55 minutes >
BAKING TIME: 25 minutes > YIELDS: 12 lasagnas

FOR THE EGGPLANT WRAPPERS

2 large globe eggplants

½ cup (120 ml) olive oil

Kosher salt and freshly
    ground black pepper

FOR THE TOMATO ANCHOVY SAUCE

6 tablespoons (90 ml)
    olive oil

2 cloves garlic, chopped,
    or 1 tablespoon garlic from
    a tube

5 anchovy fillets in oil,
    drained

1 (28-ounce / 795-g) can
    whole peeled tomatoes in
    their juice

Pinch of crushed red pepper
    flakes

1 tablespoon sugar

Kosher salt and freshly
    ground black pepper

10 leaves fresh basil

FOR THE RICOTTA FILLING

2 cups (480 ml) whole-milk
    ricotta

1 large egg

1 small clove garlic, minced,
    or 1 teaspoon garlic from a
    tube

1 teaspoon kosher salt

1 teaspoon white pepper

FOR THE BÉCHAMEL SAUCE

2 teaspoons unsalted butter

¼ cup (30 g) all-purpose
    flour

2 cups (480 ml) whole milk

1 small clove garlic, minced,
    or 1 teaspoon garlic from a
    tube

1 tablespoon chopped fresh
    flat-leaf parsley, or
    2 teaspoons parsley
    from a tube

1 tablespoon chopped fresh
    basil or basil from a tube

1 teaspoon white pepper

1 teaspoon kosher salt

Pinch of freshly grated
    nutmeg

FOR THE ASSEMBLY

Nonstick cooking spray, for
    the pan

6 sheets no-boil lasagna
    noodles

¾ cup (85 g) shredded
    mozzarella or ¾ cup (75 g)
    grated Parmesan

THIS IS POSITIVELY DELICATE, and my favorite way to enjoy lasagna. Unlike a classic casserole dish, these lasagna meals have a beginning and an end, offering you a perfect portion! I have been a guest at dinner parties given by Italian friends, and this is how they serve their pasta, too. The tomato sauce is so simple and offers a nice balance, rich but slightly tart, which cuts through the creamy béchamel sauce. These would be great as part of a larger dinner with roasted meat and vegetables.

Make Ahead The tomato anchovy sauce, ricotta filling, and béchamel sauce can all be made up to 1 day in advance. Store them in airtight containers in the refrigerator until ready to use. The béchamel sauce should be reheated before serving.

> MAKE THE EGGPLANT WRAPPERS

Preheat the broiler to high (see Note) and line 2 sheet pans with foil or Silpat mats. Slice the eggplants lengthwise into 12 (¼-inch / 6-mm) slices. Brush each eggplant slice with olive oil, then season with salt and pepper. Place the eggplant slices on the prepared pans and broil them until just brown on both sides, 1 to 2 minutes per side.

> MAKE THE TOMATO ANCHOVY SAUCE

In a 10-inch (25 cm) sauté pan over medium-high heat, combine the oil, garlic, anchovies, tomatoes and their juice, red pepper flakes, and sugar, and season with salt and pepper. Cook until slightly thickened and the tomatoes soften, about 20 minutes. Transfer to a blender or the bowl of a food processor with a blade attachment; add the basil and process until smooth. Taste and adjust the seasoning as needed.

> MAKE THE RICOTTA FILLING

In a medium bowl, mix the ricotta, egg, garlic, salt, and white pepper by hand until well combined.

MAKE THE BÉCHAMEL SAUCE

Melt the butter in a heavy medium saucepan over medium heat. Add the flour and cook, stirring constantly with a whisk, until the flour is well blended and forms a soft paste. Add the milk and continue to cook, whisking constantly, until the sauce has thickened and just begins to boil, about 15 minutes. Stir in the garlic, parsley, basil, white pepper, salt, and nutmeg. Turn off the heat and set aside.

ASSEMBLE AND BAKE THE LASAGNAS

Preheat the oven to 350°F (175°C). Spray a 12-well classic cupcake pan with nonstick cooking spray. Arrange all of the lasagna components in an assembly line. Start with the eggplant: Place 1 slice of eggplant in each well. You may want to cut the slices to better fit the wells. Leave a 2-inch (5-cm) overhang on both ends of each slice, so that the eggplant can be folded into the center of the well once the other ingredients are placed inside.

Next, layer the following ingredients in each well in this order:

    1 tablespoon ricotta filling
    1 tablespoon tomato anchovy sauce
    ½ lasagna noodle, broken into pieces to fit
    1 tablespoon ricotta filling
    1 tablespoon tomato anchovy sauce

Fold the overhanging eggplant over the filling and top each lasagna with 1 tablespoon mozzarella. Set aside the leftover tomato anchovy sauce. Bake until golden on top, about 25 minutes. Let rest in the pan for 5 minutes, then loosen the sides of each lasagna with a table knife and insert the tines of a fork between the pan and each lasagna to lift it out.

Reheat the béchamel and tomato anchovy sauces if they have cooled. Using a serving spoon, pool the béchamel on one side of each plate and the tomato anchovy sauce on the other so they meet in the middle. Center a mini lasagna on each plate of sauce. For buffet service or a family-style meal, serve the lasagnas on a large platter and garnish with fresh herbs for color. Place the sauces in bowls on the platter so guests can drizzle them on top of their servings.

Store the leftover lasagnas in an airtight container in the refrigerator for up to 5 days. The tomato anchovy and béchamel sauces can be stored in separate airtight containers for up to 3 days.

Note Alternatively, bake the eggplant slices in a 450°F (230°C) oven until slightly browned, about 15 minutes.

ASPICS

WITH ROASTED PEPPERS, EGGPLANT, & SPINACH

OVEN: 400°F (205°C) > PREP TIME: 40 minutes > BAKING TIME: 20 to 25 minutes > CHILL TIME: 2 hours or overnight > YIELD: 12 aspics

FOR THE ROASTED PEPPERS

3 bell peppers, preferably a mix of red, yellow, orange

1 teaspoon salt

2 tablespoons extra-virgin olive oil

2 tablespoons honey

Pinch crushed red pepper flakes

3 tablespoons capers, rinsed, drained, and chopped

3 tablespoons fresh oregano or marjoram

2 tablespoon red wine vinegar

FOR THE ROASTED EGGPLANT

1 eggplant, cut into 12 (¼-inch-thick / 6-mm) rounds; halve rounds if large

2 tablespoons extra-virgin olive oil

Kosher salt and freshly ground black pepper

FOR THE HERB SAUCE

2 tablespoon red wine vinegar

1 clove garlic

2 tablespoons capers, rinsed and drained

4 anchovies

½ to 1 fresh hot chile pepper, stem and seeds removed

½ cup (20 g) fresh mint leaves

½ cup (20 g) fresh basil leaves

½ cup (20 g) fresh oregano leaves

½ cup (20 g) fresh parsley leaves

⅓ cup (75 ml) extra-virgin olive oil

⅓ cup (45 g) pine nuts

FOR THE MOZZARELLA CHEESE FILLING

1 (8-ounce / 225 g) ball fresh buffalo mozzarella, cut into thin slices, then diced into ¼-inch (6-mm) pieces

¼ teaspoon kosher salt

¼ teaspoon freshly ground black pepper

1 teaspoon garlic, finely chopped, or 1 teaspoon garlic from a tube

1 tablespoon olive oil

FOR THE ZUCCHINI RIBBONS

2 large zucchini, washed

1 tablespoon olive oil

Pinch salt and pepper

Juice and zest of 1 lemon

FOR THE ASPIC

1½ cups (360 ml) vegetable or chicken stock

2 (¼-ounce) packets gelatin

1 cup (240 ml) packed spinach leaves

Lettuce leaves, for serving

FRESH SPINACH LEAVES, roasted peppers, and eggplant are encased here in a savory aspic, or gelatin. The amazing taste of this dish will turn any aspic doubter into a believer: This is an example of taking the ordinary and making it extraordinary. The flavors of this dish are bright and refreshing, the perfect combination for a summer lunch.

> MAKE THE ROASTED PEPPERS

Roast the peppers over an open flame until blistered, about 4 minutes, then place them in a zip-top plastic bag with the salt. Let steam 10 minutes, then peel the skins from the peppers but don't rinse with water. Core, seed, and cut the peppers lengthwise into 8 slices each, for a total of 24 slices.

In a medium bowl, mix the oil, honey, red pepper flakes, capers, oregano, and vinegar. Add the roasted peppers and toss to coated.

> MAKE THE ROASTED EGGPLANT

Preheat the oven to 400°F (205°C).

Brush each eggplant slice with oil, then season with salt and pepper. On a sheet pan lined with foil or a Silpat, roast the eggplant for 25 to 30 minutes, until golden in color and soft, turning once. Let cool to room temperature.

> MAKE THE HERB SAUCE

In the bowl of a food processor fitted with the blade attachment, combine the vinegar, garlic, capers, anchovies, and chile pepper (start with half the pepper, then add the other half, if desired, after tasting the sauce), along with the mint, basil, oregano, parsley, oil, and pine nuts. Pulse until smooth and set aside.

> MAKE THE MOZZARELLA FILLING

In a medium bowl, mix together the mozzarella, salt and pepper, garlic, and olive oil, then set aside until assembly.

> MAKE THE ZUCCHINI RIBBONS

Peel the zucchini into long ribbons with a T-shaped vegetable peeler or on a mandoline. Stop peeling when you reach the seeds. Place the ribbons in a medium bowl and toss with oil, salt and pepper, and the lemon juice. Set aside until assembly.

> MAKE THE ASPIC

In a small saucepan, heat the stock over medium-high heat until hot but not boiling. Sprinkle the gelatin into the stock and let sit for 5 minutes, until the gelatin dissolves. Pour the gelatin mixture into a blender, add the spinach, and blend until smooth. Transfer to a medium bowl and set aside at room temperature.

> ASSEMBLE THE MINI MEALS

Create an assembly line, with items in this order: aspic, zucchini, peppers, eggplant, herb sauce, cheese, lettuce leaves, for serving.

Line a 12-well classic cupcake pan with plastic wrap, making sure that each well is surrounded by plastic. Use 2 long pieces that overlap in the center of the pan, and leave a 3-inch (7.5-cm) border of plastic wrap overhanging all sides of the pan.

Dip 2 zucchini ribbons into the aspic and place them in a well in a cross formation.

Dip 2 pepper slices into the aspic, one red and one yellow. Add to the well, filling any negative space that remains.

Dip 1 eggplant slice into the aspic and layer it in the well. (No need to wipe off excess aspic; you will need it to hold your mold together.) Trim the eggplant to leave 2 inches (5 cm) overhanging on each side.

Repeat the layers of zucchini, peppers, and eggplant in each well, then evenly divide the herb sauce among the wells, using it all. Evenly divide the mozzarella cheese mixture among the wells. Press down on the filling in each well.

Fold the overhanging zucchini over the filling and top each well with the remaining aspic, pressing down on each mini meal to get the aspic into the layers underneath. Tightly wrap the pan in another layer of plastic wrap.

Chill in the fridge for at least 2 hours or overnight. To unpan, begin by unwrapping the top layer of plastic wrap, then lift up on the overhanging edges of the plastic wrap lining the wells of the pan to remove the terrines. They will pop out easily. Invert each terrine and plate them on a bed of lettuce, either individually or on a serving platter. Serve with a tomato salad tossed with fresh chives.

EGG ROLLS WITH SWEET & SOUR CRAB >

chapter
>FIVE<
SEAFOOD

I'VE LIVED NEAR THE OCEAN FOR SOME TIME, FIRST IN CALIFORNIA, and now in Florida. One of the major benefits of being close to the water—other than the gorgeous view and fun days at the beach with the children—is having so much fresh seafood available.

Something that never fails to surprise burgeoning cooks is how sexy seafood is. It doesn't need fancy preparations to be exquisite. I hope you'll see how easy it is to make a bland seafood meal extraordinary by adding one or two ingredients that will create different layers of flavors within a single bite.

Seafood can be served sweet or savory, chilled or hot. Try making a simple and very fresh fruit salsa with mango, lime juice and pulp, pineapple, and a spicy pepper to serve alongside. Or, go savory with chopped red onion, capers, garlic, anchovies, and olives with the zest, juice, and pulp of an orange.

Shrimp & GRITS SOUFFLÉS

OVEN: 350°F (175°C) > **PREP TIME:** 35 minutes >
BAKING TIME: 35 minutes > **YIELD:** 12 soufflés

• • •

24 slices regular or turkey bacon

FOR THE GRITS SOUFFLÉ

1 cup plus 2 tablespoons (270 ml) whole milk

½ cup (80 g) stone-ground grits

4 ounces (115 g) cheddar, grated

¼ cup (½ stick / 60 g) unsalted butter

Kosher salt and freshly ground black pepper

2 tablespoons yellow or white cornmeal

2 large egg yolks

3 large egg whites

FOR THE ASSEMBLY

1 tablespoon salted butter

½ pound (225 g) medium shrimp, peeled and deveined

4 cloves garlic, minced, or 4 teaspoons garlic from a tube

2 tablespoons chopped fresh parsley or parsley from a tube

Cayenne (optional)

Savory Tidbit **Cooking bacon on foil makes for easy cleanup. Once the bacon is cooked, transfer the slices to a paper towel to drain, then fold up the foil and toss it in the trash.**

LOW AND SLOW—that's the key to perfect grits. This baked version, similar to a soufflé, includes just enough cornmeal to hold together these naughty little packages wrapped in bacon. The flavor of the bacon melts into the grits, giving the whole dish a pleasant smokiness. You won't even notice that this recipe only uses a fraction of the butter that grits normally receive. It's more flavorful—and healthier!

Preheat the oven to 350°F (175°C).

Arrange the bacon on 2 foil-lined sheet pans and bake until it is crispy, 12 to 15 minutes. Remove the bacon to a paper towel–lined sheet pan to drain, then cut each slice of bacon in half crosswise so you have 48 short slices. Do not turn off the oven.

> MAKE THE GRITS SOUFFLÉ

In a medium saucepan over high heat, bring the milk and 1 cup (240 ml) of water to a boil, about 4 minutes. Slowly add the grits, whisking constantly. Reduce the heat to medium-low and cover the pan, stirring occasionally, until the grits are smooth and thick, about 12 minutes. Do not walk away from the grits, as they boil over easily.

Remove the pan from the heat and stir in the cheese, butter, and salt and pepper to taste. Sprinkle the cornmeal into the mixture a little at a time, stirring constantly to avoid lumps. Stir the 2 egg yolks into the grits.

In the bowl of a stand mixer fitted with the whisk attachment, beat the egg whites on medium speed until stiff peaks form, about 4 minutes. With a rubber spatula, fold the egg white mixture into the grits.

> ASSEMBLE AND BAKE THE SOUFFLÉS

Line the wells of a 12-well classic cupcake pan with the cooked bacon, using 4 half-slices per well in a crisscross formation. The bacon can peek up over the rims of the wells, which will add to the drama of this presentation.

Divide the grits among the wells, filling each well to the top. Bake until the soufflés are golden and puffed up, about 20 minutes. (They will fall when you take them out.) Let cool in the pan for 5 minutes, then use your hands to lift them from the pan, using the bacon wrappers as handles.

> MAKE THE SHRIMP

In a medium sauté pan over medium-low heat, melt the butter and sauté the shrimp and garlic just until pink, 5 to 7 minutes. Toss in the chopped parsley for color. Spoon about 3 shrimp over each soufflé and sprinkle the tops with cayenne, if you dare.

Avocado Mousses
WITH SHRIMP & MANGO

PREP TIME: 50 minutes >
CHILLING TIME: 2 to 4 hours > **YIELD:** 12 mousses

● ● ●

FOR THE AVOCADO MOUSSE

2 tablespoons boiling water

1 (¼-ounce / 7-g) packet unflavored gelatin

2 large ripe Hass avocados

Zest of 1 lime

2 tablespoons fresh lime juice

2 ounces (55 g) cream cheese

½ teaspoon kosher salt

¼ teaspoon freshly ground black pepper

FOR THE SHRIMP

2 tablespoons extra-virgin olive oil

½ pound (225 g) medium shrimp, peeled and deveined

½ teaspoon kosher salt

1 teaspoon curry powder

2 tablespoons mango chutney

2 teaspoons chopped fresh cilantro or cilantro from a tube

⅓ cup (55 g) diced fresh mango

2 teaspoons chile-lime hot sauce or your favorite hot sauce

Juice of 1 lime

FOR THE ASSEMBLY

1 avocado, halved, pitted, and cut into 24 thin slices (see Note)

3 hearts of palm, thinly sliced into 48 rounds

Note There are two basic methods for cutting an avocado: cutting the meat in the shell, or removing it from the shell and then cutting it. I prefer to cut the slices while still in the shell because this allows me to hold the avocado half in my hand, remove the pit, and then thinly slice the avocado flesh, being careful not to cut through the shell. I scoop the slices out of the shell with a large spoon. Alternatively, you can pit the avocado, scoop the flesh from each half in one piece with a large spoon, and then cut it into slices.

AMAZING. That's all I can say about this delectable mousse. It is rich, but light, and has a subtle hint of lime that cuts through the buttery avocado and cream cheese. The addition of lime-marinated shrimp adds a tart brightness. Make sure to choose avocados that are ripe and without blemish; the flesh should have a beautiful green color when sliced open.

I would serve this mousse on a bed of alternating slices of mango and avocado as the salad course for a larger meal.

> MAKE THE AVOCADO MOUSSE

Place the boiling water in a small bowl and sprinkle the gelatin over it. Stir and then let stand to bloom, about 5 minutes.

Meanwhile, pit and peel the avocados. Put the avocado flesh into a blender and add the lime zest and juice; blend until smooth. Add the cream cheese along with the salt and pepper and blend until fully combined. Add the gelatin, blending fully. Set aside at room temperature.

> MAKE THE SHRIMP

In a medium sauté pan, heat the extra-virgin olive oil over medium heat. Add the shrimp and cook, flipping them once halfway through, until they are opaque and pink, about 3 minutes. Coarsely chop the shrimp, then transfer them to a medium bowl, along with the salt, curry powder, chutney, cilantro, mango, hot sauce, and lime juice. Mix to combine, then refrigerate until cool, about 30 minutes.

> ASSEMBLE THE MOUSSES

Line a 12-well classic cupcake pan with plastic wrap by overlapping 2 long pieces along the center of the pan, leaving at least a 3-inch (7.5-cm) border of plastic wrap overhanging all sides of the pan.

Line each well with 2 overlapping slices of avocado, then 4 slices of hearts of palm per well. Add 1 heaping tablespoon of shrimp, then divide the mousse among the wells. Tap the pan to settle the mousse in the wells.

Tightly wrap the pan in another layer of plastic and chill for 2 to 4 hours. (Chilling any longer will cause the avocado to discolor.) To unpan, remove the top layer of plastic wrap, then lift up on the edges of the plastic wrap lining the wells of the pan to remove the mousses.

EGG ROLLS
WITH SWEET & SOUR CRAB

OVEN: 350°F (175°C) > **PREP TIME:** 20 minutes >
BAKING TIME: 20 to 25 minutes > **YIELD:** 12 egg rolls

FOR THE SWEET & SOUR CRAB

2 tablespoons sesame oil

1 small onion, finely chopped

½ cup (75 g) finely chopped red bell pepper

1 large clove garlic, chopped, or 1 tablespoon garlic from a tube

1 tablespoon finely chopped fresh ginger or ginger from a tube

½ cup (45 g) packed finely shredded Napa cabbage

¼ cup (60 ml) ketchup

1 to 3 tablespoons Sriracha or other hot chile sauce

1 tablespoon sugar

½ cup (120 ml) sake

2 tablespoons lime juice

2 tablespoons oyster sauce

1½ tablespoons cornstarch

8 ounces (225 g) fresh lump crabmeat, drained and picked over for shells (see Note)

FOR THE ASSEMBLY

Nonstick cooking spray, for the pan

1 (16-ounce / 455-g) package egg roll wrappers

2 scallions, sliced on a bias, for garnish

Note Fresh lump crabmeat can be found in the refrigerated section of most grocery stores.

I AM A SPICE GIRL, as you can tell by this recipe. Here a crispy wrapper is filled with the perfect blend of sweet and sour vegetables and crab. These egg rolls offer plenty of zing; if you're not a big fan of heat, cut back a little on the Sriracha or chile sauce.

> MAKE THE SWEET & SOUR CRAB

In a medium sauté pan over medium-low heat, heat the sesame oil; add the onion and let it sweat for about 3 minutes to soften (do not allow it to brown). Add the red pepper, garlic, ginger, and cabbage; turn off the heat and transfer the vegetable mixture to a medium bowl.

Using the same pan, over medium heat, bring the ketchup, Sriracha, sugar, sake, lime juice, and oyster sauce to a boil, whisking constantly. In a small bowl, dissolve the cornstarch in 2 tablespoons of water. Add this to the pan, whisking constantly until the sauce thickens, about 2 minutes. When the bubbles begin to get larger and the sauce is visibly thick, turn off the heat. Add this sauce to the bowl with the vegetables, then add the crab. Mix well and adjust the seasoning as needed.

> ASSEMBLE AND BAKE THE EGG ROLLS

Preheat the oven to 350°F (175°C).

Spray a 12-well classic cupcake pan with nonstick cooking spray and line each well with an egg roll wrapper, creating a cup. Divide the crab mixture among the wells, leaving the wrapper open. Bake until the egg roll wrapper is golden brown and crispy at the edges, 20 to 25 minutes. Let the egg rolls rest in the pan for 5 minutes, then use your hands to lift them from the pan, using the wrappers as handles. Garnish the egg rolls with fresh scallions.

CRAB & TOMATO
Napoleons
WITH TOMATO ASPIC

OVEN: 275°F (135°C) > **PREP TIME:** 15 minutes > **BAKING TIME:** 2 hours > **CHILLING TIME:** 2 hours or overnight > **YIELD:** 12 Napoleons

● ● ●

FOR THE TOMATO CONFIT

6 large ripe plum tomatoes or medium beefsteak or vine-ripened tomatoes

3 tablespoons extra-virgin olive oil

3 cloves garlic, peeled and crushed

6 sprigs fresh thyme

1 teaspoon kosher salt

FOR THE CRAB SALAD

8 ounces (225 g) fresh lump crabmeat, drained and picked over for shells (see Note, page 129)

3 tablespoons sour cream

3 tablespoons mayonnaise

Juice of 1 lemon

2 tablespoons snipped fresh cilantro

¼ cup (12 g) snipped chives

Kosher salt and freshly ground black pepper

Tabasco sauce

FOR THE TOMATO ASPIC

1 (¼-ounce / 7-g) packet unflavored gelatin

1½ cups (360 ml) V-8 juice or marinara sauce, warmed

⅓ cup finely chopped onion

1 rib celery, strings removed, very finely chopped

1 teaspoon Worcestershire sauce

½ tablespoon fresh lemon juice

½ teaspoon kosher salt

¼ teaspoon freshly ground black pepper

WHILE NAPOLEONS are traditionally desserts, this version doesn't suffer—and even improves—with the transition to savory. This Napoleon is elegant and well worth the work. To save a little time, substitute roasted tomatoes packed in olive oil and herbs, found in the deli of most markets, near the olives. These tomatoes have a bright, flavorful taste. Sun-dried tomatoes in olive oil are not a good substitute because of their earthy flavor. Using V-8 juice really makes the flavors pop.

Make Ahead The tomato confit can be made in advance, and will keep, covered in a layer of olive oil, for up to 2 weeks in an airtight container in the fridge (see "Savory Tidbit," page 131). You can also prepare the Napoleons up to a day in advance of serving, and unmold them on the day of your event.

> MAKE THE TOMATO CONFIT

Preheat the oven to 275°F (135°C). Cut the tomatoes in half and remove all of the seeds and pulp with a small spoon or knife.

Line a rimmed baking sheet with foil and drizzle with the oil, then arrange the tomatoes, cut side down, on the pan; scatter the garlic and thyme around them and sprinkle with the salt.

Bake, turning the pan from time to time, until the tomatoes are very soft and shriveled, 2 hours or more. Do not allow them to brown; if they begin to brown around the edges, turn the heat down to 250°F (120°C). When the tomatoes are cool enough to handle, cut each piece in half for a total of 24 pieces.

> MAKE THE CRAB SALAD

In a medium bowl, combine the crabmeat, sour cream, mayonnaise, lemon juice, cilantro, and chives. Season with salt, pepper, and Tabasco, then place in the fridge until assembly.

› MAKE THE TOMATO ASPIC

Pour ¼ cup (60 ml) of hot water into a medium bowl and sprinkle the gelatin over it; stir to combine. Let sit for about 5 minutes, then whisk in the warmed tomato juice, making sure you dissolve all of the lumps. If any lumps remain, reheat the mixture for a few minutes over low heat, whisking to dissolve them. Stir in the onion, celery, Worcestershire, lemon juice, salt, and pepper and set aside at room temperature.

› ASSEMBLE THE NAPOLEONS

Line a 12-well classic cupcake pan with plastic wrap by overlapping 2 long pieces of plastic wrap along the center of the pan, leaving at least a 3-inch (7.5-cm) border of plastic wrap overhanging all sides of the pan.

Distribute half of the aspic among the wells. Next place 1 piece of roasted tomato in each well. Add the crab salad, dividing it equally among the wells. Add another roasted tomato, and distribute the remaining aspic evenly between the wells.

Place another piece of plastic wrap on top of the cupcake pan and press down gently into each well to help the aspic settle, which will ensure layered Napoleons that hold their shape. Wrap the pan tightly in the plastic wrap and chill for 2 hours or overnight. Remove the top layer of plastic wrap, then lift up on the edges of the plastic wrap lining the wells of the pan to remove the Napoleons.

Savory Tidbit **When I make these, I triple the recipe for the tomato confit due to the amount of time it takes to create them. It is well worth your time, especially in the winter when tomatoes are not in season and are firm and flavorless. Creating tomato confit with those unwanted winter tomatoes will brighten their flavor, and slow roasting with olive oil and salt brings out their sweetness. I use these in salads and on wedges of bread with fresh cheese.**

Artichoke
MOUSSES
WITH SCALLOPS & MANGO

PREP TIME: 25 minutes > **CHILLING TIME:** 4 hours or overnight >
YIELD: 12 mousses

FOR THE ARTICHOKE MOUSSE

½ cup (120 ml) tomato sauce or ketchup

Juice of 1 lime

2 (¼-ounce / 7-g) packets unflavored gelatin

1 (14-ounce / 400-g) can artichoke hearts, drained

½ cup (120 ml) plain yogurt

½ cup (120 ml) sour cream

½ teaspoon curry powder

2 tablespoons mango chutney

Kosher salt and freshly ground black pepper

1 tablespoon sweet relish

FOR THE SCALLOPS

8 ounces (225 g) bay scallops, rinsed

1 teaspoon extra-virgin olive oil

½ teaspoon kosher salt

1 teaspoon curry powder

2 tablespoons mango chutney

2 teaspoons chopped fresh cilantro or cilantro from a tube

⅓ cup (55 g) diced mango

2 teaspoons hot sauce

Juice of 1 lime

FOR THE ASSEMBLY

1 avocado, halved, pitted, and cut into 24 thin slices (see Note, page 128)

3 hearts of palm, thinly sliced into 48 rounds

Several thin slices tomato, for serving (optional)

Several thin slices cucumber, for serving (optional)

2 to 3 thinly sliced hard-boiled eggs, for serving (optional)

I LOVE TO EAT NANTUCKET BAY SCALLOPS
fresh, as they are like candy, but unfortunately we don't have those in Orlando. Instead, I pick up some small, fresh bay scallops without the muscle attached. When absolutely fresh, there is no need to cook them; they are delicious simply coated in this curried dressing.

Always use caution and follow safe handling practices when preparing raw fish or shellfish. If a meal calls for raw, using it the day it's purchased is the freshest—and safest— option.

> MAKE THE ARTICHOKE MOUSSE

In a small saucepan over medium heat, heat the tomato sauce with the lime juice until just boiling. Sprinkle the gelatin over the tomato sauce, and let it sit for 5 minutes, then stir to combine. In a blender, combine the artichoke hearts, yogurt, sour cream, curry powder, chutney, and salt and pepper to taste; blend until smooth. Add the gelatin mixture to the tomato sauce mixture in the blender and stir by hand to incorporate, then stir in the sweet relish. Set the mousse aside in the blender at room temperature.

> MAKE THE SCALLOPS

Drain any liquid from the scallops. (If you prefer cooked scallops, see the Variation for cooking instructions.) Transfer the scallops to a medium bowl, then add the oil, salt, curry powder, chutney, cilantro, mango, hot sauce, and lime juice. Toss to coat the scallops thoroughly and adjust the seasoning, which should be a combination of sweet and tangy, fresh and bright.

> ASSEMBLE THE MOUSSES

Line a 12-well classic cupcake pan with plastic wrap by overlapping 2 long pieces of plastic wrap along the center of the pan, leaving at least a 3-inch (7.5-cm) border of plastic wrap overhanging all sides of the pan.

In each well, layer 2 avocado slices (pressing them into the wells), 4 hearts of palm slices, and 2 heaping tablespoons of scallops. Pour the mousse into the wells directly from the blender, dividing it equally among the wells. Tap the pan on the work surface so the mousse settles into the wells.

Wrap the cupcake pan tightly in another layer of plastic wrap and chill for 4 hours, making sure to serve the scallops the same day they were purchased if serving raw. (If the scallops are cooked, the mousses can be chilled overnight.) Remove the top layer of plastic wrap, then lift up on the edges of the plastic wrap lining the wells of the pan to remove the mousses. Serve the mousses on a bed of alternating slices of tomato, cucumber, and hard-boiled egg as a mini meal or as the salad course of a larger meal.

VARIATION For those who prefer their scallops cooked, sauté them over medium heat in I teaspoon olive oil with a pinch of salt and pepper until opaque, about 4 minutes. Then proceed with the recipe.

MAKE YOUR MEALS
Your Own

Don't think you have to make perfect creations like you see in the photographs in this book. What you create in your kitchen is exactly what your family will love. However, as you become familiar with the recipes and techniques using the cupcake pan, your dishes will naturally look better with each preparation. If you take anything from this book, let it be improved confidence in the kitchen, especially when using the cupcake pan!

SALMON
with
POTATO, PEAS, LEEKS & BROCCOLI GRATIN

OVEN: 350°F (165°C) > **PREP TIME:** 55 minutes >
BAKING TIME: 25 minutes > **YIELD:** 12 mini meals

FOR THE BROCCOLI GRATIN

2 tablespoons unsalted butter

⅓ cup (55 g) minced shallots

2 cloves garlic, minced, or 2 teaspoons garlic from a tube

½ teaspoon dry mustard

1½ cups (165 g) fresh bread crumbs (see Note, page 103) or panko

Kosher salt and freshly ground black pepper

½ cup (60 g) grated Parmesan

Florets from 1 head of broccoli, chopped small

2 tablespoons Dijon mustard

¼ cup (60 ml) whipping cream or half-and-half

1 cup (145 g) frozen peas, thawed

1 pound (455 grams) fresh salmon fillet, skin and bones removed

2 leeks

2 tablespoons unsalted butter

FOR THE POTATOES

3 tablespoons unsalted butter

4 Yukon Gold or other creamy yellow potatoes

1 cup (240 ml) heavy cream or half-and-half

1 cup (240 ml) white wine

1 tablespoon fresh thyme leaves

Salt and pepper

1 cup (115 g) grated Gruyère

Nonstick cooking spray, for the pan

THIS DISH EVOLVED from a recipe for broccoli gratin I found in *Bon Appétit* years ago and have loved ever since. What makes the combination of the gratin with the other ingredients so special is how the dry mustard and cheese of the gratin-style topping give it the feel of a strudel. Peas add a slight sweetness to the mix, while the broccoli and bread crumbs add a hearty and nutty flavor.

> ### MAKE THE BROCCOLI GRATIN

In a medium sauté pan over medium heat, melt the butter. Add the shallots and sauté until softened, about 3 minutes. Add the garlic and dry mustard; mix well. Add the bread crumbs and sauté until the crumbs are golden, 5 to 8 minutes more, tossing them back and forth in the pan to toast evenly. Season with salt and pepper. Turn off the heat. While the pan is still hot, stir in ¼ cup (30 g) of the Parmesan and continue to stir for 1 minute, scraping up any cheese that has melted on the bottom of the pan. Transfer to a medium bowl and set aside.

In a pot of boiling water, cook the broccoli florets for 2 to 3 minutes; they should be crisp and bright green. Drain the florets, rinse them under cold water to stop the cooking process, drain again, and chop them small. Place the chopped broccoli in a large bowl and toss with the Dijon mustard, cream, and the remaining Parmesan, mixing until well combined. Stir in the bread crumb mixture to combine. Set aside.

Purée the peas in a blender until smooth.

Place the salmon in the bowl of a food processor fitted with the blade and pulse until broken up but not pulverized.

Remove and discard the roots and dark green tops of the leeks. Cut the leeks crosswise into rounds and place them in a large bowl of cold water to soak for 5 minutes. Remove the rounds from the water using a slotted spoon and transfer to a colander. Rinse to remove any remaining grit. Discard the soaking water. In a large skillet over medium heat, melt the butter, then add the leeks and sauté until softened, about 4 minutes. (Do not brown.) Remove from the heat and set aside.

> MAKE THE POTATOES

Slice each potato widthwise into nine ⅛-inch (3-mm) slices, for a total of 36 pieces. In a large sauté pan over medium heat, melt the butter. Add the potatoes and cook, flipping occasionally, until golden brown, 8 to 10 minutes. Pour ½ cup (120 ml) cream and ½ cup (120 ml) white wine over the potatoes, stir in the thyme, and cook for 5 minutes. Season with salt and pepper. Add the remaining cream and wine. Increase the heat to high and bring the mixture to a boil, stirring occasionally, until the liquid is reduced by half, about 6 minutes. Reduce the heat to low, stir in the Gruyère, and heat until the cheese has melted and the mixture is well combined.

Preheat the oven to 350°F (175°C). Spray a 12-well classic cupcake pan with nonstick cooking spray.

Place 3 potato slices in the bottom of each well, forming a shell. In each well, layer the leeks, pea purée, and salmon. Distribute the cream sauce evenly over the top, then add the broccoli gratin, pressing down after each addition, until it has all been distributed evenly among the wells. Bake until the bread crumbs are golden brown and the gratin is cooked through, about 25 minutes.

Let the gratins rest in the pan for 1 minute, then loosen the sides of each gratin with a table knife and insert a fork between the pan and each gratin to lift it out. Serve with your favorite creamy soup, crusty bread, and sliced tomatoes.

Smoked Salmon
EGG SALAD SANDWICHES
ON PUMPERNICKEL

PREP TIME: 35 minutes > **CHILLING TIME:** 2 hours or up to 2 days > **YIELD:** 12 sandwiches

● ● ●

FOR THE EGG SALAD

8 large eggs

⅓ cup (75 ml) mayonnaise

2 teaspoons Dijon mustard

1 tablespoon chopped capers plus 1 tablespoon caper brine

1 tablespoon finely chopped red onion or shallot

1 tablespoon chopped fresh dill or dill from a tube

Freshly ground black pepper

1 (¼-ounce / 7-g) packet unflavored gelatin

FOR THE BREAD WRAPPER

12 thin slices pumpernickel bread

2 tablespoons unsalted butter, softened

12 sprigs fresh dill

16 ounces (455 g) Scottish or cold-smoked salmon, thinly sliced

1 tablespoon chopped fresh dill, for garnish (optional)

VARIATIONS White bread or onion-poppyseed bread are a few possible bread substitutions that would work well in this dish.

I LOVE HOW THIS grown-up egg salad is beautifully contained by the Scottish smoked salmon wrapper and sandwiched with pumpernickel on the top and bottom. Cold-smoked salmon makes an excellent substitute for the Scottish and is available in most markets. Both of these are a good choice because of their mild fish flavor. Also note that no salt is needed as the salmon already has plenty to share. These mini meals are remarkably adaptable, delicious for breakfast, lunch, or as part of a buffet. Serve with a green salad and a light dressing for a refreshingly complete meal.

> **MAKE THE EGG SALAD**

In a medium saucepan, cover the eggs by 2 inches (5 cm) with cold water and bring to a boil. Turn off the heat, cover, and let rest 10 minutes. Drain and rinse the eggs in cool water. Peel the eggs under running cool water.

Place the peeled eggs in a medium bowl along with the mayonnaise, mustard, capers and brine, red onion, dill, and pepper to taste. Whisk to bring all of the flavors together, mashing the eggs so they remain textured, not smooth (see "Savory Tidbit," page 138). Sprinkle the gelatin over the egg salad and mix thoroughly.

> **MAKE THE BREAD WRAPPER**

Using a 2-inch (5-cm) round cookie or biscuit cutter, cut each slice of bread into 2 circles, for a total of 24.

Butter 12 of the circles, on one side only, with a thin layer of butter. Place 1 sprig of dill on each buttered slice and press it so it sticks.

RECIPE CONTINUES

Line a 12-well classic cupcake pan with plastic wrap by overlapping 2 long pieces of plastic wrap along the center of the pan, leaving a 3-inch (7.5-cm) border of plastic wrap overhanging all sides of the pan.

Line the wells with the smoked salmon, allowing the salmon to hang over the edges of the pan by 2 inches (5 cm). I use 1½ slices per well, but the quantity will vary depending on the size of the slices. If the bottoms of the wells are not completely covered, cut smaller pieces of the salmon to fill them in. Add 1 round of bread, buttered side down, to each well.

Distribute the egg salad among the wells and top with the second piece of bread. Fold the salmon over the bread, and then wrap the pan in another layer of plastic wrap, pressing down on each well to compact the contents. Chill for 2 hours or up to 2 days.

Remove the top layer of plastic wrap, then lift up on the edges of the plastic wrap lining the wells of the pan to remove the mini sandwiches. To serve, invert the sand-wiches and garnish with a pinch of fresh dill, if desired.

Savory Tidbit **Instead of dirtying another dish (or three), mash the hard-boiled egg with a wire whisk in one bowl with the rest of the salad ingredients. (It's going into the salad soon enough anyway.) This also saves you the time of chopping the eggs on a cutting board.**

Lemon-Scented
CAKES
WITH SALMON, CAPER & LEMON TOPPING

OVEN: 325°F (165°C) > **PREP TIME:** 35 minutes > **BAKING TIME:** 25 to 30 minutes > **YIELD:** 12 cakes

● ● ●

FOR THE LEMON-SCENTED CAKES

Nonstick cooking spray, for the pan

1 cup (2 sticks / 230 g) salted butter, at room temperature

½ cup plus 3 tablespoons (140 g) sugar

1 tablespoon lemon extract

Zest of 5 lemons

5 large egg yolks, at room temperature

1¾ cup plus 2 tablespoons (230 g) all-purpose flour

1 cup plus 5 tablespoons (160 g) cake flour (not self-rising flour)

2 teaspoons baking powder

½ teaspoon freshly ground black pepper

1 cup (240 ml) full-fat sour cream

8 large egg whites, at room temperature

FOR THE SALMON, CAPER & LEMON TOPPING

12 ounces (340 g) cream cheese

8 ounces (225 g) crème fraîche

3 ounces (85 g) cold-smoked salmon, preferably wild sockeye, finely chopped

½ tablespoon capers in brine, drained and finely chopped

1 tablespoon lemon zest

Juice of ½ lemon

2 small bunches chives, snipped fine

COLD-SMOKED SALMON offers a delicate flavor versus traditional smoked salmon. For this cake, I prefer the subtle flavor of wild sockeye. The cake has a dominant lemon flavor and a subtle bite from the pepper.

> MAKE THE LEMON-SCENTED CAKES

Preheat the oven to 325°F (165°C). Spray a 12-well classic cupcake pan with nonstick cooking spray.

In the bowl of a stand mixer fitted with the paddle attachment, beat together the butter and sugar on medium-high speed until light and fluffy, about 4 minutes. Mix in the lemon extract and lemon zest. Add the egg yolks, one at a time, beating well after each addition.

In a medium bowl, sift together both flours, the baking powder, and pepper. Add to the egg mixture and, with the mixer on low, mix until well combined. Add the sour cream and mix until well combined.

In the stand mixer fitted a clean bowl and the whisk attachment, beat the egg whites until stiff peaks form, about 4 minutes. Gently fold the whites into the batter by hand. Fill each cupcake well with the batter. Bake until the tops are golden and a toothpick inserted in the center of a cupcake comes out clean, 25 to 30 minutes. Let the cupcakes cool completely in the pan.

MAKE THE SALMON, CAPER & LEMON TOPPING

In a stand mixer fitted with the paddle attachment, mix the cream cheese and cream fraîche until light and fluffy, about 2 minutes. Then add the salmon, capers, and the lemon zest and juice and beat to combine. Transfer the topping to a zip-top bag.

When the cupcakes are cool, loosen the edges of each and insert the tines of a fork between the pan and each cupcake to lift it out. Using a serrated knife, cut the rounded top off each cupcake and discard the top. Using an apple corer, make a 1-inch-deep (2.5-cm) hole in the center of each loaf, making sure not to cut all the way through or the filling will seep out. Snip one corner off the zip-top bag of topping. Pipe the topping into each cupcake, filling it to the top, and over the entire top of each cupcake. Smooth it with a table knife.

Place the sliced chives on a small plate and dip the top of each cake into the chives.

SMOKED SALMON *Sandwiches*

PREP TIME: 25 minutes > **CHILLING TIME:** 1 hour or overnight >
YIELD: 12 sandwiches

FOR THE RICE

1 cup (200 g) short-grain rice

2 tablespoons sake

2 tablespoons rice wine vinegar

1 tablespoon sugar

FOR THE DIJON HONEY DILL DIPPING SAUCE (OPTIONAL)

¼ cup (60 ml) Dijon mustard

2 tablespoons chopped fresh dill

2 tablespoons honey

FOR THE ASSEMBLY

1 tablespoon kosher salt

1 large handful (160 g) snow peas, ends trimmed

6 sheets nori

1 (8-ounce / 225-g) package smoked presliced salmon

1 scallion, sliced thin on the bias

2 Kirby, Japanese, baby, or pickling cucumbers, thinly sliced (see Note)

1 cup (110 g) freshly grated carrots (from 2 medium carrots)

3 tablespoons toasted sesame seeds

Note Pickling cucumbers work well here because they have less moisture. If using garden-variety cucumbers, or those with thick skins, peel them, slice in half lengthwise, and remove the seeds before slicing them crosswise.

THESE SMALL SANDWICHES have little to do with bread and a whole lot to do with rice. The layers of traditional Japanese ingredients fuse with the American flavor of the Dijon honey dill dipping sauce. I'm a fan of cold smoked salmon for this dish because of its mild fish flavor, though other excellent options include lox, Nova, peppered, or dill salmon. Serve these the day you make them or the next, as the rice becomes too firm if chilled too long.

When you're prepping the vegetables for this recipe, place them in small piles on a sheet pan so they are easily on hand when you're assembling the sandwiches (and you have fewer bowls to wash!).

Make Ahead The Dijon honey dill dipping sauce can be prepared in advance and stored in an airtight container in the refrigerator until needed. It will last for up to 1 week.

> MAKE THE RICE

Cook the rice, following the directions on the back of the package. In a small dish, combine the sake, vinegar, and sugar, stirring to dissolve the sugar. Stir the dressing into the cooked rice while it is still warm. Set aside.

> MAKE THE DIJON HONEY DILL DIPPING SAUCE

Combine all the ingredients in a small serving bowl and mix well with a spoon.

> ASSEMBLE THE SANDWICHES

Line a 12-well classic cupcake pan with plastic wrap by overlapping 2 long pieces of plastic wrap along the center of the pan, leaving a 3-inch (7.5-cm) border of plastic wrap overhanging all sides of the pan.

Bring a small pot of water to a boil with the salt. Drop the snow peas into the pot and stir once, then cook until crisp and tender but still green, 1 to 2 minutes. Drain immediately in a colander, running cold water over the peas to stop the cooking. Julienne the snow peas lengthwise; set aside.

Using scissors, cut the nori into 3-by-3-inch (9-by-9-cm) quarters, for a total of 24 squares. Place 1 piece of nori in the bottom of each well. Layer the other ingredients over the nori in each well in the following order:

1 heaping tablespoon rice

enough snow peas to cover the rice

1 slice salmon

sprinkle of scallions

3 slices cucumber

1 slice salmon

sprinkle of scallions

3 slices cucumber

generous sprinkle of carrot

sprinkle of sesame seeds

salmon to cover the surface

rice

nori

Make sure to fill the wells to the top. If you have extra of any of the layering items, press into the wells gently to make room for them. You can add extra layers as long as you end with rice and nori on top. Tuck the sides of the nori into the wells to seal the sandwiches.

Wrap the pan in another layer of plastic wrap and press down firmly to compact the ingredients; chill for 1 hour or overnight. Remove the top layer of plastic wrap, then lift up on the edges of the plastic wrap lining the wells of the pan to remove the sandwiches. Serve the sandwiches with the Dijon honey dill dipping sauce on the side.

VARIATION If you prefer to remove the "west" from this east-west fusion dish, serve the sandwiches with pickled ginger, wasabi, and soy sauce instead of the mustard dill dipping sauce. If you do this, omit the toasted sesame seeds from the recipe.

Salmon CAKES

OVEN: 350°F (175°C) > **PREP TIME:** 30 minutes >
BAKING TIME: 23 to 30 minutes > **YIELD:** 12 cakes

• • •

FOR THE LEEK WRAPPERS

6 leeks

2 tablespoons butter

1 tablespoon fresh thyme leaves

Kosher salt and freshly ground black pepper

FOR THE BREAD CRUMBS

3 slices white bread, crusts removed

3 tablespoons unsalted butter, melted

2 large cloves garlic, chopped, or 2 tablespoons garlic from a tube

FOR THE VEGETABLES

1 tablespoon unsalted butter

1 tablespoon extra-virgin olive oil

1 red onion, cut into ¼-inch (6-mm) dice

2 stalks celery, cut into ¼-inch (6-mm) dice

½ red pepper, seeded and cut into ¼-inch (6-mm) dice

2 large eggs

½ cup (40 g) chopped fresh parsley or parsley from a tube

2 tablespoons chopped capers

1 teaspoon hot sauce

1 teaspoon Worcestershire sauce

1 teaspoon Old Bay Seasoning

¼ cup (60 ml) mayonnaise

1 tablespoon Dijon mustard

1½ pounds (680 g) fresh salmon fillet, skin and bones removed

Nonstick cooking spray, for the pan

WRAPPING THE CAKES with leeks helps hold in moisture, keeping these scrumptious bites full of flavor. It doesn't hurt that they look wonderful, too. I suggest serving them chilled on a bed of greens with dressing on the side. If served for dinner, scalloped potatoes would make an excellent accompaniment.

Don't skip the homemade bread crumbs. The dusty crumbs that most people purchase from the store are not what I mean when I say bread crumbs. The difference in the final product is very different. Dust creates a dense and moistureless end result; crumbs create a fluffy and moist outcome.

Make Ahead **Impress your guests at your next luncheon by assembling the cakes a day in advance, then popping them in the oven right before serving.**

> MAKE THE LEEK WRAPPERS

Trim the rough dark green tops and the bottoms from the leeks, and remove the tough outer leaves. Cut each leek in half lengthwise, separate the inner leaves, and soak them in water to remove any grit. Remove the leeks from the water, making sure to rinse them well. You will need 24 leaves total; cut them in half so you have 4 pieces of leek for each well.

In a large sauté pan over medium heat, melt the butter, then add the leeks and thyme and sauté until the leeks are pliable, but not soft and mushy, 6 to 8 minutes. Season with salt and pepper, then taste an outer portion of leek; it should be easy to bite into.

Transfer the leeks to a sheet pan. Separate the leaves and spread them out so they don't continue to cook. Set aside until cool to the touch.

> MAKE THE BREAD CRUMBS

Preheat the oven to 350°F (175°C).

In a food processor fitted with a blade, pulverize the slices of bread. Transfer to a medium bowl and toss with the butter and garlic. Place the crumbs on a baking sheet and bake until golden brown, 8 to 10 minutes. Set aside to cool. Do not turn off the oven.

RECIPE CONTINUES

› MAKE THE VEGETABLES

Heat the butter and oil in a large sauté pan over medium heat. Add the onion, celery, and red pepper and sauté, stirring occasionally, until soft, about 8 minutes. Transfer to a large bowl to cool.

In a small bowl, whisk the eggs. Add the parsley, capers, hot sauce, Worcestershire, Old Bay, mayonnaise, and mustard, and whisk to combine. Pour the egg mixture over the cooled vegetable mixture and mix until well combined.

› ASSEMBLE THE CAKES

Place the salmon in the bowl of a food processor fitted with a blade. Pulse until just flaked; do not pulverize. Add the salmon and the bread crumbs to the vegetable mixture and stir to combine thoroughly.

Spray a 12-well classic cupcake pan with cooking spray. Line each well with 4 leek pieces, crisscrossing them on the bottom and making sure that no spaces are left uncovered. The leeks will overhang the wells. Do not trim them; they will be folded over the filling after the terrines are assembled. Working in batches, line 3 wells at a time in this way, then fill each with the salmon mixture, mounding it a little above the top; fold the ends of the leeks over the filling, pressing down gently to compact the vegetables.

Bake until cooked through, 15 to 20 minutes. Let cool in the pan for 1 minute, then insert the tines of a fork between the pan and each cake to lift it out.

Store the cakes in an airtight container in the refrigerator for up to 5 days. Reheat, wrapped in tin foil, for 15 minutes at 350ºF (175ºC).

Salads
NIÇOISE

PREP TIME: 40 minutes > **CHILLING TIME:** 2 hours or up to 2 days > **YIELD:** 12 salads

3 large eggs

8 small potatoes, such as fingerling, Russian, banana, or purple

FOR THE HERBED VINAIGRETTE ASPIC

1½ cups (360 ml) white balsamic or white wine vinegar

2 (¼-ounce / 7-g) packets unflavored gelatin

1 tablespoon capers, chopped

1 teaspoon chopped shallot

3 tablespoons chopped fresh fennel bulb

3 tablespoons chopped fresh flat-leaf parsley or parsley from a tube

3 tablespoons freshly snipped chives

Kosher salt and freshly ground black pepper

1 tablespoon Dijon mustard

¼ cup (60 ml) olive oil

**FOR THE ASSEMBLY
(SEE SIDEBAR ON PAGE 147)**

8 ounces (225 g) fresh green beans, blanched, or 1 pound (455 g) frozen green beans, thawed

2 (5-ounce / 150-g) cans Italian tonno packed in olive oil, drained

½ cup (90 g) pitted Niçoise olives

1 (2-ounce / 340-g) can oil-packed anchovies, drained

1 cup (240 g) roasted tomatoes in oil

Lettuce of your choice

Olive oil

Fresh lemon juice

THIS SALAD IS A DREAM COME TRUE. All of the classic French flavors come together in this beautifully layered presentation without the lettuce fighting for attention. The most important ingredient here is the tuna. I use Italian *tonno*, dark tuna packed in pure olive oil. The roasted tomatoes in oil have a fresh zesty flavor that is essential in bringing the dish together. Don't confuse them with sun-dried tomatoes, which have an earthy flavor. This is ideal as an hors d'oeuvre or a main-course salad.

In a small saucepan, cover the eggs by 2 inches (5 cm) with cold water and bring to a boil. Turn off the heat, cover, and let rest for 10 minutes. Rinse under cold water to cool. Peel the eggs and cut each one into 4 rounds, for a total of 12 slices.

In a medium saucepan, cover the potatoes by 2 inches (5 cm) with cold water. Bring to a boil, and cook until fork tender, about 12 minutes. Run the potatoes under cold water to cool. Cut each one crosswise into 3 slices, for a total of 24 slices.

> ## MAKE THE HERBED VINAIGRETTE ASPIC

In a small saucepan, bring the vinegar just to a boil. Sprinkle it with the gelatin, then stir to combine and let sit for 5 minutes.

In a small bowl, combine the remaining ingredients. Pour the gelatin over the herb mixture just before assembly.

RECIPE CONTINUES

› ASSEMBLE THE SALADS

Line a 12-well classic cupcake pan with plastic wrap by overlapping 2 long pieces of plastic wrap along the center of the pan, leaving at least a 3-inch (7.5-cm) border of plastic wrap overhanging all sides of the pan.

Layer the ingredients in each well in the following order, gently pressing down on each layer:

1 slice egg

1 tablespoon herbed vinaigrette

2 slices potato

4 green beans

Evenly distribute, in the following order, the tuna, olives, anchovies, and tomato in each well, then evenly distribute the remaining vinaigrette among the wells.

Wrap the pan in another layer of plastic wrap, pressing down on the wells once more, and chill for 2 hours or up to 2 days.

Remove the top layer of plastic wrap, then lift up on the edges of the plastic wrap lining the wells of the pan to remove the salads. Serve the salads together on a platter of beautiful lettuce that has been tossed with a light coating of olive oil and fresh lemon juice.

NIÇOISE
Layers

TUNA: You can substitute raw sushi-grade tuna or white albacore tuna packed in water. I recommend the Italian because the flavor is unsurpassable. If you want to use fresh tuna instead, you will need to season it. Toss it in some of the vinaigrette before layering it.

ANCHOVIES: Anchovy is traditional in this salad and can be used if you are a fan. I'd suggest that you use white anchovies.

GREEN BEANS: If you use fresh green beans, blanch them, but you could save yourself a step by using a package of thawed frozen beans.

To blanch fresh green beans, fill a medium saucepan with salted water and bring to a boil. Drop the beans into the water all at once. After 3 minutes, they will be bright green and ready to go. Drain them immediately in a colander and rinse in cold water to stop the cooking.

OLIVES: Niçoise olives are a must; there is no substitution.

ROASTED TOMATOES IN OIL: You can find these in the olive bar section of the market.

TUNA SUMMER ROLLS
WITH DIPPING SAUCES

PREP TIME: 55 minutes > **CHILLING TIME:** 1 hour or up to 1 day >
YIELD: 12 summer rolls

● ● ●

FOR THE PEANUT DIPPING SAUCE

6 tablespoons (75 g) sugar

1 Thai chile (or jalapeño), seeded and thinly sliced, or 1 tablespoon sriracha chile sauce

2 tablespoons finely chopped fresh ginger or ginger from a tube

¼ cup plus 2 tablespoons (80 ml) fresh lime juice (from 3 limes)

¼ cup (60 ml) nam pla (fish sauce)

2 tablespoons smooth peanut butter

FOR THE SOYBEAN DIPPING SAUCE

1 pound (455 g) shelled soybeans, frozen or fresh

1 bunch cilantro, washed and stemmed

2 tablespoon nam pla (fish sauce)

2 cloves garlic, chopped

1 Thai chile (or jalapeño), seeded and minced, or 1 tablespoon sriracha chile sauce

2 tablespoons lime juice

2 tablespoons peanut oil or toasted sesame oil

FOR THE ASSEMBLY

1 (12-ounce / 340-g) package Vietnamese rice paper (*bánh tráng*)

2 ripe Hass avocados, pitted and thinly sliced (see Note, page 128)

2 small Kirby or pickling cucumbers, thinly sliced into rounds (see Notes)

1 cup (110 g) freshly grated carrots (see Notes, page 113)

6 ounces (170 g) sushi-grade tuna, cut into ¼-inch (6-mm) dice

1 cup (40 g) fresh cilantro leaves, thinly sliced (see Notes), plus 12 additional cilantro sprigs for garnish

24 fresh mint leaves, thinly sliced (see Notes)

3 scallions, white and light green parts thinly sliced on the bias

Bibb lettuce leaves, for serving

ASIAN CUISINE can be a bit time consuming, but the intricate flavors of this dish make it more than worth the effort. This is honestly one of my favorite foods! I could live on rice paper filled with all things fresh, zesty, and surprising forever. This summer-roll-cum-mini-meal is a fantastic way to create an otherwise labor-intensive delight. Rolling the wrappers when making summer rolls can be a challenge, especially when they are overstuffed. Here, I've created a simple way to fill your rice paper and ensure a perfect result.

Make Ahead **The peanut and soybean dipping sauces can be made in advance and stored in airtight containers in the refrigerator until needed. They will last for up to 1 week.**

❯ MAKE THE PEANUT DIPPING SAUCE

In a small serving bowl, whisk together the sugar, chile, ginger, lime juice, fish sauce, and peanut butter. Set aside.

❯ MAKE THE SOYBEAN DIPPING SAUCE

In a blender, combine the soybeans, cilantro, fish sauce, garlic, chile, lime juice, and oil with ½ cup (120 ml) water. Blend until the sauce is smooth, using a rubber spatula to occasionally scrape down the sides. Transfer the sauce to a small serving bowl and set aside.

❯ ASSEMBLE THE SUMMER ROLLS

Line a 12-well classic cupcake pan with plastic wrap by overlapping 2 long pieces of plastic wrap along the center of the pan, leaving at least a 3-inch (7.5-cm) border of plastic wrap overhanging all sides of the pan.

In a large bowl filled with warm tap water, soak 1 rice paper wrapper for about 15 seconds or until soft. Gently swirl the wrapper in the water with your fingers, being careful not to puncture the paper. (Do not leave the wrapper in the water or it will become soggy.) Lay the wrapper on a paper towel to absorb any excess water, then fold it to fit a well of the pan. It will overhang the edges of the well. Repeat with the remaining wells.

Layer your ingredients in the rice paper–lined wells in this order: avocado, cucumber, carrots, tuna, cilantro, mint, scallions.

Fold the overhanging rice paper over the filling to seal. Wrap the pan in another layer of plastic wrap (make sure the plastic wrap is pulled tight and without holes, as the rice paper will harden if it is exposed to air). Refrigerate for 1 hour or up to 1 day.

Remove the top layer of plastic wrap, then lift up on the edges of the plastic wrap lining the wells of the pan to remove the summer rolls. Invert the rolls on beds of Bibb lettuce. Top each with a cilantro sprig, and serve the dipping sauces, side by side, in small ramekins.

VARIATION Try replacing the tuna with 6 ounces (170 g) of cooked baby shrimp or an equal amount of cooked chicken. I sometimes make a batch of the tuna version paired with pickled ginger, wasabi, and the soybean dipping sauce, and another batch with shrimp or chicken paired with the peanut dipping sauce.

If you want to avoid eating raw fish, substitute 1½ cups (265 g) soaked rice noodles (from one 6-ounce / 170-g package). To soak the noodles, cover them with boiling water in a small bowl and let them sit for 15 minutes. Drain and set aside.

Notes Kirby cucumbers are smaller and have fewer seeds than other types of cucumbers, which also means they have less moisture. That makes them perfect for working with rice paper as they won't make the papers mushy.

Layer the mint or cilantro leaves on top of one another, then thinly slice the stack.

^ CASSOULETS

chapter
>SIX<
POULTRY

NO FOOD APPEARS MORE FREQUENTLY ON DINNER TABLES around America than chicken, and for good reason. Chicken and other poultry can be adapted to numerous dishes, applications, and techniques.

It's no wonder, then, that chicken has also taken on a comforting aspect in many of the dishes in which it stars. Roasted chicken surrounded by heaps of potatoes, gravy, and other veggies is always a welcome sight. And don't forget about potpies, and the feeling of home they give you the moment you bite through their flaky crusts into velvety sauce and juicy meat.

Use this chapter to explore other varieties of poultry, from the rich, dark meat of duck to the full flavor of turkey. Some of the chicken recipes in this chapter would be excellent with turkey as a substitute, especially meals like the Vermont Chicken Potpies (page 159). Why, it's one of the first things you think of when someone mentions Thanksgiving dinner. A plump turkey likely sits at the center of your dining table as your family gathers around to celebrate the wonderful people in your lives. Let this chapter help you realize that turkey can be a creative and useful protein for many other extra-special dishes all year round!

Barbecue Chicken SANDWICHES
WITH CHILI-SPICED CORNBREAD & PIMENTO CHEESE

OVEN: 350°F (175°C) > **PREP TIME:** 1 hour >
BAKING TIME: 65 to 80 minutes > **YIELD:** 12 sandwiches

FOR THE BARBECUE CHICKEN

2 tablespoons light brown sugar

1 tablespoon freshly ground black pepper

2 teaspoons paprika

2 teaspoon cumin

1 tablespoon chili powder

1 tablespoon dry mustard

1 tablespoon kosher salt

½ teaspoon cayenne

6 bone-in chicken thighs (3 pounds / 1.5 kg), skin on

FOR THE CORNBREAD

Nonstick cooking spray, for the pan

1 cup (125 g) all-purpose flour

1 cup (160 g) yellow cornmeal

¼ cup (50 g) sugar

2 teaspoons baking powder

1 teaspoon baking soda

1 teaspoon kosher salt

2 tablespoons spice mix, reserved from the barbecue chicken

1½ cups (170 g) grated extra-sharp cheddar

1 cup (240 ml) buttermilk

2 large eggs

½ cup (1 stick / 115 g) unsalted butter, melted and cooled

FOR THE BARBECUE SAUCE

1 cup (240 ml) hot sauce

1 cup (240 ml) ketchup

2 tablespoons store-bought tamarind marinade (such as Neera's Asian Tamarind Sauce), or ¼ cup (60 ml) orange juice mixed with 2 tablespoons lime juice

1 teaspoon minced fresh garlic or garlic from a tube

3 tablespoons dry mustard

1 tablespoon Tabasco

1 tablespoon unsulphured molasses

1 tablespoon balsamic vinegar

½ cup (90 g) packed light brown sugar

¼ cup (60 ml) sweet pickle juice from the jar in your fridge

¼ cup (60 ml) steak sauce or Pickapeppa Sauce

FOR THE PIMENTO CHEESE

1 pound (455 grams) sharp cheddar

2 medium dill pickles, coarsely chopped

3 cloves garlic

1 (4-ounce / 115-g) jar pimentos with their juice

3 tablespoons mayonnaise

---

1 bunch scallions, green parts only, thinly sliced, for garnish

---

I HAVE BEEN carrying this barbecue sauce recipe around with me for years and I am happy to share it. But if you have your own cherished recipe, use that or your favorite bottled brand to save time. A rotisserie chicken would be another excellent way to cut corners; simply shred the meat from the bird before adding it to the barbecue sauce. As for the pimento cheese, this recipe has been at every potluck in my mother's family for a hundred years.

Make Ahead The barbecue sauce can be made in advance and stored in an airtight container in the refrigerator until needed. It will last for up to 2 weeks.

› MAKE THE BARBECUE CHICKEN

Preheat the oven to 350°F (175°C). Line a sheet pan with foil.

In a medium bowl, stir together the brown sugar, pepper, paprika, cumin, chili powder, dry mustard, salt, and cayenne until combined. Reserve 2 tablespoons of the spice mix for the cornbread. Rub the rest of the spice mix onto the chicken thighs to coat. Arrange the thighs in a single layer on the prepared sheet pan.

Bake the chicken until the juices run clear and a thermometer inserted into the thickest part of a thigh registers 165°F (74°C), 45 minutes to 1 hour. Do not turn off the oven.

Let the chicken rest until cool enough to handle. Remove and discard the skin and bones and shred the meat into bite-size pieces. Set aside.

› MAKE THE CORNBREAD

Spray a 12-well classic cupcake pan with nonstick cooking spray. In a large bowl, mix the flour, cornmeal, sugar, baking powder, baking soda, salt, and the reserved spice mix, then mix in the cheese. In another bowl, whisk together the buttermilk, eggs, and melted butter. Add the buttermilk mixture to the flour mixture and whisk by hand, just until incorporated; do not overmix.

Fill each well of the prepared pan to the top with the batter. Bake until golden and a toothpick inserted into the top of a cornbread comes out clean, 20 minutes. Let cool in the pan for 1 minute, then loosen the sides of each cornbread with a table knife and insert the tines of a fork between the pan and each cornbread to lift it out.

› MAKE THE BARBECUE SAUCE

Combine all the ingredients for the sauce in a small saucepan. Bring to a simmer over medium heat, and simmer for 20 minutes, stirring occasionally, until thickened. Set aside.

› MAKE THE PIMENTO CHEESE

In the bowl of a food processor fitted with a blade attachment, combine the cheese, pickles, garlic, pimentos, and mayonnaise. Pulse the cheese mixture, stopping occasionally to scrape the bowl, until mostly smooth. It should be creamy with small bits of cheese for texture.

› ASSEMBLE THE SANDWICHES

Cut each cornbread in half horizontally to create a "bun" for the sandwich. Spread the bottom piece of cornbread with a generous smear of pimento cheese. Next, add a layer of the barbecue chicken. Drizzle the chicken with barbecue sauce, then add the scallion greens, and cover with the top piece of cornbread. Repeat with the remaining cornbreads. Serve with a platter of salted fresh tomatoes and corn on the cob.

VARIATION Instead of using a full pound of cheddar in the pimento cheese recipe, substitute 8 ounces (225 g) pepper Jack mixed with 8 ounces (225 g) cheddar and swap in sweet pickle relish for the chopped dill pickles.

Carrot Loaves
WITH JERK CHICKEN

OVEN: 350°F (175°C) > **PREP TIME:** 30 minutes >
BAKING TIME: 1 hour to 1 hour 10 minutes > **YIELD:** 12 loaves

FOR THE JERK CHICKEN

6 scallions, green parts only, sliced

1 large shallot

2 small cloves garlic, or 1 tablespoon garlic from a tube

1 tablespoon finely chopped fresh ginger or ginger from a tube

½ Scotch bonnet chile, seeded (see Notes)

1 tablespoon ground allspice

1 teaspoon freshly ground black pepper

¼ teaspoon cayenne

1 teaspoon cinnamon

½ teaspoon freshly grated nutmeg

1 tablespoon fresh thyme leaves

2 tablespoons dark brown sugar or molasses

½ cup (120 ml) orange juice

½ cup (120 ml) rice wine vinegar, malt vinegar, or white vinegar

¼ cup (60 ml) red wine vinegar

3 tablespoons rum

¼ cup (60 ml) olive oil

¼ cup (60 ml) soy sauce

6 bone-in chicken thighs (3 pounds / 1.5 kg), skin on

FOR THE CARROT LOAVES

Nonstick cooking spray, for the pan

¼ cup (60 ml) unsulphured molasses

½ cup (120 ml) extra-virgin olive oil

½ cup (110 g) packed dark brown sugar

1 tablespoon honey

1 large egg

3 large egg whites

2½ cups (375 g) all-purpose flour

2 teaspoons baking powder

1 teaspoon baking soda

1 teaspoon kosher salt

2 teaspoons cinnamon

½ teaspoon freshly grated nutmeg

½ teaspoon ground cloves

2½ cups (275 g) grated carrots (from 2 large carrots; see Notes, page 113)

2 teaspoons fresh lime juice

2 teaspoons Madagascar vanilla (see Notes)

1 (8-ounce / 225-g) can crushed pineapple, or ½ cup (85 g) finely diced fresh pineapple with its juice

½ cup (60 g) salted roasted pumpkin seeds

THIS MOIST CARROT BREAD topped with crunchy pumpkin seeds makes a great bun for a sandwich filled with jerk chicken and sauce. Don't let the fancy bun stop you from trying it; just think of it as a fascinating new take on the old Sloppy Joe. If you're up for it, explore by creating your own combinations of flavorful bread and sandwich meats. It opens a whole new world of flavors for a potentially boring classic. Jerk seasoning varies from region to region; I have created my favorite spice mix here, but you can substitute 6.5 ounces (190 ml) of store-bought sauce if you prefer.

> MAKE THE JERK CHICKEN

Place all of the ingredients except the chicken in a blender and blend until smooth.

Preheat the oven to 350°F (175°C). Arrange the thighs in a single layer in a 9-by-13-inch (23-by-33-cm) Pyrex baking dish. Pour the sauce over the chicken, cover the pan with foil, and bake until a thermometer inserted in the thickest part of the thigh registers 165°F (74°C), 40 to 50 minutes. Let the chicken cool. Do not turn the oven off.

When the chicken is cool enough to handle, remove and discard the skin and bones and shred the chicken. Using a spoon, skim the fat off the surface of the jerk sauce remaining in the pan, and discard the fat. Adjust the seasoning of the remaining sauce, if necessary.

> MAKE THE CARROT LOAVES

Spray a 12-well classic cupcake pan with nonstick cooking spray.

In the bowl of a stand mixer fitted with the paddle attachment, mix the molasses, oil, brown sugar, honey, egg, and egg whites until smooth, 1 to 2 minutes. With the mixer on low speed, mix in the flour, baking powder, baking soda, salt, cinnamon, nutmeg, and cloves, just until combined. Mix in the carrots, lime juice, vanilla, and pineapple and its juice, just until combined.

RECIPE CONTINUES

Distribute the batter evenly among the wells of the prepared pan. Top with a sprinkling of pumpkin seeds, and bake until the cakes are golden brown, about 20 minutes. Let cool in the pan for 1 minute, then loosen the sides of each loaf with a table knife and pop them out of the pan.

To assemble, cut each carrot loaf in half horizontally like a bun, then spoon 1 tablespoon of the reserved sauce onto the bottom layer. Top with chicken, then turn the top of the loaf upside down and spoon a tablespoon of sauce on it. Place the top on the sandwich.

Notes If you don't have a Scotch bonnet chile, you can get equivalent heat from another pepper, such as a habanero. Whenever you're working with extremely hot chiles, it's best to wear rubber gloves and be very careful not to touch your eyes. And removing the ribs and seeds from a pepper will decrease its heat, if that's what you prefer.

Madagascar vanilla is a very special type of vanilla with a flavor unmatched by any other variety. Its taste is pure, spicy, and delicate—no substitutions will do!

Chicken Timbales
WITH SWEET RED PEPPER SAUCE

OVEN: 350°F (175°C) > PREP TIME: 1 hour 20 minutes >
BAKING TIME: 20 to 25 minutes > YIELD: 12 timbales

FOR THE CHICKEN TIMBALES

4 boneless skinless chicken
breasts (2 pounds / 910 g)

3 tablespoons extra-virgin
olive oil

1 cup (150 g) finely chopped
red pepper

½ cup (50 g) finely chopped
celery

1 small Vidalia or other sweet
onion, finely chopped

3 small finely chopped
shallots

2 cups (220 g) fresh or
store-bought bread
crumbs (see Note, page
103)

2 large eggs

¼ cup (60 ml) half-and-half

3 tablespoons chopped fresh
parsley

1 teaspoon chopped fresh
savory or thyme

1 tablespoon chopped fresh
tarragon

½ teaspoon kosher salt

¼ teaspoon freshly ground
black pepper

2 tablespoons Dijon mustard

Nonstick cooking spray, for
the pan

FOR THE SWEET RED PEPPER SAUCE

¼ cup (½ stick / 60 g)
unsalted butter

3 medium shallots, minced

3 red bell peppers, seeded,
deveined, and finely
chopped

2 (14.5-ounce / 430-g) cans
whole plum tomatoes in
their juice, chopped, or
6 fresh plum tomatoes,
peeled, seeded, and
chopped (see Note)

1 cup (240 ml) dry white wine

½ cup (20 g) minced fresh
tarragon, parsley, savory,
or thyme

Kosher salt and freshly
ground black pepper

Note To peel fresh tomatoes, cut an X on the bottom
of each tomato, submerge them in boiling water for 1
to 2 minutes, then plunge them into an ice water bath.
The skins will come right off.

THE LIGHT CUSTARD in these timbales perfectly
complements the chicken and vegetables. While a timbale
is traditionally baked in a pan shaped like a drum, the wells
of the cupcake pan are surprisingly good copies of the
original. Be mindful not to overbake these, as the moisture
will bake out and the chicken's natural juices will be lost.

I like to serve these surrounded by sautéed vegetables
and rice. They could also be served as a side dish at a
brunch without the sauce, or as a centerpiece with a luncheon salad and an herb vinaigrette.

> MAKE THE CHICKEN TIMBALES

Preheat the oven to 350°F (175°C). In the bowl of a
food processor, pulse the chicken breasts into half-inch
(12-mm) shreds. Do not pulverize.

In a 10-inch (25-cm) sauté pan, heat the oil over
medium heat. Add the bell pepper, celery, onion, and shallot and cook, stirring occasionally, until the vegetables are
tender, about 5 minutes. Transfer to a large mixing bowl
to cool slightly, about 10 minutes. Add the chicken, bread
crumbs, eggs, half-and-half, parsley, savory, tarragon, salt,
pepper, and mustard to the bowl; mix until well combined.

Spray a 12-well classic cupcake pan with nonstick
cooking spray. Fill each well to the top with the chicken
mixture. Bake until the tops are lightly golden and firm to
the touch, 20 to 25 minutes.

> MAKE THE SWEET RED PEPPER SAUCE

Melt the butter in a large skillet with high sides over
medium heat. Add the shallots and sauté until golden,
about 3 minutes, then add the peppers and sauté until
tender, about 5 minutes. Add the chopped plum tomatoes and their juices and cook, stirring occasionally, for
8 minutes longer. Stir in the wine and cook until the sauce
has reduced and thickened, about 15 minutes, then stir in
the tarragon and season with salt and pepper. Turn off the
heat and set aside.

Let the timbales cool in the pan for 1 minute, then
loosen the sides of each timbale with a table knife and
insert the tines of a fork between the pan and each timbale
to lift it out. Serve the timbales in a pool of the red pepper
sauce, or with the sauce on the side.

VERMONT *Chicken* POTPIES

OVEN: 350°F (175°C) > **PREP TIME:** 5 hours > **BAKING TIME:** 45 minutes to 1 hour > **CHILLING TIME:** 2 hours or overnight > **YIELD:** 24 potpies

1 stewing chicken (8 pounds / 3.5 kg)

3 medium onions, peeled and quartered

2 ribs celery, including the leaves and bottoms of the stalks, halved

4 sprigs fresh parsley

3 sprigs fresh sage, including stems

3 teaspoons kosher salt

1½ teaspoons white pepper

1 cup (240 ml) whole milk

½ cup (60 g) all-purpose flour

5 cups (1.2 L) chicken broth (from cooking the chicken)

½ cup (75 g) frozen peas

4 carrots, peeled and boiled, then cut into ¼-inch (6-mm) dice

Nonstick cooking spray, for the pan

3 (15-ounce / 430-g) packages ready-made pie dough (2 rounds per package), at room temperature

---

A GOOD CHICKEN POTPIE is a celebration of love itself. These little pies are worth the time you put into making them, so invite your best friends and family to enjoy this delicious take on a comforting classic. They also travel nicely in a picnic basket—even if you're only carrying them to the backyard.

Rinse the entire chicken and clean out the cavity. Place the chicken in a large pot fitted with a lid and cover with 12 cups (3 L) water. Add the onions, celery, parsley, sage, 1 teaspoon of the salt, and ½ teaspoon of the white pepper. Bring to a boil, then reduce the heat to low. Cover and simmer until a leg easily pulls away from the breast, about 2 hours, depending on the size of the bird. Remove the chicken from the pot and set it aside on a rimmed baking sheet.

Cover the pot containing the chicken broth and bring it to a simmer over medium heat. Continue simmering the broth until it is rich in color, about 2 hours more. You should have about 5 cups (1.2 L) broth; if you don't, you can add water or canned chicken broth.

Place a fine-mesh strainer or cheesecloth-lined colander over a medium-size plastic container. Pour the broth into the strainer. Using a spatula, push the solids against the strainer to squeeze out the juices; discard the remaining solids. Refrigerate the broth for 2 hours or overnight. Skim off the fat before using.

Using your fingers, remove both the white and the dark meat from the chicken, discarding the skin, fat, and bones. Transfer the meat to a cutting board and chop it into ½-inch (1-cm) pieces; place it in a bowl and set aside. Pour the remaining liquid into the broth in the fridge.

In a 16-quart (15-L) stockpot over a cold burner, whisk the milk and flour until smooth. Whisk in the broth and cook over medium heat until the sauce has thickened, about 15 minutes; season with the remaining 2 teaspoons salt and 1 teaspoon white pepper. Stir in the chopped chicken, peas, and carrots.

RECIPE CONTINUES

Preheat the oven to 350°F (175°C). Spray a 12-well classic cupcake pan with nonstick cooking spray.

Unroll the pie dough onto a flat work surface; no need to flour it. Cut each round of dough into quarters, for a total of 24 pieces. Place 1 piece of dough in each well of the prepared pan, creating a cup that overhangs the edges of the wells. Distribute the chicken filling evenly among the wells. Fold the overhanging dough into the center of each well and pinch the edges together to seal in the filling, leaving a small hole in the top of each potpie for steam to escape.

Bake until the crust is golden brown, 45 minutes to 1 hour. Let the potpies rest in the pan for 15 minutes, then loosen the sides of each potpie with a table knife and insert the tines of a fork between the pan and each potpie to lift it out. Serve the potpies hot, or allow them to cool and pack them for a backyard picnic.

Store the pies in an airtight container in the refrigerator for up to 1 week. Enjoy at room temperature or reheat, wrapped in tin foil, for 15 minutes at 350°F (175°C).

BUTTERED SAGE BREAD CRUMBS

¼ cup (½ stick / 60 g) salted butter, softened

3 tablespoons thinly sliced fresh sage leaves

2 tablespoons chopped Italian parsley

1 large clove garlic, finely chopped, or 1 tablespoon garlic from a tube

1 baguette, split in half lengthwise

Preheat the oven to 350°F (175°C). In a small bowl, mix together the butter, sage, parsley, and garlic, then spread the herb butter over both halves of the baguette. Place the baguette on a baking sheet and bake until crisp, about 25 minutes. Allow it to cool, then break the baguette into bite-size pieces. Put the bread in the bowl of a food processor fitted with a blade and pulse until the bread forms large crumbs. Do not overprocess. You should have 3 cups (330 g) of bread crumbs.

After you line each well with pie dough, trim overhanging pie dough ¼ to ½ inch (6 mm to 1 cm) above each well. Fill the wrappers and top each pie with 2 tablespoons of the crumb topping. Bake until the edges are golden brown, 35 to 45 minutes. Unpan and serve as before.

Chicken ENCHILADAS > WITH < ANDOUILLE SAUSAGE

OVEN: 350°F (175°C) > PREP TIME: 10 minutes >
BAKING TIME: 70 minutes to 1 hour 30 minutes > YIELD: 24 enchiladas

FOR THE FILLING

8 boneless skinless chicken thighs (2¼ pounds / 1 kg)

1 (1.25-ounce / 35-g) packet taco seasoning

12 ounces (340 g) andouille sausage, coarsely chopped

1 (15-ounce / 430-g) can black beans (do not drain)

2 (12-ounce / 340-g) cans enchilada sauce

2 cups (225 g) shredded cheddar

FOR THE ASSEMBLY

Nonstick cooking spray, for the pan

24 rounds frozen empanada dough, thawed, or 24 (6-inch / 15-cm) flour tortillas, any flavor

OPTIONAL TOPPINGS

Fresh salsa

Guacamole

Sour cream

Chopped fresh cilantro

REMINISCENT OF corn spoon bread and tamale pie, these enchiladas offer the perfect variation on a family classic. The hearty addition of andouille sausage imparts a smokiness to the whole dish, while the empanada dough becomes slightly crisp and flaky as it bakes. These are also excellent served with an over-easy egg placed on top.

> MAKE THE FILLING

Preheat the oven to 350°F (175°C).

In a large baking dish, arrange the chicken thighs in a single layer. Sprinkle the chicken with the taco seasoning and bake, turning once, until a thermometer inserted in the thickest part of the thigh registers 165°F (74°C), 45 minutes to 1 hour. Let cool. When the chicken is cool enough to handle, remove and discard the bones and transfer the meat to a food processor fitted with the blade attachment, making sure to include the juices from the pan. Pulse until the chicken is chopped into small pieces, but not pulverized.

In a medium bowl, mix the chopped chicken, sausage, beans and their juices, enchilada sauce, and half of the cheese.

> ASSEMBLE AND BAKE THE ENCHILADAS

Spray two 12-well classic cupcake pans with nonstick cooking spray, then line each well with either empanada dough or a flour tortilla. (If using a tortilla, gently gather the edges of the tortilla and set it into the pan, rather than pressing it down into the pan, to avoid tearing.) Do not trim the overhanging dough.

Fill each enchilada with a heaping ⅓ cup (45 g) of the filling, then sprinkle with the remaining cheese. Top with the enchilada sauce, distributing it evenly among the wells. Bake until the crust is golden brown on the edges, 25 to 30 minutes.

To unpan, loosen the sides of each enchilada with a table knife and insert the tines of a fork between the pan and each enchilada to lift it out. Serve the enchiladas with your choice of toppings.

Store the enchiladas in an airtight container in the refrigerator for up to 1 week. Reheat, wrapped in tin foil, for 15 minutes at 350°F (175°C).

CHICKEN APPLE
Hand Pies

OVEN: 350°F (175°C) ▸ PREP TIME: 55 minutes ▸
BAKING TIME: 35 to 45 minutes ▸ YIELD: 12 hand pies

FOR THE ROSEMARY CHICKEN

2 large or 3 small boneless skinless chicken breasts (1¾ pounds / 800 g)

2 bay leaves

Sprig of fresh rosemary

FOR THE SAVORY APPLE PIE FILLING

2 Granny Smith apples, peeled, cored, and cut into ¼-inch (6-mm) dice

½ cup (80 g) finely chopped red onion

3 medium cloves garlic, thinly sliced, or 2 tablespoons garlic from a tube

3 tablespoons unsalted butter

2 tablespoons finely chopped fresh rosemary

2 tablespoons light brown sugar

½ teaspoon kosher salt

¼ teaspoon freshly ground black pepper

8 ounces (225 g) grated white cheddar

FOR THE WHITE CHEDDAR BÉCHAMEL

2 tablespoons unsalted butter

¼ cup (30 g) all-purpose flour

1 cup (240 ml) whole milk

¼ teaspoon kosher salt

4 ounces (115 g) grated white cheddar

FOR THE ASSEMBLY

Nonstick cooking spray, for the pan

2 tablespoons granulated sugar

¼ teaspoon cinnamon

1 (15-ounce / 430-g) package ready-made pie dough (2 rounds), at room temperature

12 sprigs fresh thyme (optional)

REMEMBER WHEN your mom let you have the leftover pie dough and you sprinkled it with cinnamon and sugar then baked it? Well, I've taken that idea and used it to create a hand pie that will certainly serve as a surprise. Sweet apples, red onion, and rosemary with chicken are all wrapped up in cinnamon pie dough. The addition of white cheddar béchamel takes the flavor that we all love to a whole new level of taste. Yes, it has to be white cheddar! Orange cheddar just looks, feels, and tastes wrong in this dish. To save time, you could pick up a rotisserie chicken and shred the meat (you'll need 1¾ lbs / 800 g of meat).

▸ MAKE THE ROSEMARY CHICKEN

Place the chicken breasts in a large Dutch oven or stockpot and add water to cover (about 10 cups / 2.2 L). Add the bay leaves and rosemary and bring to a boil over high heat, then turn off the heat and cover. Let the chicken rest in the water for 10 to 15 minutes; it will continue to cook. Remove the chicken; it should be firm to the touch. To be certain it is cooked through, slice one piece in half; its center should not be pink. When it is cool enough to handle, after about 20 minutes, shred the meat. Reserve the broth for another recipe.

▸ MAKE THE SAVORY APPLE PIE FILLING

In a 10-inch (25-cm) sauté pan over medium heat, combine the apples, onion, garlic, and butter. Sauté until soft, 8 to 10 minutes; stir in the rosemary, brown sugar, salt, and pepper. Turn off the heat and allow to cool.

Mix 1 cup (240 ml) of the cheese and all of the shredded chicken into the cooled pie-filling mixture.

▸ MAKE THE WHITE CHEDDAR BÉCHAMEL

Melt the butter in a heavy saucepan over medium heat. Add the flour and cook, whisking constantly, until the flour is well blended and forms a paste. Add the milk and cook, whisking constantly, until thickened and just boiling, about 4 minutes. Sprinkle the sauce with the salt. Remove from the heat and mix in the cheese, whisking until smooth. Set aside.

RECIPE CONTINUES

➤ ASSEMBLE AND BAKE THE HAND PIES

Preheat the oven to 350°F (175°C). Spray a 12-well classic cupcake pan with nonstick cooking spray. In a small bowl, mix the sugar and cinnamon.

Unroll the pie dough onto a flat work surface; no need to flour it first. Sprinkle each round of pie dough with the cinnamon-sugar mixture on one side only, pressing the mixture gently into the dough. Cut each round of dough in half, and then cut each half into thirds for a total of 12 pieces. Place one piece of dough in each well of the prepared pan, cinnamon sugar side down. Don't worry if the dough doesn't line the wells evenly; there's no need to trim any overhanging dough.

Distribute the chicken mixture evenly among the wells. Distribute the béchamel evenly among the wells and sprinkle with the remaining 1 cup (115 g) cheese. Fold the overhanging pie dough toward the center of each well to form the hand pies. Bake until golden brown and bubbling, 35 to 45 minutes.

Let cool in the pan for 10 minutes, then loosen the sides of each hand pie with a table knife and insert the tines of a fork between the pan and each pie to lift it out. Serve the pies hot, garnished with a fresh sprig of thyme, or, if you can wait for it to cool to the touch, eat it out of hand.

Store the hand pies in an airtight container in the refrigerator for up to 1 week. Reheat, wrapped in tin foil, for 15 minutes at 350°F (175°C).

NACHO
Stacks

OVEN: 350°F (175°C) > PREP TIME: 15 minutes >
BAKING TIME: 25 to 30 minutes > YIELD: 12 stacks

Nonstick cooking spray, for
the pan

12 (6-inch / 15-cm) tortillas,
plain or flavored

2 tablespoons extra-virgin
olive oil

1 pound (455 g) ground meat,
such as turkey, chicken,
pork, or beef

1 (1.25-ounce / 35-g) packet
taco seasoning

1 (15-ounce / 430-g) can
black beans or kidney
beans, rinsed and drained,
or refried beans

1 (16-ounce / 455-g) jar salsa

8 ounces (225 g) grated
cheese, such as queso
fresco, sharp cheddar, or
jalapeño cheddar

OPTIONAL TOPPINGS

Black olives, sliced

Scallions, sliced

Jalapeños or other green
chiles, chopped

Additional grated cheese

Sour cream or crema

Guacamole

Fresh cilantro leaves

THIS IS A NACHO that satisfies with every bite. My children devour these stacks, which I like to serve with tortilla chips for dipping. The ingredients are blended together and melted to offer maximum flavor in every bite. This is also a great dish if you are trying to make use of odds and ends in your refrigerator.

Preheat the oven to 350°F (175°C). Spray a 12-well classic cupcake pan with nonstick cooking spray, then press a tortilla into each well.

In a large nonstick skillet, heat the oil over medium heat. Add the ground meat and taco seasoning. Cook, breaking up the meat with a wooden spoon, until crumbled and browned, about 6 minutes. Let cool slightly, then distribute the ground meat evenly among the 12 wells. Top each well with some beans.

In a medium bowl, combine the salsa and cheese and mix well. Spoon the cheese mixture on top of the beans to fill the wells.

Bake until golden brown on the edges and crisp, 25 to 30 minutes. Use your hands to lift the stacks out of the pan, using the tortilla wrappers as handles. Serve with your choice of toppings and a pile of tortilla chips on the side.

Chicken
TAMALE PIES

OVEN: 350°F (175°C) > **PREP TIME:** 45 minutes >
BAKING TIME: 45 minutes to 1 hour > **YIELD:** 12 pies

FOR THE TOMATO SAUCE

8 plum tomatoes, chopped small

1 (14.75-ounce / 430-g) can creamed corn

1 medium red onion, finely chopped

1 tablespoon powdered chile

1 tablespoon kosher salt

FOR THE CHICKEN

1 tablespoon extra-virgin olive oil

1½ pounds (680 g) boneless skinless chicken breasts, cut in half lengthwise

Juice of 1 lemon

½ teaspoon kosher salt

¼ teaspoon freshly ground black pepper

FOR THE TAMALES

1 cup (240 ml) whole milk

1 cup (155 g) cornmeal

3 large eggs

1 cup (180 g) black olives, cut into ¼-inch-thick (6-mm) slices

FOR THE ASSEMBLY

Nonstick cooking spray, for the pan

12 small red, yellow, or orange bell peppers (make sure they are skinny enough to fit in the wells of the pan)

3 ounces (85 g) shredded Monterey Jack or pepper Jack

3 ounces (85 g) sharp cheddar

I LOVE THE creamy texture of these chicken tamale pies. Bake them in various bell peppers—red, yellow, and orange—for a splash of color, then serve them on a bed of sautéed corn and sprinkle the tops with cilantro and scallions. Selecting the right powdered chile for your pies can be fun as there are so many to try: smoked, hot, ancho, and then some. Shave some time off the preparation by using the meat from a rotisserie chicken (you'll need 1½ to 2 cups / 210 to 280 g shredded meat), or make these pies vegetarian by omitting the meat altogether.

Make Ahead The tomato sauce can be made up to 2 days in advance and stored in an airtight container in the refrigerator until needed. It will last for up to 1 week.

> MAKE THE TOMATO SAUCE

In a 10-quart (10-L) pot, combine the tomatoes, creamed corn, onion, powdered chile, and salt. Cook over medium heat, stirring occasionally, until thickened, about 10 minutes. Set aside.

> MAKE THE CHICKEN

In a large skillet, heat the oil over medium heat, then add the chicken breasts. Cook, flipping once, until no longer pink in the center, 8 to 10 minutes. Sprinkle with the lemon juice, salt, and pepper. Cut into ¼-inch (6-mm) dice. Set aside.

> MAKE THE TAMALES

In a medium bowl, combine the milk, cornmeal, and eggs; whisk until smooth. Add this mixture to the tomato sauce and cook over medium heat, stirring constantly, until thickened, 10 to 15 minutes. Remove from the heat and stir in the chicken and olives.

> ASSEMBLE AND BAKE THE PIES

Preheat the oven to 350°F (175°C). Spray a 12-well classic cupcake pan with nonstick cooking spray.

Cut the top off of each pepper to make a cup and remove the seeds. Place 1 pepper in each well. Distribute the chicken mixture evenly among the wells. Bake until the peppers soften and the edges begin to brown, 45 minutes to 1 hour. About 10 minutes before the end of the cooking time, sprinkle each pepper with the two kinds of shredded cheese.

Let the pies rest in the pan for 3 minutes, then insert the tines of a fork between the pan and each pepper to lift it out. Serve with a warm succotash of lima beans, kidney beans, or butterbeans, corn, tomatoes, and sweet peppers sautéed in butter.

Store the pies in an airtight container in the refrigerator for up to 1 week. Reheat, wrapped in tin foil, for 15 minutes at 350°F (175°C).

Chilled
CHICKEN SALADS
> WITH GRAPES <

PREP TIME: 1 hour 5 minutes > **CHILLING TIME:** 2 hours or overnight > **YIELD:** 12 salads

FOR THE SOUTHERN CHICKEN SALAD

4 boneless skinless chicken breasts (2 pounds / 910 g)

1 small onion, chopped

1 carrot, peeled and cut into thirds

½ cup (20 g) celery leaves or 1 rib celery

½ cup (50 g) thinly sliced scallions, green parts only

2 sprigs fresh parsley

2 bay leaves

2 tablespoons kosher salt

10 whole black peppercorns

4 hard-boiled eggs, finely chopped

½ cup (50 g) finely chopped celery

1 apple, peeled, cored, and cut into ¼-inch (6-mm) dice

1 cup (250 g) red or green seedless grapes, quartered

2 tablespoons finely chopped fresh tarragon, or to taste

½ cup (50 g) walnuts, finely chopped

2 tablespoons fresh lemon juice

FOR THE BOILED DRESSING

3 tablespoons sugar

1 tablespoon all-purpose flour

2 teaspoons dry mustard

1 teaspoon kosher salt

½ cup (120 ml) tarragon white vinegar, white vinegar, or white balsamic vinegar

1 tablespoon unsalted butter

2 large eggs, lightly beaten

FOR THE LEMON ASPIC

Juice and zest of 2 lemons

2 (¼-ounce / 7-g) packets unflavored gelatin

FOR THE ASSEMBLY

6 ripe Hass avocados, halved, pitted, and cut into 16 slices each (see Note, page 128)

WRAP CHICKEN SALAD up in a whole new way with these beauties. Avocado slices serve as the unusual wrappers here. While you're welcome to use your own recipe for chicken salad, this one is a bit special, as it was given to me by Toby, a real Southern belle. Any chicken salad left over would make great sandwiches for lunch the next day.

> MAKE THE SOUTHERN CHICKEN SALAD

In a heavy 4- to 5-quart (4- to 5-L) pot, combine the chicken, onion, carrot, celery leaves, scallions, parsley, bay leaves, salt, and peppercorns with enough water to cover. Bring to a boil, then turn off the heat and cover the pot. Let the chicken rest for 10 to 15 minutes in the water; it will continue to cook. Remove the chicken from the pot; it should be firm to the touch. To be certain it is cooked through, slice one piece in half; its center should not be pink. When it is cool enough to handle, after about 20 minutes, shred the meat. Reserve the broth for another recipe.

Place the shredded chicken in a large bowl and stir in the eggs, celery, apple, grapes, tarragon, walnuts, and lemon juice. Set aside.

> MAKE THE BOILED DRESSING

In a small saucepan, combine the sugar, flour, mustard, and salt. Whisk in the vinegar, ½ cup (120 ml) water, and the butter and cook over medium heat, whisking occasionally, until the mixture comes to a boil and thickens slightly, about 6 minutes. Whisk 2 tablespoons of this hot mixture into the beaten eggs, then pour the egg mixture into the saucepan and whisk until smooth. Turn off the heat and let the dressing cool, about 20 minutes. Toss the dressing with the chicken salad. Refrigerate until needed.

> MAKE THE LEMON ASPIC

In a small saucepan over medium heat, bring ¾ cup (180 ml) water and the lemon juice just to a simmer. Stir in the gelatin and lemon zest, turn off the heat, and let sit for 5 minutes. Stir again, then transfer the aspic to a medium bowl.

› ASSEMBLE THE SALADS

Line a 12-well classic cupcake pan with plastic wrap by overlapping 2 long pieces of plastic wrap along the center of the pan, leaving at least a 3-inch (7.5-cm) border of plastic wrap overhanging all sides of the pan.

Line each well with 4 avocado slices, creating a wrapper on the bottom and sides of the well. Fill each well to the top with the chicken salad mixture, then press down to make room for more avocado slices. Cover the top of the chicken salad in each well with 4 more avocado slices, then spoon 2 tablespoons of aspic into each well, pressing down to make sure the aspic seeps through. Wrap the pan tightly in another layer of plastic wrap and refrigerate for 2 hours or overnight.

Remove the top layer of plastic wrap, then lift up on the edges of the plastic wrap lining the wells of the pan to remove the salads.

CURRIED
Chicken Salads
> WITH MANGO <

PREP TIME: 50 minutes > CHILLING TIME: 2 hours or overnight > YIELD: 12 salads

FOR THE CHICKEN SALAD

4 boneless skinless chicken breasts (2 pounds / 910 g)

1 carrot, peeled and cut into thirds

1 rib celery

1 small onion, chopped

1 bay leaf

Sprig of fresh thyme

2 tablespoons kosher salt

1 green apple, peeled, cored, and finely sliced (leave the peel on if you prefer)

1 bunch chives, finely snipped

½ cup (75 g) raisins

1 cup (250 g) green or red seedless grapes, quartered

¼ cup (10 g) chopped fresh flat-leaf parsley leaves

FOR THE CURRY SAUCE

1 tablespoon extra-virgin olive oil

1 small onion, cut into ¼-inch (6-mm) dice

1 tablespoon finely chopped fresh ginger or ginger from a tube

1 large clove garlic, minced, or 1 tablespoon garlic from a tube

¼ cup (25 g) curry powder

1 (13.5-ounce / 385-g) can coconut milk

2 tablespoons honey

2 tablespoons peanut butter

Kosher salt and freshly ground black pepper

FOR THE ORANGE ASPIC

2 cups (480 ml) orange juice

2 (¼-ounce / 30-g) packets unflavored gelatin

---

4 large ripe mangos, peeled

Bibb lettuce (optional)

Toasted coconut (optional)

Mango chutney (optional)

Cilantro leaves (optional)

Pistachios, chopped (optional)

I'VE TAKEN TWO of my grandma Hazel's favorite things—aspic and curried chicken salad—and brought them into a savory tidbit to die for. This meal works great with whatever curried chicken recipe you use, your family's favorite or mine. The key is the aspic-dipped mango slices, which keep this whole meal together. I think Grandma Hazel would approve. If you prefer, you can easily use meat from a rotisserie chicken, using both dark and light meat, or even canned chicken meat (you'll need 3 cups / 420 g of meat total). Any leftover chicken salad would make a perfect addition to a bowl of greens or a sandwich.

> MAKE THE CHICKEN SALAD

In a heavy 4- to 5-quart (4- to 5-L) pot, combine the chicken breasts, carrot, celery, onion, bay leaf, thyme, and salt with enough water to cover. Bring to a boil over high heat, then turn off the heat and cover the pot. Let the chicken rest in the water for 10 to 15 minutes; it will continue to cook. Remove the chicken from the pot; it should be firm to the touch. To be certain it is cooked through, slice one piece in half; its center should not be pink. When it is cool enough to handle, after about 20 minutes, shred the meat. Reserve the broth for another recipe

In a large bowl, stir together the chicken, green apple, chives, raisins, grapes, and parsley. Set aside.

> MAKE THE CURRY SAUCE

Heat the oil in a small pan over medium heat; add the onion, ginger, and garlic and cook, stirring occasionally, until soft, about 4 minutes. Stir in the curry powder, coconut milk, honey, and peanut butter and simmer, about 3 minutes. Season with salt and pepper and add more curry powder if you like a stronger curry sauce. Turn off the heat and let the sauce cool, about 20 minutes. Stir the sauce into the chicken salad. Refrigerate until needed.

> MAKE THE ORANGE ASPIC

Bring the orange juice to a simmer in a small saucepan over medium heat. Whisk in the gelatin, making sure there are no lumps, and let it sit 5 for minutes. Transfer to a medium bowl and set aside at room temperature.

› ASSEMBLE THE SALADS

Cut each mango in half (see Note) and cut each half into very thin slices, about 12 slices per half. Add the mango slices to the bowl of orange aspic.

Line a 12-well classic cupcake pan with plastic wrap by overlapping 2 long pieces of plastic wrap along the center of the pan, leaving at least a 3-inch (7.5-cm) border of plastic wrap overhanging all sides of the pan.

Line each well with 4 to 6 mango slices, enough to cover the bottom and sides. Fill each well to the top with the chicken salad mixture. Cover the top of the chicken salad in each well with the remaining mango slices, then spoon 2 tablespoons of aspic into each well, pressing down to make sure the aspic seeps through. Wrap the pan tightly in another layer of plastic wrap and refrigerate for 2 hours or overnight.

Remove the top layer of plastic wrap, then lift up on the edges of the plastic wrap lining the wells of the pan to remove the mini meals.

Invert each salad on a leaf of Bibb lettuce. Serve sprinkled with toasted coconut, with mango chutney (plain or mixed with Greek yogurt), a few cilantro leaves, and chopped pistachios on the side.

Note **A mango pit runs vertically through the center of the fruit. To halve the mango, cut a small piece from each end, and then stand the fruit upright on your cutting board. Use the tip of your knife to find the pit, then cut downward along the edge of the pit to remove the mango half. Repeat on the other side of the pit to remove the remaining half.**

CASSOULETS

OVEN: 350°F (175°C) > PREP TIME: 1 hour > BAKING TIME: 25 minutes >
YIELD: 12 cassoulets

FOR THE CASSOULET FILLING

1 (8-ounce / 225-g) package
duck breast, preseasoned
and fully cooked (see Note)

Kosher salt

1 pound (455 g) lamb shanks,
preseasoned and fully
cooked, with their juice
(see Note)

3 tablespoons olive oil

3 large cloves garlic, chopped,
or 3 tablespoons garlic
from a tube

1 small onion, cut into ¼-inch
(6-mm) dice

2 carrots, peeled and cut into
¼-inch (6-mm) dice

1 tablespoon chopped fresh
oregano or oregano from a
tube

2 tablespoons fresh thyme
leaves

3 bay leaves

Pinch ground cloves

Freshly ground black pepper

1 cup (240 ml) dry white wine

3 tablespoons tomato paste

1 cup (240 ml) chicken broth

1 (15.5-ounce / 430-g) can
cannellini beans or navy
beans, rinsed and drained

FOR THE BREAD CRUMBS

2 tablespoons unsalted
butter

1 cup (110 g) panko bread
crumbs

1 large clove garlic, chopped,
or 1 tablespoon garlic from
a tube

FOR THE ASSEMBLY

Nonstick cooking spray, for
the pan

¼ cup (½ stick / 60 g)
unsalted butter

12 thin slices white bread,
such as Pepperidge Farm's
Very Thin White Bread

2 tablespoons fresh thyme
leaves

Note **Preseasoned and fully cooked lamb shanks and
duck breasts are available in the freezer sections of
most supermarkets. To use them, all you have to do is
thaw or warm them according to the package directions.**

IN MY OPINION, cassoulet is the best of French cuisine.
I grew up living on it and then eating leftovers for a full
week. My father labored over this dish for three hours, and
I always went with him to select the meat from the butcher.
This dish has been modified over its existence. Lamb,
duck, pork, sausage, turkey thighs, or chicken—the choice
is yours. This time-saving version makes a laborious dish
into something manageable by using preseasoned and
precooked duck breast and lamb shanks. All you need to do
is pull together the aromatics and the vegetables, and you
have an amazing mini meal in one hour.

> MAKE THE CASSOULET FILLING

Heat a medium ovenproof skillet over medium heat until
hot. Place the duck breast, skin side down, in the skillet
and sear it until the fat begins to render and the skin is just
golden brown, 2 to 3 minutes.

Transfer the duck breast to a cutting board, setting
the skillet on the stovetop—you will reuse it in a minute.
Use a knife to remove the fat layer from the duck. Return
the fat to the skillet and cook over medium heat until both
sides are browned and crisp, 2 to 3 minutes. Set aside.

Discard any fat from the lamb and shred the meat
from both the lamb and the duck into a bowl.

In a small saucepan over medium heat, reduce the
juice from the lamb package by half, about 6 minutes.
Remove from the heat and set aside.

In a 12-inch (30-cm) sauté pan, combine the oil, garlic, onion, carrots, oregano, thyme, bay leaves, and cloves.
Season with black pepper. Sauté over medium heat until
the vegetables are softened, about 5 minutes. Add the
wine, tomato paste, and broth. Bring to a simmer and cook
until reduced by half, about 15 minutes. Remove the bay
leaves. Add the beans and meat and cook, stirring occasionally, until the sauce has thickened, about 5 minutes.
Turn off the heat and set aside.

❯ MAKE THE BREAD CRUMBS

Melt the butter in a small saucepan over low heat, then add the garlic and bread crumbs, tossing to combine.

❯ ASSEMBLE AND BAKE THE CASSOULETS

Preheat the oven to 350°F (175°C). Spray a 12-well classic cupcake pan with nonstick cooking spray.

Butter the bread on one side only. Sprinkle the buttered side with the fresh thyme leaves and press down gently so they stick to the butter. Place 1 slice, buttered side down, in each of the wells of the prepared pan, firmly pressing the bread into the wells. The edges of the bread may peek over the top of the pan. Distribute the cassoulet filling evenly among the wells and sprinkle the bread crumbs on top. Bake on the lower oven rack until the tops are golden brown and the bread wrapper is toasted, about 25 minutes. Let rest in the pan for 1 minute, then loosen the sides of each cassoulet with a table knife and insert the tines of a fork between the pan and each cassoulet to lift it out. Drizzle each cassoulet with the reserved juices. Serve immediately.

CHICKEN & VEGETABLE
Rice Vermicelli Cups
IN SZECHUAN SPICES

OVEN: 350°F (175°C) > **PREP TIME:** 45 minutes >
BAKING TIME: 15 minutes > **YIELD:** 24 mini meals

FOR THE CHICKEN & VEGETABLE FILLING

3 boneless skinless chicken breast (2 pounds / 910 g)

4 ounces (115 g) snow peas, trimmed and julienned

6 scallions, thinly sliced

2 carrots, freshly grated

½ red bell pepper, cut into ¼-inch (6-mm) dice

1 (8-ounce / 225-g) can bamboo shoots, drained and chopped

1 (8-ounce / 225-g) can baby corn, drained and cut into ¼-inch (6-mm) pieces

½ cup (20 g) fresh cilantro leaves, chopped

FOR THE RICE NOODLES

4 ounces (115 g) dried rice vermicelli, from 1 (6-ounce / 170-g) package

2 tablespoons toasted sesame oil

2 tablespoons toasted sesame seeds

FOR THE SAUCE

½ cup (120 ml) mayonnaise

1 tablespoon Dijon mustard

2 tablespoons toasted sesame oil

¼ cup (60 ml) soy sauce

1 to 2 tablespoons hot chile oil

¼ cup (60 ml) peanut oil

1 teaspoon Szechuan spice mix or Chinese five-spice powder (see Note)

FOR THE ASSEMBLY

Nonstick cooking spray, for the pan

2 (16-ounce / 280-g) packages egg roll wrappers

3 tablespoons toasted sesame seeds

THE BAKED AND CHILLED versions of this dish are quite different, though equally delicious. With the baked, a crispy egg roll wrapper is used to cradle the filling, while the chilled version uses soft rice paper instead. The Szechuan spices are *hot*, so don't be afraid to adjust them to your taste buds. I like to include them rather than hold back. The possible variations on this recipe are plentiful. Shrimp or extra-firm tofu can take the place of the chicken. For even more variety, prepare half of the meals baked and the other half chilled, and serve them both ways. I like to serve these with a hot and sour soup and a platter of thinly sliced mango with lime juice.

> MAKE THE CHICKEN & VEGETABLE FILLING

Place the chicken breasts in a large pot with enough water to cover. Bring to a boil, then turn off the heat and cover the pot. Let the chicken rest for 10 to 15 minutes; the chicken will continue to cook. Remove the chicken from the pot; it should be firm to the touch. To be certain it is cooked through, slice one piece in half; its center should not be pink. When the chicken is cool enough to handle, after about 20 minutes, chop it into ¼-inch (6-mm) dice.

Bring a small saucepan of water to a boil and drop in the snow peas. Blanch until crisp-tender and bright green, 1 to 2 minutes. Drain and rinse under cold water.

In a medium bowl, combine the chicken, snow peas, scallions, carrots, pepper, bamboo shoots, baby corn, and cilantro. Mix gently with your hands and set aside.

> MAKE THE RICE NOODLES

In a medium bowl, soak the noodles in boiling water for 15 minutes, then drain, run under cold water, and return to the bowl. Toss with the sesame oil and sesame seeds.

> MAKE THE SAUCE

In a small bowl, combine the mayonnaise, mustard, sesame oil, soy sauce, chile oil, peanut oil, and spice mix, and whisk until well combined.

> ASSEMBLE AND BAKE THE CUPS

Preheat the oven to 350°F (175°C). Spray a 12-well classic cupcake pan with nonstick cooking spray.

Place 1 egg roll wrapper in each well of the pan, creating a cup that fills the well. Layer the noodles on the bottom of each well and the chicken and vegetable filling on top. Sprinkle with the sesame seeds. Lightly spray the top edges of the egg roll wrappers with the cooking spray. Bake until the wrappers are golden brown, about 15 minutes. Let cool in the pan for 5 minutes, then use your hands to lift them from the pan using the egg roll wrappers as handles.

VARIATION

This version should be served the same day it is made, as the noodles are likely to get soggy in this no-bake version.

FOR THE WRAPPER

> 2 (12-ounce / 340-g) packages Vietnamese rice paper (*bánh tráng*)

Prepare the chicken and vegetable filling, rice noodles, and sauce as directed previously.

Line the wells of a cupcake pan with plastic wrap by overlapping two long pieces of plastic wrap along the center of the pan, leaving at least a 3-inch (7.5-cm) border on all sides of the pan.

In a large bowl filled with warm tap water, soak 1 rice paper wrapper for about 15 seconds or until soft. Gently swirl the wrapper in the water with your fingers, being careful not to puncture the paper. (Do not leave the wrapper in the water or it will become soggy.) Lay the wrapper on a paper towel to absorb any excess water, then fold it to fit a well of the pan. It will overhang the edges of the well. Repeat with the remaining wells.

Fill each well three-quarters full with the chicken and vegetable filling. Evenly distribute the rice vermicelli noodles among the wells, then fold the overhanging rice paper over the noodles. Tightly wrap the pan in another layer of plastic wrap.

Chill for 2 hours or overnight. To unpan, unwrap the outer layer of plastic wrap, then lift up on the overhanging edges of the plastic wrap lining the wells of the pan to remove the meals. Serve each meal on an individual bed of Bibb lettuce or on a platter as part of a larger meal.

Note **Szechuan spice mix is composed of ground Szechuan pepper, crushed red pepper, garlic, ginger, sugar, and salt, while Chinese five-spice powder is composed of star anise, cloves, cinnamon, Szechuan pepper, and ground fennel. Both spice mixes can be purchased in the spice section of your grocery store. You can also purchase the ingredients separately and make your own spice mixes, tailoring them to your tastes.**

TURKEY, APPLE &
Sweet Potato
PIES

OVEN: 400°F (205°C) > PREP TIME: 25 minutes >
BAKING TIME: 35 to 45 minutes > YIELD: 24 potpies

FOR THE FILLING

2 tablespoons unsalted
butter

1 yellow onion, cut into
¼-inch (6-mm) dice

3 apples, cored and cut into
¼-inch (6-mm) dice

1 medium sweet potato or
yam, peeled and cut into
¼-inch (6-mm) dice

1½ pounds (680 g) frozen
turkey sausage patties or
links, crumbled (see Note)

1 tablespoon chopped fresh
sage

1½ teaspoons caraway seeds

1⅓ cups (315 ml) chicken
broth

⅔ cup (165 ml) dry sherry

3 tablespoons cornstarch

Kosher salt and freshly
ground black pepper

FOR THE ASSEMBLY

Nonstick cooking spray, for
the pan

2 (15-ounce / 430-g)
packages ready-made pie
dough (2 rounds per
package), at room
temperature

2 (17.3-ounce / 485-g)
packages (2 sheets) puff
pastry, at room
temperature

3 cups (345 g) grated sharp
cheddar

Note To crumble the sausage for this recipe, choose
turkey sausage patties or links that are frozen, then
thaw them slightly. Put them in the bowl of a food
processor with the blade attachment and pulse until the
pieces are small but not pulverized.

I FIND IT IMPOSSIBLE to resist this potpie, with its
yummy turkey sausage and sweet potatoes. You will not
believe how easy and delicious this is. If you dice the sweet
potatoes small enough, your children won't even know
they're there. I like to serve this with a bountiful mixed green
salad and a bowl of steaming hot butternut squash soup.

> MAKE THE FILLING

In a medium sauté pan over medium heat, melt the butter
and sauté the onions, apples, and sweet potato until softened, 10 to 12 minutes. Add the sausage, sage, caraway
seeds, broth, sherry, and cornstarch, and season with salt
and pepper. Stir to combine and cook until the mixture
thickens, about 4 minutes. Turn off the heat and let rest
until ready to assemble.

> ASSEMBLE THE PIES

Preheat the oven to 400°F (205°C). Spray two 12-well
classic cupcake pans with nonstick cooking spray.

Unroll the pie dough onto a flat work surface; no need
to flour it. Cut each round of dough in half, and then cut
each half into thirds for a total of 24 pieces. Place 1 piece
of dough in each well of the prepared pans. There may be
small spaces where the pan shows through. Using kitchen
scissors, trim any excess dough overhanging the edges of
the wells. Fill each well three-quarters full with the potpie
filling.

Unroll the puff pastry sheets and cut each sheet into
12 even pieces, for a total of 24 pieces. Top each well with
1 piece of puff pastry, tucking the pastry into the well if
it overlaps the pie dough; don't handle it too much or it
won't puff. Sprinkle each pie with cheese, about 2 tablespoons per pie.

Bake until golden brown and puffed, 35 to 45 minutes.
Let the potpies rest in the pan for 15 minutes, then loosen
the sides of each potpie with a table knife and insert the
tines of a fork between the pan and each potpie to lift it out.

Store the potpies in an airtight container in the refrigerator for up to 5 days. Reheat, wrapped in tin foil, for 15
minutes at 350°F (175°C).

THANKSGIVING
> DINNER <

OVEN: 350°F (175°C) > PREP TIME: 30 minutes >
BAKING TIME: 25 minutes > YIELD: 12 mini meals

USING LEFTOVERS

Nonstick cooking spray, for the pan

Leftover turkey, thinly sliced

Leftover stuffing

Leftover gravy

Leftover cranberry sauce

Leftover mashed potatoes

OR, USING PURCHASED INGREDIENTS

2 Idaho russet potatoes, peeled and cut into 2-inch (5-cm) pieces

¼ cup (60 ml) heavy cream

2 tablespoons unsalted butter

Kosher salt and freshly ground black pepper

1 (6-ounce / 170-g) package seasoned stuffing mix

1 (14-ounce / 400-g) can whole cranberry sauce

½ pound (228 g) sliced turkey in gravy, plus extra gravy for serving

Nonstick cooking spray, for the pan

TURKEY DINNER is delicious any time of year, as my family well knows. We have Thanksgiving in Cape Cod in July every year because our large clan of thirty-two family members can't always get together during the holidays. No matter the time of year, turkey dinner with the family is always a special occasion. Now you can create a Thanksgiving feast whenever you like, and all of it in a perfect mini meal. These recipes are a great way to use up Thanksgiving leftovers, but don't fret if the turkey and stuffing are long gone—the recipe includes a method using purchased ingredients.

Preheat the oven to 350°F (175°C).

If you are using homemade leftovers: Spray the wells of a 12-well classic cupcake pan with nonstick cooking spray. Cut 12 pieces of turkey to fit into the wells of the pan. Fill the wells one-quarter full of stuffing; lay a slice of turkey on top with some of the gravy and 1 tablespoon of the cranberry sauce per well. Top with mashed potatoes and a bit more stuffing to fill the wells. Press down to compact and bake until heated through, about 25 minutes. Let rest in the pan for 5 minutes, then loosen the sides of each meal with a table knife and pop them out of the pan. Serve in a pool of gravy.

———————————

If you are using purchased ingredients: Place the potatoes in a medium saucepan and cover with cold water. Bring to a boil over high heat and boil until fork tender, about 13 minutes. Drain the potatoes and return them to the pot. Use a potato masher to mash the potatoes.

In a small saucepan, heat the cream and butter over medium-high heat until just about boiling, about 3 minutes. Pour the hot cream mixture over the potatoes and stir to combine. Season with salt and pepper.

Meanwhile, prepare the stuffing as per package directions.

Assemble, unpan, and serve the mini meals as described above.

BARBECUE PORK HAND PIES ^

chapter
>SEVEN<
MEAT

AMERICAN MEALS MADE WITH MEAT ARE NOTORIOUS FOR

being heavy and laden with grease, but it doesn't need to be that way. As your ideas about what a meal should be begin to shift, so should the way you view certain ingredients. Instead of loading up meat dishes with salt and gravy, consider how herbs, spices, and other ingredients can make the meal healthy and flavorful. Eating smart doesn't have to mean making your dishes taste bland.

One problem I often see involves the huge portions of meat we serve ourselves each night. Triple-stacked burgers weigh you down. Instead, use a variety of vegetables, sauces, and wrappers to fill out your meal. A serving of meat should be no larger than a deck of cards or the palm of your hand, which is exactly why the cupcake pan is one of your best tools for eating well. Serving size isn't a problem when the whole meal fits in the palm of your hand!

While fast-cooking cuts of beef can serve as a good standby in case of dinner emergencies, broaden your scope a bit to include other delicious meats, including lamb and pork. I've tried to present enough variety in the dishes in this section to show the multitude of ways meat can be prepared and enjoyed.

Southwestern
BEEF PIES
IN FLOUR TORTILLAS

OVEN: 350°F (175°C) > PREP TIME: 25 minutes >
BAKING TIME: 20 to 25 minutes > YIELD: 12 pies

FOR THE BEEF PIE FILLING

2 teaspoons extra-virgin olive oil

1 small onion, cut into ¼-inch (6-mm) dice

1 small zucchini, grated

3 to 5 chipotle peppers in adobo sauce (from a 7-ounce / 200-g can), finely chopped, or 1 tablespoon powdered smoked chile

1 teaspoon cumin seed or ground cumin

1 (14.5-ounce / 430-g) can stewed tomatoes with oregano, with their juice, chopped

1 (14.5-ounce / 430-g) can yellow hominy, drained

1 (1-pound / 455-g) package cooked beef pot roast with gravy, shredded (see Note)

2 tablespoons cornstarch

Kosher salt and freshly ground black pepper

FOR THE ASSEMBLY

Nonstick cooking spray, for the pan

12 (6-inch / 15-cm) flour tortillas

2 ounces (55 g) grated cheddar

1 bunch scallions, green parts only, thinly sliced, for garnish

Note Prepared meals like pot roast with gravy are great in a dinner emergency. When combined with a spectacular recipe like this one, no one will know you cheated even a little. Prepared meals can be found in the refrigerated or freezer section of most grocery stores.

THE SEMI-HOMEMADE nature of these beef pies is a godsend on busy days. No one will ever know that you cut a corner—they will just marvel at how clever you are. Serve this with a sauté of corn and red peppers as a dinner entrée, or with a green salad for lunch.

> MAKE THE BEEF PIE FILLING

In a large sauté pan, heat the oil over medium heat and sauté the onion and zucchini until softened, about 3 minutes. Then stir in the chipotle peppers, cumin, tomatoes, hominy, and shredded beef. In a small bowl, combine the cornstarch with 2 tablespoons water, then add the cornstarch slurry to the pot. Simmer, stirring occasionally until the liquids begin to bubble and create a gravy, 8 to 10 minutes. Season to taste with salt and pepper, then set aside.

> ASSEMBLE AND BAKE THE PIES

Preheat the oven to 350°F (175°C).

Spray a 12-well classic cupcake pan with nonstick cooking spray.

Line each well with a flour tortilla. The edges of the tortilla will peek over the top of the pan. Distribute the beef pie filling evenly among the wells of the pan, and then sprinkle with the grated cheese.

Bake until bubbling and golden, 20 to 25 minutes. Let the pies cool in the pan, then use your hands to lift them out of the pan using the tortilla wrappers as handles. Sprinkle with the scallions and serve immediately.

Mom's
> BEST <
MEAT LOAF

OVEN: 350°F (175°C) > **PREP TIME:** 15 minutes >
BAKING TIME: 45 minutes > **YIELD:** 12 meat loaves

2¼ pounds (1 kg) ground beef

1 (4-ounce / 115-g) container fried onions or shallots, crumbled

½ teaspoon freshly ground black pepper

3 tablespoons chopped fresh garlic or garlic from a tube

2 teaspoons seasoning salt

2 large eggs

1 cup (240 ml) ketchup, divided

2 tablespoons Worcestershire sauce

2 tablespoons hot sauce (I like smoked chipotle)

1 tablespoon honey

1 tablespoon blackstrap molasses

3 tablespoons finely chopped fresh parsley or parsley from a tube

Nonstick cooking spray, for the pan

3 slices bacon

THIS MEAL IS FAST! When my son says he wants meat loaf, this is always my go-to recipe! By the time the children get home, I have dinner ready to serve. If I have learned anything about meat loaf, it's this: The flavors need to be bold, because they can get lost in the cooking. This is a perfect portion of meat when served with a larger meal.

Preheat the oven to 350°F (175°C).

In a medium bowl, combine the ground beef, crumbled fried onions, pepper, garlic, seasoning salt, eggs, ¼ cup (60 ml) of the ketchup, the Worcestershire, hot sauce, honey, molasses, and parsley. Mix well by hand or with a wooden spoon.

Spray a 12-well classic cupcake pan with nonstick cooking spray. Using a ½-cup (120-ml) measure, fill each well to the top with the meat loaf mixture. Cut each piece of bacon into 4 pieces, for a total of 12. Top each loaf with 2 tablespoons ketchup and a bacon piece.

Bake the meat loaves for 45 minutes, making sure the bacon has browned. If the bacon is not browned, turn on the broiler and brown the tops of the meat loaves for no more than 20 seconds, keeping a close watch. As soon as they come out of the oven, remove the meat loaves from the pan using the tines of a fork.

Store the meat loaves in an airtight container in the refrigerator for up to 5 days. Reheat, wrapped in tin foil, for 15 minutes at 350ºF (175ºC).

SHORT RIBS
Braised with
MUSHROOMS, ONION & BACON

OVEN: 375°F and 350°F (190°C and 175°C) > PREP TIME: 45 minutes >
OVEN TIME: 1 hour 55 minutes to 2 hours 25 minutes > YIELD: 12 mini meals

FOR THE SHORT RIBS

2½ pounds (1.2 kg) beef short ribs

Kosher salt and freshly ground black pepper

2 tablespoons extra-virgin olive oil

2 tablespoons unsalted butter

1 medium onion, cut into ¼-inch (6-mm) dice

1 large carrot, peeled and cut into ¼-inch (6-mm) dice

1 large stalk celery, cut into ¼-inch (6-mm) dice

¼ cup (35 g) fresh minced garlic or garlic from a tube

2 cups (480 ml) dry red wine

3 sprigs fresh thyme

2 bay leaves

5 stems fresh parsley

FOR THE MUSHROOM SAUCE

4 slices bacon, coarsely chopped

1 tablespoon unsalted butter

1½ cups (105 g) sliced button mushrooms

1 (10-ounce / 280-g) package frozen pearl onions, thawed and drained

FOR THE ASSEMBLY

Nonstick cooking spray, for the pan

1 (16-ounce / 455-g) package egg roll wrappers

12 frozen latkes, thawed, from 2 (12-ounce / 340-g) boxes

I LOVE SHORT RIBS because they can be seasoned with just about any flavor and will be different every time you make them. I've used citrus rind, cinnamon, and anise with great success. Here, I use the classic flavor of braised ribs and combine it with egg roll wrappers for amazing results. Pie dough could be used instead to give the dish a potpie style.

> MAKE THE SHORT RIBS

Preheat the oven to 375°F (190°C).

Season the ribs with salt and pepper to taste. In a Dutch oven, heat the oil over medium-high heat. Add the meat in two batches and brown on all sides, about 8 minutes. Transfer the meat to a plate.

Reduce the heat to medium. Add the butter, onion, carrot, celery, and garlic and sauté until the onions are translucent, about 4 minutes. Return the short ribs to the pot and add the red wine, thyme, bay leaves, and parsley. Bring to a boil, cover, and transfer the pot to the oven. Braise the ribs until the meat is falling off of the bone, 1½ to 2 hours. Remove from the oven and set aside. Don't turn off the oven.

> MAKE THE MUSHROOM SAUCE

In a medium skillet over medium heat, cook the bacon until crisp, about 6 minutes. Transfer to a paper towel–lined plate. Drain all but 1 tablespoon of the bacon fat from the skillet.

Add the butter, mushrooms, and onions to the skillet and sauté, stirring occasionally, until just brown, about 8 minutes. Add the bacon to the mushroom sauce and stir to combine. Transfer to a large bowl.

❯ ASSEMBLE AND BAKE THE SHORT RIBS

Reduce the oven temperature to 350°F (175°C).

Remove the meat from the pot and shred it, reserving the braising liquid. Add the shredded meat to the mushroom sauce. Using a fine-mesh sieve set over a medium heatproof bowl, strain the meat and mushroom mixture and reserve the resulting liquid. Remove and discard the parsley, thyme, and bay leaves. Add the onion, carrots, and celery from the Dutch oven to the meat and mushroom mixture. Skim the fat from the braising liquid and add the liquid from the meat and mushroom mixture to the braising liquid.

Spray a 12-well classic cupcake pan with nonstick cooking spray. Line each well with 1 egg roll wrapper. Fill each well to the top with the meat and mushroom mixture and drizzle each with 2 tablespoons of the reserved braising liquid. Fold over the edges of the egg roll wrappers and top each packet with a latke.

Bake until the latkes are golden on top, about 25 minutes. Let rest in the pan for 5 minutes, then loosen the sides of each meal with a table knife and pop them out of the pan.

BEEF
STROGANOFF

OVEN: 350°F (175°C) > PREP TIME: 30 minutes >
BAKING TIME: 25 minutes > YIELD: 12 mini meals

FOR THE CREAM SAUCE

¼ cup (½ stick / 60 g) salted
   butter

2 tablespoons all-purpose
   flour

1½ cups (360 ml) chicken
   broth

6 tablespoons (90 ml) sour
   cream

2 teaspoons Dijon mustard

¼ cup (10 g) chopped
   fresh dill

Kosher salt and freshly
   ground black pepper

FOR THE BEEF

1½ pounds (680 g) beef
   tenderloin, trimmed of all
   fat and cut into ½-inch
   (1-cm) cubes

1 teaspoon kosher salt

½ teaspoon freshly ground
   black pepper

1 tablespoon unsalted butter

1 tablespoon extra-virgin olive
   oil

FOR THE MUSHROOM CAPS

2 tablespoons unsalted
   butter

12 large whole white
   mushrooms, stems
   removed

1 tablespoon fresh thyme
   leaves

1 large clove garlic, minced,
   or 1 tablespoon garlic from
   a tube

½ teaspoon kosher salt

¼ teaspoon freshly ground
   black pepper

FOR THE MUSHROOM SAUTÉ

2 tablespoons olive oil

½ cup (80 g) minced shallots
   (from 3 large shallots)

4 cups (380 g) button
   mushrooms, roughly
   chopped

1 large clove garlic, chopped,
   or 1 tablespoon garlic from
   a tube

Nonstick cooking spray, for
   the pan

1 (16-ounce / 455-g) package
   egg roll wrappers

BEEF STROGANOFF is one of those dishes that can easily become an over-indulgence. With the cupcake pan, you can enjoy it in individually sized wrapped packages. So you can feel good about enjoying the sour cream for once! The egg roll wrapper is a stand-in for the noodles traditionally served with this dish. Usually, you use a beef stew meat, but that only works when you are cooking the meat for a long time. This needs to be made with tenderloin of beef so you get a tender texture in a short cooking time.

> MAKE THE CREAM SAUCE

In a medium saucepan over medium heat, melt the butter, then add the flour, whisking for 1 minute to make a paste. Pour in the broth in a slow stream, whisking, then turn the heat to high and bring to a boil. Stir in the sour cream, mustard, dill, and salt and pepper to taste. Transfer to a large bowl.

> MAKE THE BEEF

Season the beef with the salt and pepper. Heat the butter and oil in a large sauté pan over medium heat and sauté the beef until medium-rare, about 4 minutes. (It will continue to cook in the oven so you don't want to overcook it now.) Transfer the beef to the bowl containing the cream sauce.

> MAKE THE MUSHROOM CAPS

In a 12-inch (30-cm) sauté pan, melt the butter over medium heat and sauté the mushroom caps with the thyme, garlic, and salt and pepper until just softened and the juices are cooked off, about 5 minutes. Set aside.

RECIPE CONTINUES

In the same sauté pan, heat the oil over medium heat and add the mushrooms, shallots, and garlic. Cook until the mushroom liquid has cooked off and the mushrooms begin to brown, about 10 minutes. Add this to the beef mixture.

Preheat the oven to 350°F (175°C).

Spray the wells of a 12-well classic cupcake pan with nonstick cooking spray. Fill each well with 1 egg roll wrapper. The edges of the wrapper will peek over the top of the pan. Fill the egg roll wrappers to the top with the beef mixture and fold the wrapper in to create a neat package. Top each with a sautéed mushroom cap.

Bake for about 25 minutes, until the wrappers are crispy and golden in color. Let rest for 5 minutes, then remove each stroganoff from the pan by gently pulling on the egg roll wrappers.

TACOS

OVEN: 350°F (175°C) > PREP TIME: 20 minutes >
BAKING TIME: 25 minutes > YIELD: 12 tacos

Nonstick cooking spray, for
  the pan

12 (6-inch / 15-cm) flour
  tortillas

2 tablespoons plus
  1 teaspoon extra-virgin
  olive oil

1 onion, thinly sliced

1 (4.25-ounce / 125-g) can
  mild chopped green chiles,
  drained

1 teaspoon kosher salt

1 pound (455 g) lean ground
  beef

1 (1.25-ounce / 35-g) package
  taco seasoning

1 (16-ounce / 455-g) can
  refried beans

1 cup (115 g) grated sharp
  cheddar

OPTIONAL

Fresh tomatoes, chopped

Fresh romaine lettuce,
  shredded

Canned pinto beans, drained
  and rinsed

Sour cream

Salsa

Jalapeños, chopped

WHEN I USED TO CATER for actors and crews at the studios in Hollywood, taco day was always a huge hit. Studio execs especially liked the mix-and-match options to create a personalized meal. This classic family meal works beautifully in the cupcake pan. The flour tortilla creates a little bowl for the ingredients, which eliminates the mad dash to eat from both ends of the taco before the filling and toppings fall out. Flour tortillas are pliable. Regular corn tortillas won't work for this recipe because they break when placed in the well. The sharp cheddar brings out the other flavors, making these tacos a perfect ensemble.

Preheat the oven to 350°F (175°C).

Spray a 12-well classic cupcake pan with nonstick cooking spray. Line each well with a flour tortilla. The edges of the tortilla will peek over the top of the pan.

Heat 2 tablespoons of the oil in a medium skillet over medium heat. Add the onions and cook, stirring occasionally, until golden, about 8 minutes. Stir in the chiles and salt. Transfer the onion mixture to a medium bowl.

In the same skillet, heat the remaining 1 teaspoon oil over medium heat. Add the beef, breaking it up with the back of a wooden spoon, and the taco seasoning; cook until browned and crumbled, about 8 minutes. Add the refried beans to the meat; turn off the heat, and stir to combine. Adjust the seasoning, if needed.

Distribute the meat and bean mixture evenly among the wells, then top each with the onion mixture and sprinkle with the cheese. Bake until heated through and the edges of the tortilla are golden, about 25 minutes. While the tacos bake, fill the wells of an empty cupcake pan with the optional toppings. Let the tacos cool for 1 minute, then use your hands to lift from the pan using the tortilla wrappers as handles. Serve with the pan of toppings alongside and allow everyone to pick their own toppings.

FLANK STEAK
Mexican Bake

OVEN: 350°F (175°C) > PREP TIME: 15 minutes >
BAKING TIME: 30 to 40 minutes > YIELD: 12 mini meals

FOR THE STEAK

Nonstick cooking spray, for
the pan

2½ pounds (1.2 kg) flank
steak

1 teaspoon kosher salt

½ teaspoon freshly ground
black pepper

FOR THE RICE AND BEANS

1 cup (250 g) uncooked rice

1 (16-ounce / 455-g) can
refried beans

FOR THE ASSEMBLY

15 slices pre-sliced pepper
Jack

1 (16-ounce / 280-g) jar salsa
of your choice

THE TITLE OF THIS RECIPE ALONE is enough to make me salivate. Although the recipe is simple, the flavors are not. The filling is rich and cheesy with a slight tanginess from the salsa.

> MAKE THE STEAK

Place the steak on a cutting board. Cover the steak with a piece of plastic wrap and use a mallet to pound the meat until it is ¼ inch (6 mm) thick. Season the meat with the salt and pepper. Cut the steak into 12 pieces, approximately 4 by 4 inches (10 by 10 cm).

> MAKE THE RICE AND BEANS

Cook the rice according to the directions on the back of the package. In a medium bowl, mix the cooked rice and the refried beans until well combined.

> ASSEMBLE AND BAKE THE MINI MEALS

Preheat the oven to 350°F (175°C). Spray a 12-well classic cupcake pan with nonstick cooking spray.

Press 1 piece of steak into each well of the prepared pan. Press 1 slice of cheese into each well on top of the steak. Cut the remaining 3 slices of cheese into quarters, for a total of 12 pieces. Divide half of the rice mixture evenly among the 12 wells. Top each well with 1 tablespoon salsa. Divide the remaining rice mixture evenly among the wells, then add another tablespoon of salsa and a quarter-slice of cheese to each well.

Bake until the meat is cooked through but not dry and the cheese is melted, 30 to 40 minutes. Let cool in the pan for 2 minutes, then loosen the sides of each mini meal using a table knife and insert the tines of a fork between the pan and each mini meal to lift it out. Serve immediately alongside the salsa of your choice.

Upside-Down
GREEN APPLE
HAM LOAVES

OVEN: 350°F (175°C) > PREP TIME: 30 minutes >
BAKING TIME: 20 minutes > YIELD: 12 loaves

FOR THE HAM LOAVES

2 tablespoons extra-virgin
olive oil

1 medium onion, chopped

1 pound (455 g) ham steak,
cut into large chunks

½ pound (225 g) ground veal

½ pound (225 g) ground pork
sausage

2 large eggs

1 cup (240 ml) whole milk

1 cup (110 g) panko
bread crumbs

1 tablespoon dry mustard

2 tablespoons chopped fresh
flat-leaf parsley

Freshly ground black pepper

FOR THE BROWN SUGAR–MUSTARD GLAZE

¼ cup (½ stick / 60 g)
unsalted butter

½ cup (125 g) condensed
tomato soup (see Note)

¼ cup (60 ml) Dijon mustard

½ cup (120 ml) apple cider
vinegar

½ cup (110 g) packed light
brown sugar

Freshly ground black pepper

FOR THE ASSEMBLY

Nonstick cooking spray, for
the pan

¾ cup (165 g) packed light
brown sugar

2 green apples, peeled, cored,
and cut into to ¼-inch
(6-mm) slices

Chopped fresh flat-leaf
parsley, for garnish

Note If you don't have condensed tomato soup on
hand, you can substitute tomato sauce or ketchup.

SWEET-TART APPLES combine exquisitely with salty ham in these delectable little loaves, but it's the glaze that takes them over the top. The glaze is supposed to be sweet and tangy, so don't be surprised by its flavor, which is similar to the sauce used for Swedish meatballs.

> MAKE THE HAM LOAVES

In a small sauté pan over medium heat, heat the oil and sauté the onion until soft, about 10 minutes. Set aside.

In a food processor fitted with a blade, pulse the ham several times until it is chopped but not pulverized. Add the veal, sausage, eggs, milk, panko, mustard, and parsley. Season with pepper and process, scraping down the sides occasionally with a rubber spatula, just until the mixture comes together. Do not overmix. Transfer the ham mixture to a large bowl and mix in the sautéed onion.

> MAKE THE BROWN SUGAR–MUSTARD GLAZE

In a small saucepan over medium-low heat, melt the butter, then add the tomato soup, mustard, vinegar, brown sugar, and a few grinds of black pepper. Bring to a boil, stirring occasionally, and cook until thickened slightly, about 15 minutes.

> ASSEMBLE AND BAKE THE LOAVES

Preheat the oven to 350°F (175°C). Spray a 12-well classic cupcake pan with nonstick cooking spray.

Sprinkle the bottom of each well with 1 tablespoon brown sugar, then add 2 or 3 slices of green apple, enough to line the bottom of the pan. Distribute the ham mixture evenly among the wells, making sure to even out the tops so they bake flat. Spoon on some of the brown sugar–mustard glaze.

Bake until the loaves are cooked through, about 20 minutes. Do not exceed 20 minutes or the loaves will dry out. Insert the tines of a fork between the pan and each loaf to lift it out. If any apple has stuck to the pan, scrape it out and use it to top the loaves. Serve drizzled with additional glaze and sprinkled with parsley. Store the loaves in an airtight container in the refrigerator for up to 5 days. Reheat, wrapped in tin foil, for 15 minutes at 350°F (175°C).

BEEF TAMALE PIES

OVEN: 400°F and 350°F (205°C and 175°C) > PREP TIME: 45 minutes >
BAKING TIME: 1 hour 10 minutes (this includes preparing the squash
and empanada dough) > YIELD: 24 pies

FOR THE CHILES

2 poblano chiles

1 teaspoon kosher salt

FOR THE BUTTERNUT SQUASH

1 pound (455 g) butternut
squash, peeled and cut
into ¼-inch (6-mm) dice

2 tablespoons extra-virgin
olive oil

1 tablespoon honey

Kosher salt

Freshly ground black pepper

FOR THE BEEF

Nonstick cooking spray, for
the pan

1 pound (455 g) lean ground
beef

½ teaspoon ground cumin

¼ cup (35 g) currants or
raisins, chopped

½ teaspoon kosher salt

¼ teaspoon freshly ground
black pepper

FOR THE CORN

2½ cups (340 g) frozen corn
kernels

1 green or red jalapeño,
seeded and finely chopped

2 cloves garlic, minced

1½ teaspoons ground cumin

1½ teaspoons ground
oregano

4 plum tomatoes, cut into
¼-inch (6-mm) dice

2 tablespoons olive oil

1 teaspoon kosher salt

½ teaspoon freshly ground
black pepper

⅓ cup (35 g) thinly sliced
scallions

⅓ cup (15 g) chopped
cilantro

FOR THE POLENTA AND YOGURT MIXTURE

1 teaspoon kosher salt

1 cup (160 g) yellow cornmeal

½ cup (120 ml) plain yogurt

FOR THE ASSEMBLY

1½ cups (175 g) grated sharp
cheddar

1½ cups (175 g) shredded
Monterey Jack

Nonstick cooking spray, for
the pan

3 packages (10 rounds per
package) empanada dough
rounds

12 sprigs fresh cilantro

THE ADDITION OF SQUASH AND POLENTA
to this beef tamale pie imparts a rich, sweet flavor to a simple
dish. The poblano chiles add a nice, mild heat. To give the
tamales a lovely orange color, use empanada dough made
with annatto (see Note, page 189). You can purchase
pre-roasted butternut squash in some markets.

> MAKE THE CHILES

Roast the chiles over an open flame on the stovetop until
blistered, about 4 minutes. Or preheat a broiler to high
and blister the chiles under the broiler, positioned on the
top rack, about 3 minutes per side. Watch carefully, as
they can burn quickly under the broiler.

Place the chiles and salt in a zip-top bag or a bowl
covered with plastic wrap to steam off the skin. Let steam
for 10 minutes, then peel off the skin. (Don't rinse under
water.) Seed and dice the chiles. Set aside.

> MAKE THE SQUASH

Preheat the oven to 400°F (205°C).

Arrange the squash on a foil-lined sheet pan, then
brush with the oil and honey. Season with salt and pepper.
Bake until the squash is softened and slightly browned,
about 30 minutes. Transfer to a large bowl. Reduce the
oven temperature to 350°F (175°C).

> MAKE THE BEEF

Spray a medium skillet with nonstick cooking spray and
set it over medium heat. Place the beef in the pan, stir in
the cumin, currants, salt, and pepper. Sauté, breaking up
the beef with a wooden spoon, until the beef is browned,
8 to 10 minutes. If fat has accumulated in the pan, drain
the meat in a paper towel–lined colander set over a bowl.
Transfer the beef to the bowl with the squash and toss to
combine.

> MAKE THE CORN

Using the same skillet, heat the oil over medium heat. Add the corn, jalapeño, garlic, cumin, oregano, and tomatoes and sauté until softened, about 4 minutes. Season with the salt and pepper. Turn off the heat and add the scallions, cilantro, and chopped poblano chiles. Transfer the corn mixture to the bowl containing the beef and squash; mix until well combined.

> MAKE THE POLENTA AND YOGURT MIXTURE

In a medium stockpot, bring 3½ cups (840 ml) water to a boil with the salt. Whisk in the cornmeal, then bring the mixture back to a boil for 2 minutes. Turn the heat to low and cook an additional 8 minutes, until the polenta has thickened. Turn off the heat and stir in the yogurt.

> ASSEMBLE AND BAKE THE PIES

In a large bowl, mix the cheddar and Monterey Jack together; stir in half of the polenta mixture, mixing until combined.

Spray a 12-well classic cupcake pan with nonstick cooking spray. Line each well of the pan with 1 empanada dough round. Layer each well with some polenta, then the beef and squash mixture, then more polenta, and finally top with the remaining cheese, making sure to fill the well fully to the top.

Bake until the empanada dough is cooked through, the filling is hot, and the cheese is melted, 35 to 40 minutes. Let cool for one minute in the pan, then loosen the sides of each pie using a table knife, and insert the tines of a fork between the pan and each pie to lift it out. Serve each pie garnished with a sprig of cilantro.

Note Be sure to look for Goya brand empanada dough in your market's freezer section. The discs are 5-inch (12.5-cm) rounds and come in a 14-ounce (390-g) package of ten discs. The dough rounds fit perfectly into the wells of the pan and do not need to be cut or rolled. (Note that Goya "Discos Grandes" are too big for the cupcake pan, and Fargo Tapas de Empanadas and Goya Tapa Empanada dough shells are used for frying, not baking.) The dough will either be white or orange—the orange discs have been seasoned with annatto and can be substituted for plain dough as you prefer. Take the dough out of the freezer 20 minutes prior to cooking to thaw. Store any unused dough rounds in your freezer in an airtight plastic zip-top bag or wrapped tightly in plastic wrap.

> BEEF <
EMPANADAS

OVEN: 350°F (175°C) > PREP TIME: 30 minutes >
COOKING TIME: 35 to 45 minutes > YIELD: 12 empanadas

● ● ●

¼ cup (60 ml) olive oil

2 New York strip steaks (1¼ pounds / 570 g), trimmed of fat and cut crosswise into ¼-inch- (6-mm) slices

1 teaspoon kosher salt

½ teaspoon freshly ground black pepper

2 tablespoons freshly grated ginger or ginger from a tube

2 tablespoons minced fresh garlic or garlic from a tube

2 teaspoons Chinese chile paste, or ½ teaspoon cayenne, or 1 tablespoon powdered chile

1 small onion, minced

2 cups (480 g) canned plum tomatoes in their juice, chopped

¼ cup (35 g) dried cherries, finely chopped

1 teaspoon cinnamon

1 teaspoon cumin

1 teaspoon ground coriander

½ cup (70 g) pine nuts, toasted

Nonstick cooking spray, for the pan

2 (14-ounce / 400-g) packages empanada dough (see Note)

1 (8-ounce / 225-g) package queso de mano or other creamy white melting cheese, grated (see Note)

Note With the rising popularity of Southwestern cuisine—as well as the rising population of those who cook it—these ingredients are becoming easier to find. Many grocery stores are starting to carry a wider variety of Hispanic foods, including empanada dough and queso de mano. If you can't find empanada dough, you can use 6-inch (15-cm) flour tortillas, and if queso de mano is not available, sub in mozzarella or provolone.

THESE ARE DROP-DEAD AMAZING and a meal on their own. While not common to empanadas, cherries provide a wonderful sweetness that contrasts with the flavor of the chiles. I like to prepare these with preformed empanada dough rounds colored with annatto (see Note), so when they come out of the oven, they are a Santa Fe red earth color. My trick here for cooking the meat quickly is to trim the fat from the steak and then slice the steak crosswise into ¼-inch (6-mm) strips.

Preheat the oven to 350°F (175°C).

In a large sauté pan over high heat, heat 2 table-spoons of the oil and add the strips of steak. Cook to medium rare, about 1 minute per side. Remove the beef to a cutting board and chop it into small pieces. Transfer the beef to a medium bowl and season with the salt and pepper, ginger, garlic, and chile paste; set aside.

In the same pan over medium heat, heat the remaining 2 tablespoons oil and sauté the onion until golden, 10 minutes. Stir in the plum tomatoes, cherries, cinnamon, cumin, coriander, and toasted pine nuts. Turn off the heat. Stir the onion mixture into the beef mixture.

Spray a 12-well classic cupcake pan with nonstick cooking spray and line each well with 1 empanada round. The edges of the dough will peek over the top of the pan. Fill each well halfway with the beef filling, then layer half the queso de mano in the center of the well. Top with the remaining beef filling and then the cheese.

Bake until the empanada dough is cooked through and the filling is hot and bubbling, 35 to 45 minutes. Loosen the sides of each empanada using a table knife, then insert the tines of a fork between the pan and each empanada to gently lift it out. Serve with rice, beans, and a salad of orange segments, romaine, and avocado.

Store the empanadas in an airtight container in the refrigerator for up to 5 days. Reheat, wrapped in tin foil, for 15 minutes at 350°F (175°C).

PORK

Pot Stickers

IN EGG ROLL WRAPPERS

OVEN: 350°F (175°C) > PREP TIME: 20 minutes >
BAKING TIME: 12 to 15 minutes > YIELDS: 12 pot stickers

¼ cup (60 ml) sherry

2 tablespoons cornstarch

2 tablespoons freshly grated ginger or ginger from a tube

2 teaspoons sugar

1 tablespoon minced garlic or garlic from a tube

2 tablespoons soy sauce

2 teaspoons minced fresh lemongrass or lemongrass from a tube

1 tablespoon chile paste or bottled Asian chile sauce

2 tablespoons sesame oil

½ teaspoon white pepper

6 scallions, thinly sliced on the bias

1½ pounds (680 g) ground pork

½ cup (¾ ounce / 85 g) fresh shiitake mushrooms, stemmed and thinly sliced

⅓ cup (35 g) freshly grated carrot

⅔ cup (100 g) bamboo shoots, drained, from 1 (8-ounce / 225-g) can

Nonstick cooking spray, for the pan

1 (16-ounce / 455-g) package egg roll wrappers

1 (6-ounce / 170-g) jar mango chutney

THE ADDITION OF LEMONGRASS to these tasty pot stickers offers the perfect balance to the sweet carrots and earthy mushrooms. Shrimp or chicken serve as excellent substitutions for the pork, or you may combine the flavor of different meats and seafood, as is often done in Asian cuisine. You may want to double this recipe because one pan was not enough for me.

In a small bowl, whisk together the sherry, cornstarch, ginger, sugar, garlic, soy sauce, lemongrass, chile paste, sesame oil, and white pepper. Stir in the scallions and set aside.

In a large skillet over medium heat, brown the pork in the sesame oil, breaking up the meat with the back of a wooden spoon, 8 to 10 minutes. Use a slotted spoon to transfer the pork to a plate, leaving the juice in the pan.

Raise the heat to medium-high, add the shiitakes, carrot, and bamboo shoots to the pan, and cook until the mushrooms are soft, about 3 minutes. Add the sherry mixture, stirring constantly, just until a glossy sauce forms, about 2 minutes. Remove from the heat.

Preheat the oven to 350°F (175°C). Spray the wells of a 12-well classic cupcake pan with nonstick cooking spray, and then line each well with an egg roll wrapper to create a fluted cup. The edge of the wrapper will peek over the top of the pan.

Using a ⅓-cup (75-ml) measure, fill each well with the pork mixture, using it all. Fold in the edges of the wrapper and lightly spray the tops with cooking spray. Bake until the wrappers are golden, 12 to 15 minutes. Let the pot stickers cool in the pan for 3 minutes, then insert the tines of a fork between the pan and each pot sticker to lift it out. Serve with miso soup and sautéed baby bok choy with garlic.

BARBECUED PORK HAND PIES

OVEN: 325°F and 350°F (165°C and 175°C) › PREP TIME: 4 hours 25 minutes ›
BAKING TIME: 5 hours 40 minutes › YIELD: 24 hand pies

●●●

FOR THE SLOW-COOKED PORK

4 quarts (3.8 L) beef broth

¾ cup (160 ml) red wine vinegar

1 tablespoon smoked paprika

1 teaspoon cayenne

1½ tablespoons cumin

3 tablespoons chipotle Tabasco sauce

2 large cloves garlic, minced, or 2 tablespoons garlic from a tube

1 tablespoon ground ginger

1 cup (260 g) tomato paste

¼ cup (60 ml) molasses

4 to 4½ pounds (1.8 to 2 kg) pork shoulder

FOR THE BARBECUE DIPPING SAUCE

2 tablespoons canola oil

1 tablespoon unsalted butter

1 cup (160 g) chopped onion

2 large cloves garlic, minced, or 2 tablespoons garlic from a tube

1 (28-ounce / 1-L) can tomatoes, in juice

1 cup (240 ml) ketchup

½ cup (120 ml) fresh lemon juice (from 3 lemons)

½ cup (120 ml) apple cider vinegar

3 tablespoons molasses

1 tablespoon soy sauce

2 tablespoons Worcestershire sauce

4 whole cloves

1 teaspoon cinnamon

3 dried chiles

2 teaspoons dry mustard

2 teaspoons ground ginger

2 teaspoons smoked paprika

FOR THE MOLASSES APPLES

1 cup (240 ml) apple juice or cider

⅓ cup (75 ml) molasses

1 tablespoon brandy

½ teaspoon cinnamon

⅛ teaspoon ground cloves

⅛ teaspoon freshly grated nutmeg

8 large Granny Smith apples, peeled, cored, and cut into ¼-inch (6-mm) dice

FOR THE ASSEMBLY

Nonstick cooking spray, for the pan

2 (14-ounce / 400-g) cans buttermilk biscuit dough

2 tablespoons cinnamon

2 tablespoons sugar

BISCUITS ARE FILLED with slow-cooked pork shoulder with barbecue sauce and apples for a robust take on this summer classic. As always, semi-homemade substitutions make this a quick and easy meal.

Make Ahead The barbecue dipping sauce can be made in advance and stored in an airtight container in the refrigerator until needed. It will last for up to 2 weeks. The molasses apples can also be made in advance, and stored in an airtight container in the refrigerator. They will last for up to 1 week.

› MAKE THE SLOW-COOKED PORK

Preheat the oven to 325°F (165°C).

In a large roasting pan with a lid, whisk together the broth, vinegar, smoked paprika, cayenne, cumin, Tabasco, garlic, ginger, tomato paste, and molasses. Add the pork shoulder and cover the pan. Bake until the meat falls apart, about 5 hours. While the meat is roasting, prepare the dipping sauce and molasses apples.

When the meat is done, transfer it to a rimmed baking sheet to cool for easy handling, about 1 hour. If the braising liquid has not thickened, place the roasting pan on two burners and reduce the liquid over high heat until it reaches a thick consistency, about 40 minutes. At this point, add additional molasses, salt, pepper, or spices, if you like your barbecue sauce spicy.

Shred the meat, making sure to discard any bones and fat. Mix the meat with 3 cups of the reduced sauce.

› MAKE THE BARBECUE DIPPING SAUCE

In a medium saucepan, heat the oil and butter over medium heat. Add the onion and garlic and cook, stirring constantly, until caramelized, 18 to 20 minutes, reducing the heat if they begin to burn. Add the tomatoes, ketchup, lemon juice, vinegar, molasses, soy sauce, Worcestershire, cloves, cinnamon, chiles, mustard, ginger, and paprika. Reduce the heat to low; cover and cook, stirring occasionally, for about 2 hours. Let cool, about 1 hour, then pour the sauce into a blender and puree.

> MAKE THE MOLASSES APPLES

In a large pan, combine the juice, molasses, brandy, cinnamon, cloves, and nutmeg with 1 cup (240 ml) water; bring to a boil over high heat and boil for 5 minutes. Add the apples and return to a boil for 3 minutes. Reduce the heat and simmer, stirring, until the apples are tender but still chunky and the mixture has thickened, about 25 minutes. Set aside.

> ASSEMBLE AND BAKE THE HAND PIES

Preheat the oven to 350°F (175°C). Spray two 12-well classic cupcake pans with nonstick cooking spray.

Slice each uncooked biscuit round in half, for a total of 48 rounds. Place one piece of dough in the bottom of each well. Fill each well with the pork mixture and 1 heaping tablespoon of the molasses apples. Top with the other biscuit half. Sprinkle the tops with the cinnamon and sugar. Reserve any remaining apple mixture for serving. Bake until golden brown, 35 to 40 minutes, rotating the pans between oven racks halfway through baking.

To unpan, loosen the sides of each hand pie with a table knife, then insert the tines of a fork between the pan and each pie to lift it out. Serve with the barbecue dipping sauce and molasses apples.

Store the leftover hand pies in an airtight container in the refrigerator for up to 5 days. Reheat, wrapped in tin foil, for 15 minutes at 350°F (175°C). Store the barbecue dipping sauce and leftover molasses apples in separate airtight containers in the refrigerator.

PÂTÉS
with Bacon
& BAY LEAF

OVEN: 350°F (175°C) > PREP TIME: 1 hour 25 minutes >
BAKING TIME: 1 hour > YIELD: 12 pâtés

FOR THE CUSTARD

2 tablespoons unsalted butter

2 tablespoons all-purpose flour

1 cup (240 ml) half-and-half

¼ cup (60 ml) Dijon mustard

4 large egg yolks

FOR THE PÂTÉ

2 tablespoons unsalted butter

½ pound (225 g) ham steak or deli ham, chopped

1 cup (160 g) chopped onion

3 bay leaves

1 tablespoon fresh thyme leaves

1 (2-ounce / 55-g) can anchovies packed in oil, drained

1½ pounds (680 g) chicken livers

¼ cup (60 ml) Cognac

FOR THE ASSEMBLY

12 bay leaves

12 slices bacon, halved lengthwise to create 24 long, skinny slices

I WAS RAISED on this rich pâté, and it holds much of the responsibility for developing my palate. The mustard and Cognac give these meals a savory flavor while mellowing out the stronger taste of liver. These mini pâtés would be excellent shared as part of a ploughman's luncheon with cornichons, quince chutney, Dijon and pommery mustards, toast points, crackers, or French bread. And they work so well during holiday celebrations and spontaneous fêtes!

Make Ahead The pâtés can be made up to 1 week in advance of serving. Store them in an airtight container in the refrigerator until ready to serve.

> MAKE THE CUSTARD

In a medium saucepan over medium heat, melt the butter, then whisk in the flour to create a paste. Cook for about 1 minute, then slowly pour in the half-and-half and add the Dijon, whisking constantly to mix thoroughly, about 2 minutes.

In a small bowl, whisk the 4 yolks. Slowly add ½ cup (120 ml) of the warmed cream mixture to the yolks, whisking constantly, then add the egg-cream mixture to the saucepan, whisking constantly for about 3 minutes. (Do not let the mixture boil.) Transfer to a bowl set over another bowl filled with ice water. Allow to cool completely, stirring occasionally, about 1 hour.

> MAKE THE PÂTÉ

In a large skillet over medium heat, melt the butter, then add the ham, onion, bay leaves, thyme, and anchovies; cook until the onion is translucent, about 6 minutes. Add the livers and cook, stirring occasionally, until they are no longer pink inside, about 8 minutes. Pour the mixture into a sieve to drain off any liquid. Allow the mixture to cool completely, then remove the bay leaves.

Place the cooled custard, the cooled chicken liver mixture, and the Cognac in the bowl of a food processor fitted with the blade attachment and puree until smooth.

❯ ASSEMBLE AND BAKE THE PÂTÉS

Preheat the oven to 350°F (175°C). Place 1 bay leaf in the bottom of each well of a 12-well classic cupcake pan. Place 2 slices of the bacon, side-by-side, over the bay leaf in each well. The bacon should overhang the wells of the pan. Distribute the pâté mixture evenly among the wells, then fold the bacon over the filling.

Bake the pâtés until the bacon is golden, about 1 hour. Let cool in the pan for 10 minutes, then insert the tines of a fork between the pan and each pâté to lift it out. Set the pâtés on a wire rack set over a baking sheet to let the excess fat drip off. Transfer the pâtés to an airtight plastic container and chill for 1 hour or up to 1 week before serving. To serve, invert the pâtés so the bay leaf is on top.

Prosciutto POCKETS

WITH ZUCCHINI, TOMATO CONFIT & BUFFALO MOZZARELLA

OVEN: 275°F and 350°F (135°C and 175°C) > PREP TIME: 20 minutes >
BAKING TIME: 2 hours and 25 minutes > YIELD: 12 pockets

FOR THE TOMATO CONFIT

2 pints (600 g) cherry tomatoes

⅓ cup (75 ml) extra-virgin olive oil

1½ teaspoons kosher salt

6 cloves garlic, thinly sliced

6 sprigs fresh thyme

FOR THE PARSLEY AND CAPER SALSA

⅓ cup (45 g) capers

2 tablespoons caper brine from the jar

6 cloves garlic

1 cup (40 g) packed fresh flat-leaf parsley leaves

½ cup (120 ml) extra-virgin olive oil

1 ounce (25 g) anchovy fillets packed in oil, drained

Juice and zest of ½ lemon

FOR THE ASSEMBLY

Nonstick cooking spray, for the pan

24 slices prosciutto (12 ounces / 340 g)

3 large zucchini, about 7 inches (17 cm) in length, ends trimmed

1 pound (455 g) buffalo mozzarella, very thinly sliced

1 cup (100 g) grated Parmesan

THIS VERSATILE DISH can be prepared either baked or chilled. When baked, the mozzarella melts temptingly over the stacked layers. The chilled version macerates beautifully, presenting fresh and vibrant flavors and colors, like an antipasto in a prosciutto shell. If you're short on time, jarred sun-dried tomatoes in oil or fresh oven-roasted Italian tomatoes from your grocery store deli can be used as substitutes for the tomato confit.

Make Ahead The tomato confit can be made in advance and stored in an airtight container in the refrigerator until needed. It will last for up to 2 weeks.

> MAKE THE TOMATO CONFIT

Preheat the oven to 275°F (135°C). Line a rimmed baking sheet with foil or a Silpat mat. Place the tomatoes on the pan and drizzle with the oil. Sprinkle with the salt and add the garlic slices and thyme. Bake for 2 hours, turning the tomatoes every 30 minutes to prevent browning. The long cooking time and the low heat will allow the tomatoes to caramelize in their own sugar.

Let the tomatoes cool on the pan. Using a rubber spatula, transfer them to a small bowl with the oil and any juices from the pan.

> MAKE THE PARSLEY AND CAPER SALSA

In a blender or a food processor fitted with the blade attachment, combine the capers, brine, garlic, parsley, oil, anchovies, and lemon juice and zest, and blend until smooth.

> ASSEMBLE AND BAKE THE POCKETS

Preheat the oven to 350°F (175°C). Spray a 12-well classic cupcake pan with nonstick cooking spray. Line each well with 2 slices of prosciutto in a cross pattern. The prosciutto will overhang the edges of the well.

Using a vegetable peeler, preferably a T-shaped peeler, thinly peel each zucchini into long ribbons, stopping when you reach the seeds.

Top the prosciutto in the wells with 2 ribbons of zucchini in a cross pattern, covering any spaces not covered by the prosciutto. Add 1 thin slice of mozzarella; top with 4 roasted tomatoes and a bit of juice from the confit. Continue layering zucchini, mozzarella, and tomatoes, ending with the mozzarella. Fold the overhanging prosciutto and zucchini over the filling and top each pocket with the grated Parmesan.

Bake uncovered until the Parmesan is golden, 25 minutes. Let cool in the pan for 10 minutes, then loosen the sides of each pocket with a table knife and pop them out of the pan. Invert the pockets onto plates or a platter and drizzle with the parsley and caper salsa.

Store the pockets in an airtight container in the refrigerator for up to 5 days. Reheat at 350°F (175°C).

VARIATION To make a chilled version, line the cupcake pan with plastic wrap before layering the ingredients. Assemble as for the baked version, omitting the Parmesan. Wrap the pan in plastic wrap, stack another cupcake pan on top of the filled pan to compact the pockets, and refrigerate for 4 hours or overnight.

Westphalian Ham

> & GRUYÈRE <

GRILLED CHEESE

OVEN: 350°F (175°C) > **PREP TIME:** 15 minutes >
BAKING TIME: 20 to 25 minutes > **YIELD:** 12 sandwiches

Nonstick cooking spray, for the pan

18 slices thin white bread, such as Pepperidge Farm's Very Thin White Bread

8 ounces (225 g) thinly sliced deli ham

12 ounces (340 g) thinly sliced Swiss or Gruyère

THIS IS A DELIGHTFUL WAY to reinvent a childhood favorite! These adult grilled cheeses are chic little sandwiches with several thin layers of pure delicious flavors. Play with the cheese and meat combinations to create flavors that will excite your guests. Try tuna salad with a slice of pepper Jack, turkey and smoked Gouda with a side of applesauce for dipping, or roast beef and cheddar with a red pepper relish. The variations are endless!

You can use any extra bread scraps to make bread crumbs, and the ham and cheese scraps would work perfectly in an omelet. Try using the tomato jam from page 105, the apple ketchup from page 48, or the apple compote from page 108 in one of these sandwiches. Delicious!

Preheat the oven to 350°F (175°C). Spray a 12-well classic cupcake pan with nonstick cooking spray.

Using a 2-in (5-cm) round biscuit cutter or cookie cutter of any shape, cut out 36 pieces of bread. Do the same with the ham and cheese.

To assemble, place a piece of bread into each well. Next place one slice of ham, one slice of cheese, and another slice of bread. Repeat twice more, ending with cheese on top.

Bake for 20 to 25 minutes, until the cheese is melted and the bread is toasted. Loosen the sides of each sandwich with a table knife and pop them out of the pan. Serve with a dollop of your favorite mustard, or dip in tomato soup!

LAMB
Tagine
HAND PIES

OVEN: 350°F (175°C) > PREP TIME: 25 minutes >
BAKING TIME: 25 to 30 minutes > YIELD: 12 pies

FOR THE RICE

1 cup (160 g) rice

2 cups (480 ml) chicken broth

1 cinnamon stick

FOR THE LAMB

3 tablespoons olive oil

1 small onion, finely chopped

1 pound (455 g) ground lamb

3 tablespoons minced fresh garlic or garlic from a tube

Generous pinch of saffron strands or annatto (see Note)

1 teaspoon cinnamon

1 tablespoon freshly grated ginger or ginger from tube

Kosher salt and freshly ground black pepper

1 tablespoon chopped fresh cilantro or cilantro from a tube

½ cup (120 ml) lamb or beef stock

1 tablespoon brown sugar

FOR THE ASSEMBLY

Nonstick cooking spray, for the pan

½ cup (70 g) whole almonds, toasted, for garnish

8 pieces crystallized ginger, julienned, for garnish

12 sprigs fresh cilantro, for garnish

Note Saffron is the dried stigma of the crocus flower. One of the world's most costly spices, it lends a deep golden color and distinct flavor to many dishes. Annatto, a less expensive (and less flavorful) alternative, is found in the international foods aisle or spice section of the grocery store, or at specialty food shops. It is commonly used in Mexican cuisine and will lend a similar color but slightly different flavor to food.

YEARS AGO ON A TRIP TO SPAIN, I was trying to decide whether to make a side trip to Morocco. Some Dutch travelers told me I needed a green card to enter the country, and fool that I was, I took them at their word. Little did I know that the rule only applied to Europeans—my passport was enough to get me there! Needless to say, I never made it to Morocco, but I love the colors and fragrances of the country and its cuisine, especially lamb and Moroccan and tagine spices. Here, I've created a hand pie that uses an empanada dough wrapper colored and flavored with annatto to mimic the color of the red clay in Morocco.

> MAKE THE RICE

In a medium saucepan, cook the rice following the directions on the package but substituting the chicken broth for water and adding the cinnamon stick. Set aside.

> MAKE THE LAMB

Heat the oil in a medium sauté pan over medium heat. Add the onion and cook, stirring constantly, until golden brown, 8 to 10 minutes. Add the lamb, garlic, saffron, cinnamon, ginger, salt and pepper, cilantro, stock, and brown sugar. Cook until the lamb is no longer pink, 8 to 10 minutes. Turn off the heat.

Remove the cinnamon stick from the rice and transfer the rice to a large bowl. Add the lamb to the rice and mix.

> ASSEMBLE AND BAKE THE HAND PIES

Preheat the oven to 350°F (175°C). Spray a 12-well classic cupcake pan with nonstick cooking spray. Line each well with 1 disc of empanada dough colored with annatto. The edges of the dough will peek over the top of the pan. Fill each well to the top with the lamb mixture.

Bake for 25 to 30 minutes. Immediately loosen the sides of each pie using a table knife and insert the tines of a fork between the pan and each pie to lift it out. Garnish each hand pie with the toasted almonds, candied ginger, and a cilantro sprig. Serve alongside couscous that has been tossed with dried apricots, pistachios, cilantro, and orange zest.

Store the hand pies in an airtight container in the refrigerator for up to 5 days. Reheat, wrapped in tin foil, for 15 minutes at 350°F (175°C).

ACKNOWLEDGMENTS

NO BOOK OF THIS SIZE AND SCOPE is accomplished by the author alone (I can't believe I am an author!). Many people helped me on this journey, and we will be linked together forever over the stove because of it. Everyone challenged me and pushed me beyond the borders of the cupcake pan to move from dilet tante to first-time author. Chief among those were the SweetByHolly team who were with me the entire way and contributed consistency and commitment to keeping my SweetByHolly shops up and running while I tested and wrote the book in the middle of the night and filmed *Cupcake Wars* in between recipes. If it were not for Ashton, Kayla, Krista, Malory, and all of the Sweeties, this book never would have happened.

Thank goodness for my editor, Natalie Kaire, who happened to be channel surfing one night and saw my win on the Food Network's *Cupcake Wars*, I will be forever grateful for her phone call and how it changed the course of my sweet and savory journey forever. Thanks, too, to the team at Stewart, Tabori & Chang, especially Dervla Kelly, who stepped in as my editor and showed great enthusiasm for my book. A thank-you to the most delightfully indefatigable literary agent, Alison Fargis of Stonesong, for pushing me to be the very best that I can be.

I was fortunate to have amazing writing help from the talented Michelle Witte and solid recipe testing knowledge from Vanessa Seder. Both held my hand for over a year and offered many hours of devoted work.

Many thanks to Tina Rupp, the book's photographer, Marianna Velazquez, the food stylist, and Leslie Siegel, the prop stylist, for creating such gorgeous photos. Their creations perfectly capture and bring to life the spirit of the book.

Less readily apparent but extremely important work was done by: Max Mutchnick and Erik Hyman for direction, Sheraton Kalouria for his vision, Mark Danielewski, Blair and Gail, for showing me how it's done, the family farm, church suppers, and potluxe™ dinners everywhere. Peter Maiers, Gussie, Andrew Bush, Joel and Christina Wilder, Susan, David, Tom, Karen and Katherine Wilder, Andrea Murdoch-Cohen, SweetByHolly supporters, Jeannie Lee, Emily Elun, Maria Martinez, Dani Caird, Priscilla and Walter Cane, Maureen Flannigan, and every guest who has dined on my food since I was five years old.

Special thanks to my husband, for always having my back and for going to the grocery at midnight, and to my children, Georgia and Whitman, for having really good palates and being so good-spirited and energetic.

CONVERSION CHARTS

WEIGHT EQUIVALENTS: The metric weights given in this chart are not exact equivalents, but have been rounded up or down slightly to make measuring easier.

VOLUME EQUIVALENTS: These are not exact equivalents for American cups and spoons, but have been rounded up or down slightly to make measuring easier.

AVOIRDUPOIS	METRIC
¼ oz	7 g
½ oz	15 g
1 oz	30 g
2 oz	60 g
3 oz	90 g
4 oz	115 g
5 oz	150 g
6 oz	175 g
7 oz	200 g
8 oz (½ lb)	225 g
9 oz	250 g
10 oz	300 g
11 oz	325 g
12 oz	350 g
13 oz	375 g
14 oz	400 g
15 oz	425 g
16 oz (1 lb)	450 g
1½ lb	750 g
2 lb	900 g
2¼ lb	1 kg
3 lb	1.4 kg
4 lb	1.8 kg

AMERICAN	METRIC	IMPERIAL
¼ tsp	1.2 ml	
½ tsp	2.5 ml	
1 tsp	5.0 ml	
½ Tbsp (1.5 tsp)	7.5 ml	
1 Tbsp (3 tsp)	15 ml	
¼ cup (4 Tbsp)	60 ml	2 fl oz
⅓ cup (5 Tbsp)	75 ml	2.5 fl oz
½ cup (8 Tbsp)	125 ml	4 fl oz
⅔ cup (10 Tbsp)	150 ml	5 fl oz
¾ cup (12 Tbsp)	175 ml	6 fl oz
1 cup (16 Tbsp)	250 ml	8 fl oz
1¼ cups	300 ml	10 fl oz (½ pint)
1½ cups	350 ml	12 fl oz
2 cups (1 pint)	500 ml	16 fl oz
2½ cups	625 ml	20 fl oz (1 pint)
1 quart	1 liter	32 fl oz

OVEN MARK	F	C	GAS
Very cool	250–275	130–140	½–1
Cool	300	150	2
Warm	325	170	3
Moderate	350	180	4
Moderately hot	375	190	5
	400	200	6
Hot	425	220	7
	450	230	8
Very hot	475	250	9